'MANAGING' STRESS

'MANAGING' STRESS

Emotion and Power at Work

Tim Newton

with Jocelyn Handy
and Stephen Fineman

SAGE Publications
London • Thousand Oaks • New Delhi

First published 1995
Reprinted 1996

SAGE Publications Ltd
6 Bonhill Street
London EC2A 4PU

SAGE Publications Inc
2455 Teller Road
Thousand Oaks, California 91320

SAGE Publications India Pvt Ltd
32, M-Block Market
Great Kailash – 1
New Delhi 110 048

British Library Cataloguing in Publication Data

A catalogue record for this book is available from the
British Library.

ISBN 0 8039 8643 2
ISBN 0 8039 8644 0 pbk

Library of Congress catalog card number 94–69147

Typeset by Photoprint, Torquay, Devon
Printed and bound in Great Britain by
Biddles Ltd, Guildford and King's Lynn

Contents

Preface

This book has two main aims. Firstly, it will present a critical understanding of the experience of stress and distress in employment. Secondly, it will use this critical analysis to explore broader debates relating to discourse, agency and subjectivity. We hope that this book will be of interest to a variety of readers. For students and practitioners, such as managers, social workers, psychologists and nurses, we aim to present an alternative to what we see as a very narrow current conceptualization of stress. At the same time, the book should also have some interest for sociologists and social psychologists who are trying to untangle the complex issues surrounding discourse, agency and subjectivity. Finally, though we are rather critical of mainstream psychology – and especially organizational psychology – we hope that researchers in these areas will find this book of interest.

Note on the Authors

Tim Newton is a lecturer in organization studies, in the Department of Business Studies at the University of Edinburgh.

Jocelyn Handy is a lecturer in the Psychology Department at Massey University, Palmerston North, New Zealand.

Stephen Fineman is reader in organizational behaviour in the School of Management at the University of Bath.

1

Introduction: Agency, Subjectivity and the Stress Discourse

Stress is a subject that is hard to avoid. Wherever you turn there are a multiplicity of guides on the nature of stress from psychologists, epidemiologists, therapists, consultants, journalists and so on. In academic texts, or in popular media articles, we learn how stress is a fact of our busy modern lives, and how we should watch for the 'danger signs' of stress. We must monitor our 'stress levels', analyse our 'coping strategies', and learn how to become 'stress-fit' through a range of 'stress management techniques'. As a social science discourse, stress displays the rare ability to interest both researcher/practitioner and lay public. There are few other issues which cross so easily between academic and lay concerns, where both academic and lay publics appear to actively theorize about the subject.

In this book we shall explore these different aspects of stress, and what they tell us about ourselves, and how we should be. Our particular focus is upon stress in employment, and the ways in which employees are said to feel and cope with stress. Yet this is not a conventional book on work stress, one simply concerned to explore the relation of organizational 'stressors' to individual 'strains', or the effectiveness of coping strategies and stress management. Rather our primary interest in stress, and work stress, is because it does represent a very popular social science discourse, seemingly written into and over all of our daily lives. Stress does appear to be 'everywhere'. From being a subject which was barely referenced a century ago, it has become so prevalent that for most people in the West it is 'unavoidable', an undeniable fact of the modern condition. Our concern is with how this has come about, and also with the way in which stress 'speaks' to us, with the kind of 'subject' that is created in stress discourse. Examining stress thus provides a focused vehicle by which to explore how our sense of ourselves relates to a particularly modern and widespread discourse.

Through this project we also hope to challenge the way in which we presently think about stress. To us, the terms of such thinking are currently very narrow, and we hope that this book will help to place what we now think of stress within wider debates about power, emotion and subjectivity. Part of the appeal of the stress discourse may lie in the way in which it seems to say that the distresses we feel in our everyday lives are chiefly a function of ourselves. To this extent, current thinking about stress can appear empowering in telling us that it is up to us to change our lives: the key to dealing with stress lies in the way in which *we* approach and manage it. Though this is a positive and appealing message, in this book we shall continually seek to question it. We shall try to illustrate how a concern with stress does not necessarily represent a concern with either the welfare or the empowerment of the individual; how stress is not just about the individual and her coping patterns, but can reflect power relations between men and women, employer and employee, superior and subordinate; how both the appraisal of stress, and coping with it, can be a collective process dependent on a number of people, rather than just an individual concern; how the definition of stress represents a rather narrow perspective on emotion, and how stress needs to be seen in relation to differing tacit codes of emotional restraint within private, public and organizational settings; how though the language of stress is of relatively recent historical origin, it is one which can be seen to rearticulate older senses of ourselves.

By way of an introduction to stress, I shall turn to the way in which it is represented in the popular media. Analysis of popular media treatment of stress has a number of advantages. Firstly, for those unfamiliar with the stress discourse, it provides an outline of its central ideas (and as I shall also argue, the popular media presentation of stress is not very different from its treatment by either academics or stress practitioners and consultants). Secondly, the simplified language of journalism makes the discourse more transparent, and also reminds us of how commonly the concepts are utilized (most readers should recognize at least some parts of the media discoursew). Thirdly, this analysis also helps in illustrating how social science discourses like that of stress present a particular image of ourselves, seeming to want to both explain and define our subjectivity.

Stress in Popular Media

Stress has covered almost every corner of the media, from television series, to articles in the quality press, to management journals, to the tabloids, and even local freebies. In the West, the stress capital tends to be women's glossies, especially those that focus more on human relationships (as distinct from 'homes and gardens'). In order to introduce the stress discourse, the content of this literature will be examined below. Deconstruction of popular representations in the media is of course not an entirely new subject, and it has received a fair amount of attention from feminist writers, in relation to both the media portrayal of women (e.g. Tuchman et al., 1978) and their employment in the media (e.g. Creedon, 1989).[1] The concern for the present though is more narrowly focused on the stress discourse itself.

Copy on stress would seem to be located in almost every editor's filing cabinet. Production is easy; include a stress check questionnaire, offer a ten-point plan to help readers attain 'stress-fitness', and make a few telephone calls to some academic luminaries on file. A typical feature of these articles is the argument that stress is quintessentially a problem that must be borne by management and those in senior positions, whether captains of industry or leaders of government. An article by Cal McCrystal on 'prime ministerial stress' in *The Independent on Sunday* (25 October 1992: 23) epitomizes this image. The article represented an elaboration of themes previously appearing in a report in *The Times*, which suggested that the current British prime minister, John Major, had shown the strain of cumulative woes through eating habits which had led to weight loss, as well as other symptoms such as dyeing his hair. McCrystal argues that such prime ministerial stress is not a new thing; rather he portrays it as an almost inevitable consequence of this demanding office. Thus although 'Disraeli is remembered for his gaudy performances . . . stress did surface.' Apparently, the 'dead giveaway' of stress was a behavioural 'twitch' under stress whereby he moved his leg 'twice or three times, then curved his foot upwards'. According to McCrystal, increasingly bizarre but unmistakable signs of stress afflicted other British prime ministers such as Gladstone (whose symptom was visiting brothels), Asquith (whose stress 'came out' in writing love letters), Churchill (who floated 'on alcohol through every day'), Eden (given away by gall bladders), Lloyd George (who sought sexual comfort from his mistress in order to get over the horrors of 'pre-speech nerves'), Macmillan (who 'vomited in the lavatory before major speeches') and even the 'iron lady' herself, Margaret Thatcher, who surely must have been showing signs of stress when she 'borrowed whiskey from the Irish delegation at a summit'.

Though stress grew to a big seller in the 1980s, it does not appear to have lost its popularity. For example, *Good Housekeeping* (hereafter *GH*) ran articles on stress in August, September and October of 1992 (and also has a resident stress researcher, Jenny Firth-Cozens, as its 'agony aunt'). They tell us that 'stress is an epidemic with work and money worries the leading cause.' It apparently affects us all and, perhaps not surprisingly therefore, 'it may account for up to 50% of absenteeism at work' (*GH*, August 1992: 80–1). The August to October *GH* stress articles are worth examining further. Whilst they are in no sense a representative sample, they do illustrate easily recognizable themes in the popular media *and* academic treatment of stress.[2] They therefore provide a quick and convenient introduction to predominant assumptions of the stress discourse.

Throughout these articles the emphasis is on 'fitness', namely the ability to live with and control this 'modern-day menace'. For example, the August article offered 'The complete de-stress guide', designed to help readers recognize stress symptoms, identify the sources of stress and apply coping strategies. They are told firstly to remain vigilant for the symptoms of stress: 'Perpetual tiredness is a clear indication of stress', whilst 'other danger signs' include 'depression, panic attacks, drinking or eating too much, overuse of tranquillisers . . . insomnia or other sleeping problems, headaches' (*GH*, August 1992: 81). If such self-surveillance shows the danger signs then 'you need to work out whether the real problem lies in your psyche or in your way of life.' So whether it's your psyche or your lifestyle, the need is to examine yourself since that is where the sources of stress lie. For example, let's say you are: 'overloaded? Take some tips from industry and look at time management, delegation and prioritising' (*GH*, August 1992: 81). There is no suggestion in this article (or in most others like it) that you should see work overload as a source of legitimate grievance, or say to your superiors that your workload is impossible. No, you should 'buckle down' and 'own your own stuff', but in our modern world this can be helped by stress management techniques such as time management, prioritizing or delegation. The likelihood that you may be so overloaded that time management and prioritizing are an irrelevance is not seriously considered (nor is the possibility that delegation simply may not be available or practically feasible).

Stress guides legitimate their advice through the continual calling up of experts. The September stress-related article in *GH* starts by calling on Britain's best-known agony aunt, Marjorie Proops, then quotes the advice of a medical doctor, an educationalist, a geriatrician and a psychologist, before ending the article with a 'last witness' the magazine's modern-day agony aunt, namely '*GH* Consultant Psychologist, Dr Jenny Cozens'. There is also an emphasis that we should not be surprised to be stressed since, after all, stress is an 'epidemic' and 'life is now so stressful' (Dr Ruth Lever quoted in the *GH* September issue): it is so common that it is *normal* to feel stressed. In this way, the media discourse problematizes stress but also normalizes it, and asserts that you shouldn't feel odd to be stressed *unless* it reaches 'maladaptive' or 'abnormal' levels. To prevent the latter danger, a number of techniques, or 'coping strategies', are offered. For example, other than the time management and delegation advice noted above, *GH* regularly offers readers advice through the agony aunt column of Dr Cozens, which advises readers to, say, 'try gestalt therapy' (*GH* October issue). Elsewhere the stress articles suggest the Alexander technique, aromatherapy, colour therapy, meditation and health farms. The October issue also has an article largely devoted to therapy and counselling, which notes that 'The modern way to solve a problem is to treat it as a challenge, so more people are turning to counselling.' The article provides a number of vignettes describing how individuals have benefited from counselling, such as 'Pauline, 38, a divorcee' who 'learnt a lot about myself'. Some therapists are described in glowing, almost magical terms: 'she was marvellous – wise, full of common sense and she listened to us.'[3]

Though the language here is that of journalism rather than 'scientific' psychology, these *GH* articles manage to convey much of the *academic* stress discourse. For example, a common theme to be found in both popular media and academic stress is the supposed close correlation between stress and both psychological and physical health. Thus the October *GH* issue notes that:

'A lot of diseases we see are stress-related', says GP Anne Dyson. The Essex group practice where she is a partner now has a psychologist who can spend 45 minutes at a time with a patient – rather than the 10 minutes a GP can afford. 'If we can teach stress management techniques rather than dishing out tranquillisers, everyone will benefit.' (*GH*, October 1992: 76)

Such assumptions are not just confined to mainstream women's magazines but are also to be found in more feminist-oriented magazines such as *Everywoman*. The November 1992 issue explains the problems of 'stress breakdown'; where 'fear, frustration and fatigue overwhelm the body's capacity to meet stress' (p. 30). Similar concerns are to be found in the academic literature through attention to epidemiology (Fletcher, 1988), through the prospective 'type A' studies and other approaches suggesting stress–health links (e.g. Karasek et al., 1987) as well as through the evaluation of the efficacy of stress management techniques (Murphy, 1988). Though there is still debate about the nature of the stress–health link, it would generally appear to be assumed by researchers that stress is a major health risk. Together with the generally assumed prevalence of stress, the health link helps to legitimate the discourse because of the potentially dire consequences of stress for individuals and organizations (e.g. health services, employers).

Yet another theme shared by the popular and academic stress discourse is the naturalism of stress, whereby its inevitability and prevalence reflect the fact that it is part of nature, a taken-for-granted aspect of the living world:

> You only have to watch a wildlife programme to realise that a certain level of stress is natural. Most animals have to check their surroundings carefully for predators before they eat or drink, something most of us would find intolerably stressful. (*GH*, August 1992: 80)

The same image appears in the academic literature, dating from the argument that stress is resultant from our 'animal response' of either 'fight or flight' when confronted with threats or danger. As we shall see in chapter 2, such responses are seen as 'phylogenetically outdated', inappropriate to the modern age, so that it is the anachronistic nature of our responses to fear and anxiety that are portrayed as causing present-day stress.

To sum up, stress is an epidemic plaguing modernity. It is shown as closely linked to health, mental and physical, and because of these links and its prevalence it becomes vitally important to distinguish abnormal from normal levels of stress. Stress experts are said to provide an essential role both in defining unacceptable/abnormal stress levels, and in devising and evaluating stress management techniques to help the individual cope with stress. Stress is depicted as an inevitable part of the natural world, and within the popular media is seen as a particular malaise of those in high position.

The question that remains is that of why the stress discourse receives such attention from the popular media. Assuming that editors are right in thinking that it does sell magazines and newspapers, why is the stress discourse so saleable? Why does it seem so successful? Why are we interested in it, and why does it speak to us? Do we believe in it? As Gergen notes, 'newspapers, magazines, and television provide a barrage of new criteria of self-evaluation' (1991: 76). But do we really explain ourselves to ourselves in terms of media rhetoric, or through other forms of discursive bombardment? Do we use and act on these new criteria of self-evaluation? Are we so easily enrolled through new discursive practices, such as the stress management practices of employee counselling, relaxation, meditation and bio-feedback?

The rest of this chapter will examine debates that relate to this kind of question, namely how our subjectivity relates to discourses like that of stress. But before we can begin to address these questions, it is necessary firstly to define what we mean by discourse and by subjectivity.

Discourse and Subjectivity

The word 'discourse' is generally used in this book in its Foucauldian sense to refer to assemblages of knowledge which create 'truth effects', or 'how effects of truth are produced within discourses which in themselves are neither true nor false' (Foucault, 1980: 198). Examples of such bodies of knowledge are those deriving from medicine, psychiatry, physiology, psychology, sociology and so on. Their power comes not from their ability to give us 'real truth', but from their claims to truth, their claims to know the world. Within the stress discourse, these effects of truth are produced by the way in which it proclaims stress as a major problem (an epidemic), and through its definition of the 'stressed subject'. Like other discourses, its proclamation of the truth of stress is aided by an array of discursive practices which allow researchers, practitioners and lay publics to analyse and manage stress, to know and show its existence as a major twentieth century problem, and to proffer techniques by which it can be assessed and governed.

Following Foucault, the truth of stress is seen within this book as an effect, as a representation of the world through claiming to know it, rather than as some objective reality. As in other Foucauldian work, I am concerned to deconstruct the text of stress in a loosely Derridean sense whereby the 'deconstruction of the subject is, among other things, the genealogical analysis of the trajectory through which the concept of the subject has been built, used and legitimised' (Derrida, 1992: 7). I wish to explore how the stressed subject has been created, historically developed and validated within stress discourse, and what image it produces of someone who is stressed: for example, often this appears as someone whose stress is chiefly a function of themselves (their personality, behaviour style, 'appraisal process', coping pattern etc.), largely unrelated to wider social and power relations. Since stress is a product of the individual, the solutions to the stress 'problem' are also reliant on individual rather than social/collective intervention. The stressed subject is expected to 'conquer' stress through their own autonomy and enterprise.

To this extent this book has similarities with other work drawing on Foucault such as that of Hollway (1991) and Rose (1990), and their exploration of the relationship between discourses such as social Darwinism, human relations, management studies and psychotherapy, and our sense of our selves as animalistic, self-actualizing and autonomous subjects. Yet, though I draw on a Foucauldian sense of discourse, this book is not a Foucauldian text; it draws theoretically as much if not more on labour process theory, radical structuralist accounts, and the work of those concerned with the sociology of emotion such as Elias and Hochschild (see chapter 3 in this book).

Within this book, I use the term 'subjectivity' to collectively refer to three senses of how we come to know ourselves. Firstly, I employ it as it is often applied in Foucauldian accounts, namely as understanding how the subject is constituted within academic and lay discourse, and how this is reflected in discursive practices and the kind of rhetorical devices used by individuals in everyday conversation (e.g. Rose, 1990; Hollway, 1991; Knights and Morgan, 1991; Wetherell and Potter, 1992). I shall also refer to more traditional views of subjectivity as denoting feeling, sentiments and so on, particularly where we undertake social constructionist analysis of feeling rules in relation to reported stress (Hochschild, 1983; see especially chapters 3, 6 and 7). In addition, there is also an interest in Marxist concerns with subjectivity, traditionally represented by the problem of false consciousness. Here subjectivity is primarily viewed within the conflict between capital and labour, such as the concern exhibited in recent Marxist analyses in explaining how people buy into repressive ideologies which support capitalist domination (see below). As Hall argues, 'it is clear that the discourses of the New Right have been engaged . . . in the production of new subject positions and the transformation of subjectivities' (S. Hall, 1988: 49).

Having outlined our sense of discourse and subjectivity, we can now return to my earlier questions, namely, 'Do we believe in stress?', 'Do we use it and act on it?' and 'How does our sense of ourselves relate to it?'

Stress Discourse and Subjectivity

There is currently one study which has tried to examine the way in which people use the concept of stress in understanding themselves. This is the anthropological analysis of Pollock (1988). The aim of her study was to explore people's ideas about health and illness with particular attention to multiple sclerosis, schizophrenia and 'nervous breakdown'. She interviewed 114 white adults living in Nottingham, 48 of whom came from families affected by multiple sclerosis, 33 from those affected by schizophrenia, and 33 from ' "ordinary" families' (1988: 382). The limitation of her study is that it was skewed towards particular kinds of illness associated with particular groups of respondents. But what is interesting is how stress appeared as a dominant theme in explaining illness, being most commonly used to explain nervous breakdowns, heart attacks, and minor complaints such as headaches and stomach-aches. Of particular interest is the way in which her respondents cited many of the themes observed in the media. Firstly, there was the general belief that stress was a cause of illness and that 'a severe headache or recurrent stomach pains had been brought on by "stress" or "worry" ' (1988: 382). Secondly, there was a perception that stress had increased over the past few decades to the extent that it was now an 'inevitable and ubiquitous condition of modern living' (1988: 382). As in the popular media, it was leaders and managers who were seen as most likely to be 'felled' by stress, with the 'paradigm heart-attack case' being the 'pressurised executive or businessman' (1988: 382). Her respondents explained the link to illness through the way in which stress 'resulted in a gradual wearing out of the body's defences', whilst some referred to 'the "scientific" theory of adrenalin' (1988: 382). Whilst stress was ubiquitous, *individual* 'make-up' determined whether one 'succumbed' to it, depending on innate differences, as well as whether one had learnt the right 'attitude of mind' and self-control.

Analysis of the media representation of stress, as well as the work of Pollock, begs the question of whether there is some deterministic relation between discourse and subjectivity so that, like it or not, we all become to some extent constituted within new discourses. This is the conclusion that Pollock formed, arguing that her observations resulted from 'the rather spectacular success of the steady diffusion and popularisation over the last few decades of the various theories about stress put over by numerous behavioural and social scientists, who have taken up the subject for research' (1988: 383). For Pollock, stress is 'not something naturally occurring' but instead represents 'a product of social and behavioural science research' (1988: 390). Her argument in effect is that we have all become stressed not so much because life really is more stressful, but because social science has had a spectacular success in persuading us that stress is a 'scientific' and 'objective' fact. But are we so open to discourse? Do we simply follow the regimes of social science? Do we become stress believers through a mixture of academic/media evangelicism and the spread of stress management practices (like counselling and relaxation)? Is our sense of ourselves so easily reconstituted through the claims to truth of powerful discourses like that of stress? In short, why do we believe in stress?

The conventional answer to this last question is that we believe in stress because we have, 'in reality', become more stressed throughout the twentieth century. But there are two notable problems with this argument. One is that there is no way of knowing if we have all become more stressed, even if stress surveys do suggest increasing stress. To put this another way, stress surveys may just be measuring the power of the stress discourse, rather than the real experience of stress. We cannot assess whether stress itself really exists since an individual may *primarily* report it because of his or her participation in the stress discourse. For example, imagine that you could research the work experience of a person doing a job in 1904, and a person who did exactly the same job in 1994 (admittedly something of a fictitious example). The person doing the job in 1904 would probably not report stress; the one doing it in 1994 well might. Does that mean the 1904 job was not stressful? Clearly the ability to express stress depends on the ability to learn the language of stress and the parameters of the stress discourse. Since the largely social science formulation of this language was hardly articulated in 1904, it is unlikely that a stress survey could measure it. By the same token, apparent increases in stress in surveys, say, conducted between 1944 and 1994, may simply reflect the increasing post-war spread of the discourse. This does not mean that people are necessarily any more stressed.

The other problem with saying that we believe in the current stress discourse because we have become more stressed is that it implicitly assumes that there are no major problems with present explanations of stress. People adopt the stress discourse both because they feel stressed, and because the explanations of the stress discourse are 'right'. But as chapter 2 of this book will argue, present accounts of stress give a very narrow view of the stressed subject as someone who is apolitical, ahistorical, individualized, decontextualized. This implies that even if for the sake of argument we accept that stress has 'really' increased in the twentieth century, this does not explain why we have adopted a particular kind of explanation of stress (see chapter 3). In other words, the question of interest is not so much that of why we believe in the *reality* of stress, as why we believe in current *representations* of stress (Newton, 1994c). Are they really so right, so apt to our experience of ourselves? Are we so passive that we just (relatively) uncritically absorb the promulgations of stress academics, practitioners and journalists? Or do we play a far more active role in relation to stress discourse? One way of beginning to answer these questions is by taking a foray into thorny issues of how human agency relates to discourse.

Agency and Discourse

A conventional way to approach this issue is to consider the depiction of human agency in *traditional* Marxist accounts. If we follow such interpretations, people tend to appear as fairly passive, dupes of a 'false consciousness' whereby we come to believe in ideas convenient to the ruling class. Discourse is largely synonymous with the ideology by which the ruling class maintains its position through presenting its own interests as though they were exactly the same as those of everyone else. For example, ideas such as egalitarianism may be ideologically fortuitous in encouraging the notion of a society where everyone has an equal chance, but where there must inevitably be some winners and losers, some at the top of the heap and some at the bottom. It articulates with the promotion of individualism, wherein whether you're a winner or a loser is primarily up to you, whether you are, say, an ambitious, on-your-bike go-getter or a security-conscious plodder (or at worst a lazy workshy 'scrounger').

In this context the language of stress, with its emphasis on individualism, apoliticism, ahistoricism and so on, can be seen as just one further reflection of a pervasive ideology which glosses over the inequalities of power reflected in existing social structures, and lays the blame primarily on the individual, rather than their position in relation to, say, class, race or gender. People believe in the language of stress primarily because they have swallowed capitalist ideology, and the current stress discourse articulates fairly well with this ideology (see chapters 2 to 5). The stress discourse therefore just represents one more promotion of a false consciousness that prevents us from discovering our true selves (Hochschild, 1983).

As a number of writers have noted, the problem with the above traditional kind of Marxist critique is that it posits some notion of truth, of the real underlying hidden reality, against the false consciousness swallowed by the masses. Ideological representation such as egalitarianism is a veneer to hide the *truth* of the economic interests that prevail under capitalism. The most ardent or at least the best publicized critic (of late) of such a notion of truth is probably Michel Foucault. Since, for Foucault, all is potentially discourse, and notions of the latent underlying truth are but further forms of discourse, there can be no privileged position saying, 'We are right', and any such attempts are themselves but further illustration of the relation between power and knowledge, of how the discovery of any supposed truth is intimately related to power. Power is not simply repressive in, say, the sense of the domination of 'management' over labour, but it is productive since it 'traverses and produces things, it induces pleasure, forms knowledge, produces discourse' (Foucault, 1980: 119). The implication of Foucault's work is not simply that we are dupes of false ideology, passive victims of the economic interests of capital and the ruling class. Rather power works through us by telling us about ourselves and our world through, say, the discourses of psychiatry, psychology, biology, medicine, economics which reveal the secret of our selves. For example, we learn that we are normal, what our IQ is, how we can be healthy, the benefits of the free market and so on. With the stress discourse we can learn some secrets of our subjectivity, whilst stress questionnaires can comment on the stress levels of individuals, occupations or organizations. Yet for all this productiveness, Foucault would not want us to think that it revealed any ultimate truth, or that 'our liberation is in the balance' (Foucault, 1981: 159), so that the discovery of, say, the secrets of stress might *truly* empower us, makes us into stress-fit super-beings liberated from the onslaughts of the modern age. The stress discourse provides only one way of seeing, through a repertoire of practices that enable us to define the stressed subject, and via procedures which can adjust the subject back to 'normal' stress levels. There is no ultimate secret, no true reality, and any notion of liberation or self-actualization can never make any sense outside the terms of the discourse.

The contrasting images of our subjectivity in Marxist and Foucauldian accounts can be further illustrated through comparing the images of the self-contained in the work of Frankfurt School writers, and that exampled by more recent Foucauldian work. Erich Fromm provides a Frankfurt School example in his application of a loosely neo-Marxist account to a consideration of the self. For Fromm, our understanding of ourselves was directly tied to the development of capitalism, which appears as the engine driving us all away from the former certainties of medieval feudalism:

> While competition was certainly not completely lacking in medieval society, the feudal economic system was based on the principle of cooperation and was regulated – or regimented – by rules which curbed competition. With the rise of capitalism these medieval principles gave way more and more to a principle of individual enterprise. Each individual must go ahead and try his luck. He had to swim or sink. (1942: 51)

Whilst we have gained a freedom from feudal bondage, we have also lost security and certainty in our lives:

> The individual is freed *from* the bondage of economic and political ties. He also gains in positive freedom by the active and independent role which he has to play in the new system. But simultaneously he is freed from those ties which used to give him security and a feeling of belonging . . . By losing his fixed place in a closed world man [sic] loses the answer to the meaning of his life; the result is that doubt has befallen him concerning himself and the aim of life. He is threatened by powerful suprapersonal forces, capital and the market. (1942: 52)

Within this kind of analysis, stress would probably be seen as the consequence of the lack of belonging that individuals feel through a suppression of meaning in life, a direct consequence of a capitalist system which denies the individual a fixed place, and at the same time emphasizes individual enterprise rather than cooperation and collaboration.[4] Stress would appear as the logical fallout of capitalism and the need of the individual to continually fight to survive, to swim rather than sink (see above). With some Foucauldians there are somewhat similar images of subjectification to those exhibited by the Frankfurt School. For example, Parker argues that 'a *subjectivity* is produced in discourse as the self is *subjected* to discourse' (1989: 64), and where the individual is implicated 'in the reproduction of relations of domination' (1989: 57). More faithful servants of Foucault have however avoided the repressive implications entailed in the idea of domination, instead drawing on a more positive, productive account of power, and arguing for the free constitution of the individual through discourse. For example, Rose and Miller have argued that contemporary Western governments do not dominate their subjects in a repressive sense; rather, modern discourses have aligned the subjectivity of individuals with the political rationales of government (e.g. Rose, 1990; Miller and Rose, 1990; Rose and Miller, 1992). Yet as with writers like Fromm, Reich or Sennett, there is still an image of an individual who is only seemingly liberated, where freedom, if not illusory, only makes sense in terms of adherence to discourse, is only a truth effect. For example, Rose provides an interesting analysis of self-growth and psychotherapy discourse through attention to Rogers's client-centred therapy, transactional analysis, gestalt therapy, as well as feminist growth books such as Louise Eichenbaum and Susie Orbach's (1984) *What do Women Want?* (a book which promises to 'change lives'). After analysing this discourse of growth and fitness, Rose notes that:

> It promises to make it possible for us all to make a project of our biography, create a style for our lives, shape our everyday existence in terms of an ethic of autonomy. Yet the norm of autonomy secretes, as its inevitable accompaniment, a constant and intense self-scrutiny, a continual evaluation of our personal experiences, emotions, and feeling in relation to images of satisfaction, the necessity to narrativize our lives in a vocabulary of interiority. *The self that is liberated is obliged to live its life tied to the project of its own identity.* (1990: 254, my italics)

But here the illusion of freedom does not result from the repression of capitalism. Rather we have freely chosen our own subjectification:

> If the new techniques for the care of the self are subjectifying, it is not

because experts have colluded in the globalization of political power, seeking to dominate and subjugate the autonomy of the self through the bureaucratic management of life itself. Rather, it is that modern selves have become attached to the project of freedom, have come to live in terms of identity, and to search for means to enhance that autonomy through the application of expertise. (1990: 258)

Thus we may search for the secrets of our identity in discourse such as that of the stress discourse, but this search is not the consequence of capitalism. Rather we identify with the sense of freedom, of gaining autonomy through, say, therapy, through transactional analysis, through reading the stress discourse and practising stress management.[5] In Foucauldian accounts, we are seen to actively participate in the stress discourse through our allegiance to the seeming truth of the discourse, and through our enrolment in its discursive practice. As Rose and Miller put it: 'Personal autonomy is not the antithesis of political power, but a key term in its exercise, the more so because most individuals are not merely the subjects of power but play a key part in its operations' (1992: 174).

To sum up, if we follow traditional Marxism, we appear as rather passive victims of false consciousness, and to the extent that the stress discourse is reflective of such false consciousness we might be expected to swallow it more or less wholesale. In contrast, with Foucault, we do have more of a sense of our own agency in relation to the stress discourse, of how it works through us and gives shape to new forms of subjectivity. Chapter 3 will further explore these varying images of the subject presented in neo-Marxist and Foucauldian accounts (with the former illustrated by the considerably refined neo-Marxist analysis produced within *current* labour process theory). It will also examine the work of Elias as a way of beginning to address some of the problems of dealing with human agency which can be seen to occur with neo-Marxist and Foucauldian treatments.[6] At the same time, chapter 3 will try to produce a far wider theoretical background than that usually applied in thinking about stress and distress in the workplace.

The rest of the book plan is described below.

Book Plan

At the beginning of this chapter, I stated that I was concerned to explore how discourses such as that of stress relate to our subjectivity and our sense of ourselves, *and* also to critique and challenge the way in which we think about stress. The chapters that follow variously focus on one or other or both of these aspects of our project. Chapter 2 presents a historical analysis of the stress discourse through a detailed analysis of the development of the stressed subject. In so doing, it will attempt to substantiate the argument put forward in this chapter that the stressed subject is one who appears as largely ahistorical and decontextualized. At the same time, chapter 2 will provide a detailed introduction to those unfamiliar with the academic stress discourse, as well as asking those who are familiar with it to consider a rather different version of its history to that which is conventionally presented.

Chapter 3 will then attempt to develop a theoretical domain by which we can consider the stress discourse, viewing it from the perspective of labour process theory, Foucault and Elias. This chapter should also be of particular interest to those concerned with the issues of discourse, agency and subjectivity. It will not however try to produce some new all-encompassing meta-theory (a project which would in any case be contrary to the loosely deconstructionist tone of this book: Newton, 1994c). Rather the theoretical analysis forms a backdrop to discussions elsewhere in the book.

In chapter 4, we present a sharp contrast to the conventional image of the stressed subject. In this chapter, Jocelyn Handy draws on radical structural critique to show how different the text of the stress discourse might look if it were *not* written from an individualistic, and in consequence apolitical, perspective. This chapter particularly attends to the alternative image of stress that arises once we adopt a *collective* view of the subject. Chapter 5 analyses the stress management practices associated with the discourse, such as those of employee counselling, meditation, relaxation and bio-feedback. It also shows the constraints on the ability of the employee to manoeuvre in relation to such practices, and thus provides a further examination of the relationship between discourse, practice, power and agency. It particularly focuses on the manipulation and coercion of individuals and collectives that may accompany the deployment of employee counselling in employment settings. Together, chapters 4 and 5 present particularly criticial accounts of both stress discourse and practice.

Chapter 6 develops the discussion of emotion codes provided in chapter 3 (through reference to Elias). In this chapter, Stephen Fineman presents a social constructionist critique of the stress discourse by showing how it pays insufficient attention to the emotion codes that surround the expression of stress and distress at work. Through reference to examples drawn from the health service, social work, and the entertainment and airline industry, he illustrates both the explicit and implicit feeling rules which apply in different employment contexts, and the difficulties of intervening to try and change feeling rules.

Chapter 7 draws on all the preceding chapters to consider how we might write a different image of the stressed subject. The aim of this chapter is to show how this subject might be historicized, politicized, emotionalized, gendered and so on. At the same time, it will develop the arguments presented in chapter 6 in order to demonstrate how change and intervention in relation to work stress, distress and emotion are fraught and difficult affairs. Chapter 7 will also emphasize how the stress discourse needs to be seen in the context of related contemporary discourse (e.g. that relating to 'human growth'), and will try to explore further the question of why the stress discourse has been so successful.

Notes

1   Examining gender issues immediately raises the question of the kind of sociopolitical context in which discourse is established, a subject we shall return to in chapter 4. Certainly there does still seem to be something in old feminist critiques of women's magazines – for example, that of Faulder who argued that the difference between traditional women's magazines and those aimed at the more modern women such as *Cosmopolitan* is that the latter are 'just a more expensive and sexier version of the little woman out to get her man and keep him' (1977: 186). Though this is not true of every article, it is a theme that has hardly entirely disappeared.

2   In sampling theory terms, the methodology I followed was less than perfect. My 'sampling' was based on a few magazines that were lying around in my university department office and a few others belonging to friends, as well as scanning the magazine racks of my local Safeway. Nevertheless, I would argue that most of the themes presented are far from exclusive to these particular articles.

3   There are many similarities between the popular media treatment of stress and the way articles on sex are presented. Indeed, as the premier feature of many women's magazines, sex articles illustrate the parameters in which second-tier issues like stress and diet are set. In the glossy magazines, sexual normality is defined by our capacity both for (hetero)sexual desire and for fulfilment, both to have the flames of passion and to revel in their satisfaction. Glossy magazine articles ask questions such as 'Are you fit for sex?' (*She*, October 1992), or 'Can you psych yourself into sex?' (*Company*, March 1992). In order to avoid the abnormal and undesirable position of being non-sex-fit, they provide advice such as: 'Almost any aerobic exercise can produce benefits in the bedroom' (*She*, supplement, October 1992: 17). The suggestion here is not to actually use such exercise in the bedroom, but rather as a literal and metaphorical warm-up, since physical exercise and workouts are 'becoming the favoured method of foreplay for more and more people'. Obviously it is imperative that you join these more and more people, so that you too can have a normal, healthy, happy and liberating sex life. And to help you, nearly all of these monthly sex guides have a welter of experts in the field of sexuality ready to advise on 'what controls our sexual desire' (*Company*, March 1992: 50). The phrase 'according to experts' appears again and again, with articles calling on sex therapists, sex psychologists, endocrinologists and physiologists to account for our sexuality. If we follow their advice, we shall attain the land of healthy, happy, heterosexual coupledom, surely an ideal which we all aspire to: 'He puts his hand on her thigh and she

winks. At parties they like to flirt – with each other. You'd never guess that Tom, 33, and Sue, 30, have been together for seven years. Arms entwined, their body language says "passionate affair" not "married with children" ' (*She*, supplement, October 1992: 14). Though the normality of practice is usually portrayed as falling slightly short of these glowing ideals, the glossy magazines portray a normality of striving, of the need to be ever vigilant to the possibility of sexual slothfulness and flagging desires, encapsulated in phrases such as 'Are you fit for sex?" They are ever concerned to define what is completely normal. For example, they note how sex is related to stress: 'Sometimes, of course, the sheer stress of life is enough to make sex seem less interesting. Experts note that such fluctuations in desire are completely normal' (*Company*, March 1992: 52). Through these articles a holy triangle of normality, fitness and experts appears, with the last playing the role of both prescribing sexual behaviour and soothing away anxieties over our performance, the fluctuations on the road to the health, fulfilment and happiness which will come when we are sexually fit. It is exactly the same kind of conjunction that appears in the media representation of stress.

4 It's interesting to note that similar arguments about the modern lack of belongingness appear in the work of nco-human-relations writers such as Likert and McGregor, except that their accounts are not based on an extension of Marxist notions of alienation.

5 However, this self-examination and scrutiny is *not* such a thoroughly modern affair, and can just be seen as a process of secularization of the soul-searching which the educated classes have long undertaken in the hope of growth and salvation (symbolized perhaps by the monastic cell). In the spirit of the Protestant work ethic, the modern era may be more concerned with creating heaven on earth, or, in human growth terms, working on yourself so that you become all that you can be, self-actualize and so on.

6 The actor network theory of Callon and Latour can be seen as a step in this direction, albeit that their analysis tends to downplay power relations (Newton, 1994d).

2

Knowing Stress: From Eugenics to Work Reform

This chapter will analyse the subject that has been created within twentieth century stress discourse, and how this subject is expected to know stress. This analysis will lean towards a genealogy in that it will *not* assume that there is any linear (one historical building block upon another) development; yet it will also lean towards a more conventional history in that it will also *not* assume that 'accidents . . . accompany every beginning' (Foucault, 1984: 80). In sum, the stress discourse is seen as developing somewhat haphazardly, but each new twist is seen not as accidental but rather as being conditioned by, and established within, existing discourse and social relations.

The subject created within stress discourse appears as that of a person whose stress is chiefly a function of their own self, whether this is because of their instincts, their stress appraisal, their outmoded physiology or their sense of their psychological environment. Such a creation denies a number of alternatives, and in particular is decontextualized, apolitical, ahistorical and decollectivized. In displaying the rather heavy individualization inherent in the stress discourse, this chapter can also be seen as a specialized illustration of many of the themes of the 'psy' discursivities (e.g. psychology, psychotherapy, psychiatry: Rose, 1985; 1990).

Contrary to the impression created within celebratory histories of stress (e.g. Selye, 1950; 1956; 1976), as well as by historians of psychology (e.g. Hearnshaw, 1987), the discourse is seen here to very largely represent development since World War II. It is true that the word 'stress' has been in use for some time, as analyses of sources in the *Oxford English Dictionary* suggest.[1] However, the development of academic theories of stress remains largely confined to the post-war period. Whilst this chapter will attempt to demonstrate that stress is largely a post-war construction, particularly in its psychological sense, it will also examine the earlier sources that are cited in current celebratory histories of stress. Such accounts create the illusion that the major themes of stress discourse have a lengthy pedigree, and they help to foster the impression that current conceptions of stress represent the natural way to see stress. I shall start by focusing on two of these themes, namely the naturalization and individualization of stress discourse, and show how these themes link to particular writers celebrated within stress discourse.

Eugenics, Social Darwinism and Stress

Within existing histories of stress, the earliest figure associated with the establishment of stress as a legitimate subject for academic study is that of Walter Cannon, who used the term 'stress' to refer to patterns of physiological response of 'organisms' to emotional stimuli (e.g. Beehr and Franz, 1987). In some histories of stress, Cannon appears almost as a founding father, but this seems in many ways a strange choice. The problem with using Cannon in this way is that he hardly refers to stress at all. It is true that in his 1914 paper Cannon does refer to problems of 'great emotional stress', but his primary concern was with developing a physiological theory of emotions and of instincts. In relation to the former, there is some reference to stress, but it was not central to his theorizing. For example, in a 1935 paper entitled the 'Stresses and strains of homoeostasis', 'stress' refers to disruptive stimuli such as 'cold, lack of oxygen, low blood sugar, loss of blood' (1935: 6). It can be argued that such work represents a 'physiology of stress' (Mason, 1975), but even this seems misleading since the primary concern is with the physiology of *homoeostasis*, not with physiological stress *per se*. Certainly there is little concern with formulating any kind of psychosocial account of stress, either for its own sake, or to legitimate an interest in the physiology of stress.

That Cannon is referenced as a founding father is partly a reflection of his frequent citation by a figure who did go some way to popularizing a psychological notion of stress, namely Hans Selye (whose work is discussed below). Yet in spite of lying in the shadow of a later celebrant of stress, Cannon's work is still worth examining because of the way in which it is currently used in order to portray stress as a struggle between our 'outmoded' biological nature and the complexity of a modern and rapidly changing society, drawing on the argument that social problems are fundamentally about the limitations of our biology. This image of stress still represents a central theme in present stress conceptualization, and it is therefore worth paying some detailed attention to its historical antecedents. This will be done through outlining the work of Cannon, as well as that of an influential social psychologist contemporary, Graham Wallas.

Cannon, a Harvard Medical School professor, became interested in the physiology of instincts, an interest conditioned by ideas within social Darwinism, eugenics and the emerging social psychology (particularly the instinct theory of William McDougall).[2] Referencing Darwin, Cannon argued that instincts, such as fear and anger, arose because 'during the long course of racial experience they have developed for quick service in the struggle for existence' (1939: 195). Like eugenicists, he was concerned to prevent the degeneration of the population, and he believed that exercising certain instincts was vital to maintaining a healthy race, particularly the 'fighting instinct': 'We are concerned with the question of the fighting instinct and thus assuring the physical welfare of the race' (1939: 391). Influenced by writers such as Angell (1933), Cannon saw social problems deriving from the difficulty of satisfying instincts such as fighting instincts without recourse to war. Such a view appears as a logical corollary of a concept of social life as being both largely predicated on, and in continual struggle with, biology and nature. Thus he cites writers such as Angell who argued that: 'man's [sic] ultimate struggle is not with man but with nature, which includes human nature. Broadly speaking, to the degree that man fights man, he becomes a victim of nature' (1933: 160). The problem of fighting and wars is thus rooted *not* in social relations but in nature and biology, and it is here that the struggle must take place. In further support of this kind of argument Cannon cites the 'interesting suggestion . . . that nervous strain and restlessness [are] due to balked disposition' (1939: 380). Here Cannon is directly referencing another, less acknowledged, early twentieth century academic reference to stress from the work of the then prominent social psychologist, Wallas. The psychology historian Hearnshaw argues that, 'Far rather than McDougall, Graham Wallas deserves to be regarded as the first considerable British social psychologist' (1964: 116), and the ideas of Wallas are indeed worthy of some attention.

In his book *The Great Society*, Wallas argued that instinctual dispositions such as 'Curiosity, Property, Trial and Error, [and] Sex' had to be stimulated, for otherwise 'a state of nervous strain will result'. In illustrating the stress associated with unstimulated or balked dispositions, Wallas drew firmly on eugenicist and social Darwinist arguments. For example, he illustrated what he saw as the social problems of the 'casual labour quarters in London' where 'modern civilisation has so disastrously failed' (1914: 62). This failure of civilization arose because of weak and capricious stimulation of instincts such as hunger, love and heroism. In the uncivilized parts of London:

The babies are tugging at dirty india-rubber teats. The sweet-shops are selling hundredweights of bright-coloured stuff, which excites the appetite of the children without nourishing their bodies. That pale-faced boy first knew love, not when he looked at a girl whom later he might marry, but when a dirty picture post-card caught his eye or he watched a suggestive film. His dreams of heroism are satisfied by halfpenny romances, half criminal and half absurd. (1914: 62–3)

Appropriate stimulation of the instincts thus not only is an academic concern, but is vital to preventing a further degeneration of the population, particularly among the lower classes. Similar concerns of potential evolutionary calamity were noted by Cannon, who cited the argument of 'militarists' that 'without wars nations become effete, their ideals become tarnished, the people sink into self-indulgence, their wills weaken and soften in luxury' (1939: 379). Although Cannon argued against such an inevitability of war, he nevertheless agreed with the argument that people must struggle for their existence through stimulating and satisfying instincts, as otherwise population degeneration would result. Both Wallas and Cannon argued that social engineering was vital in preventing population degeneration. Social control was necessary in order to maintain the health of the race; and since, for Cannon, the social was itself predicated on the biological, the methods of biology and physiology could be productively applied in the service of 'social homoeostasis'.[3]

To sum up, the primary concern of Cannon and Wallas lay with instincts, and the question of whether or not instincts were appropriately satisfied, a crucial issue given the dangers of war and population degeneration. Throughout they present an image of the naturalism of human behaviour, wherein the social is largely dependent on the biological. And what is striking about subsequent stress discourse is how it has continued and reinforced this naturalism. I shall explore this elsewhere in this chapter, but for now it can be graphically illustrated through analysing the way in which Cannon is currently applied in stress discourse and practice. He is now most commonly cited in relation to the 'fight/flight' instinct, where the 'emotion of fear is associated with the instinct for flight, and the emotion of anger or rage with the instinct for fighting or attack' (Cannon, 1914: 264).[4] A common part of present-day introductions to stress fitness programmes is some reference to the fight/flight instinct, noting how, whilst this instinct may have been appropriate to Stone Age people, it is highly inappropriate to the modern age. The stress management guide of Arroba and James provides one illustration: 'Modern offices and factories may be very different from the environments our ancestors inhabited, but our bodies are still programmed to cope with primitive and dangerous places' (1987: 6). Benson gives us another:

> Although the fight-or-flight response is still a necessary and useful physiologic feature for survival, the stresses of today's society have led to its excessive elicitation; at the same time, its behavioral features, such as running or fighting, are usually socially inappropriate or unacceptable . . . Those who experience greater environmental stress and, therefore, more frequent elicitation of the fight-or-flight response have a greater chance of developing chronic hypertension (that is, chronic high blood pressure). (1979: 143)

This idea of Stone Age man suffering in the modern-day office is very popular, with an intuitive appeal and the advantage of simplicity. However there are a number of limitations to it deriving from its glorification of nature and natural instincts. Firstly, the image it presents of 'primitive societies' is one where a social world almost ceases to exist. What is portrayed is a society where life is very simple, and the only stressors are from the occasional meeting with a dangerous animal. In this society there are few social stressors, and one can only assume either that people did not talk to each other, or that they lived in peaceful harmony because somehow or another life was socially extremely simple. In contrast, modern society is so complex that for today's individuals, 'the benefits of a good night's sleep may elude them owing to the brain's furious activity in trying to deal with its problems' (De Board, 1978: 113). We are now caught up in a far more complex *and* social world, yet the explanation for our stresses does not fundamentally lie in this social complexity but is a result of our natural, but outmoded, animal instincts.

Although often cited in the stress literature, this kind of argument is extremely tenuous. As Pollock noted, 'it is hard to see on what grounds we could be justified in assuming that the populations of non-industrialized societies carry a lighter burden of stress' (1988: 388). Certainly anthropological research indicates that pre-industrial societies are just as complex in their social nature as industrial societies (Sahlins, 1972). Yet what the current Stone Age theme in stress discourse does is to reinforce Cannon's argument that social life is largely predicated on, and is in continual struggle with, biology and nature – an argument which, as we have seen, echoes eugenicist and social Darwinist concerns. Whilst we have developed technologically and socially, we are still animals underneath, and to understand our psyche we must understand our true nature, our instinctual needs.[5] The implication is that if our nature had evolved sufficiently, we would have no problems with the modern age. Conflict in organizations would be a thing of the past, because anger and rage, or anxiety and fear, would no longer be aroused by unpleasant and outmoded instincts. We would experience no stress from our work tasks, or from working with our colleagues, or from the struggles between capital and labour, because the *internal* mechanisms causing stress would have been eliminated.

This biological explanation of stress also provides for an individualization of stress, since it firstly places responsibility for stress on our (biological) selves, and secondly tells us that there is nothing we can do about it except for trying to modify our outmoded instincts (by, say, stress management exercises which may reduce the 'cumulative effects' of anger and anxiety). The complexity of the modern age is taken as given, as an inevitable aspect of human evolution and the rapid development of tools and technology. Individuals are seen as having very little part in the reproduction of this society, but rather must buckle down and address the problems in themselves and their unfortunate inheritance of outworn instincts. In sum, the Stone Age argument has notable parallels with the assumptions of the popular media presentation of stress, with its onus on the *individual* to deal with the seeming inevitability of a natural stress (see chapter 1).

Creating Stress: Hans Selye

Most writers credit the academic emergence of the stress concept as lying partly with the work of Walter Cannon, but most importantly with that of Hans Selye (e.g. Mason, 1975; Hearnshaw, 1987). For example, Hearnshaw argued that 'the wider concept of stress was not clearly formulated until 1926 when a Prague medical student, H. Selye, introduced it' (1987: 209).

That Selye should have formulated a stress theory prior to World War II seems surprising since, as we shall see, the war was highly significant in energizing discourse relating to mental health and stress. Before the war, stress received very little attention from what might be expected to be its natural constituency, psychology and occupational psychology. The closest to stress theorizing that one can come in pre-war occupational psychology is fatigue studies which long formed a central part of its subject matter (Munsterberg, 1913; Muscio, 1920), and Hearnshaw has argued that fatigue studies were the earliest precursors of current stress discourse (1987: 208–9). Yet fatigue studies were primarily concerned with issues relating to job tasks and to performance and 'industrial efficiency' (e.g. the effect of rest pauses), so providing a psychological answer to Taylor's scientific management and to the problem of ensuring the efficiency of munitions workers in World War I (Muscio, 1920: 46). Furthermore, the closest one comes in fatigue studies to anything resembling stress is reference to nervous fatigue. But this was very limited in theorizing, and largely just constituted a defensive posture against the impact of the Hawthorne studies, which had suggested that performance might be about more than just the design of rest pauses, lighting and so on.[6]

Similarly it seems inappropriate to credit Selye with a pre-war theory of stress, particularly if one is concerned with the history of *psychological* stress. It is true that he did use the word 'stress' in a paper in 1935, but at this stage its use was not associated with a theory (Selye and McKeown, 1935; Selye, 1952: 20). In his most detailed account of the 'history of stress', Selye (1976) notes that the first formulation of what *later* became his stress *theory* lay in a very brief article published in *Nature* in 1936 (Selye, 1936a). He also documents three other articles published before the war (Selye, 1936b; Selye and Collip, 1936; Selye, 1937). Yet, what is most noticeable about these pre-war articles is that none of them make any reference to stress.

So why did Selye historically construct his interest in stress theorizing as lying before the war when, in the critical papers laying out (what is *later* labelled) a stress theory, there is no mention of stress? Selye gives us an answer in the 1952 publication of a series of his stress lectures, *The Story of the Adaptation Syndrome*. There he explains that he abandoned the term before the war because it created 'adverse public opinion', and because 'there was too much criticism of my use of the word "stress" for endocrine and other non-specific somatic reactions' (1952: 33).[7] Selye argued that gradually reference to stress became more acceptable: 'through habit rather than logic . . . the term slipped into common usage, as the concept itself became a popular subject for research' (1952: 41). What Selye did not explain however was quite why this habit appears to have been learnt sometime in the period between 1937 and 1946. For by 1946 Selye is again using the dreaded term 'stress' (e.g. 1946: 119), and by 1950 Selye has happily titled his 1025 page epic *Stress*.

In effect, Selye does not outline any stress theory until immediately after the war (in his 1946 article), supposedly because his public had not formed the habit of it, which seemingly is 'learnt' during the war. His comments therefore suggest that the war was critical to public acceptance of the relevance of stress as a legitimate explanatory concept (an argument which I shall further support below). For now, the question that remains is whether Selye's theorizing does deserve the label 'stress' (i.e. whether his pre-war critics were right:

see above). To answer this question a brief account of the basics of his stress theory, the general adaptation syndrome (GAS), is necessary.

The GAS is essentially a physiological theory which asserts that animals exhibit a *non-specific* physiological response to the stressful demands, or stressors, placed upon them, namely that there is a commonality of response to a diverse range of demands such as cold, heat and exercise (a theory which has been subject to some criticism[8]). The impetus for his theory came from research into scx hormones, in the process of which he observed a very similar pattern of morphological changes from both the injection of the extracts of cattle ovaries and the injection of formalin. He further found that other extracts, such as from kidneys or from the spleen, produced the same pattern of response. The message therefore in Selye's research was that there was a common 'non-spccific' physiological response to 'noxious agents' which he summarized in his theory of the GAS. The question again is whether these noxious agents deserve the label 'stress'. Certainly, in his immediate post-war work there is only limited theorizing about stressors; rather they just appear as the noxious things in the environment which lead to non-specific physiological response. And the GAS has remained essentially the same in having a poorly differentiated notion of stress (Selye, 1976). But what did change was that Selye began to wrap the GAS up in implicit psychosocial explanations of stress. For example he opened his 1956 book, *The Stress of Life*, with the following little homilies:

> The soldier who sustains wounds in battle, the mother who worries about her soldier son, the gambler who watches the races, the horse and the jockcy he bet on; they are all under stress.

> The beggar who suffers from hunger and the glutton who over-eats, the little shopkeeper with his constant fears of bankruptcy and the rich merchant for yet another: they are also under stress.

> The housewife who tries to keep her children out of trouble, the child who scalds himself – and especially the particular cells of the skin over which he spilled the boiling coffee – they too, are under stress.

> This is a fundamental question in the life of everyone; it touches closely upon the essence of life and disease. (1956: 4)

In developing these psychosocial images of stress, it seems likely that Selye was influenced by the growing post-war attention to the psychology of stress. For example, he was a contributor to a volume edited by Wolff et al. in 1950 (*Life Stress and Bodily Disease*) where, though much of the concern remains physiological, several papers also explored psychological stress in relation to 'life events',

'anxiety factors', 'emotions' and 'personality factors'. But as significant as the psychological legitimation of stress provided by Selye
was his attempt to create the perfect truth effect around stress (see
chapter 3). Increasingly he portrayed stress in essentialist terms as a
natural semi-instinctive response. For example, he declared that
'the concept of stress is very old', so that 'it must have even occurred
to prehistoric man' who would surely have known stress when he
'realized that he had exceeded the limits of what he could reasonably handle' (1976: 3).

In sum, whilst Selye's GAS theory remained essentially a theory
of *physiological* non-specific response patterns, attached to his
theorizing was the promotion of stress as *the* significant sociological,
and especially psychological, problem of the mid to late twentieth
century.[9] Selye cannot be credited with creating the stress concept
which, as we shall see, appears significantly related to the experiences of the war (and his promotion of the concept is in any case
almost exclusively post-war). Yet he could not be blamed for *not*
trying to promote it as the fundamental question, and have us
believe that it is almost as significant as sex in achieving healthy lives
(see chapter 3). And with psychologists, this propaganda does
appear to have been effective. For example, Appley and Trumbull
argued that after Selye's 1955 *invited* address to the American
Psychological Association, his use of the 'stress' term and his stress
theory were 'applied widely, though largely uncritically by clinical
and experimental psychologists alike' (1986: 5). This positive
reception by psychologists is not surprising given certain central
implicit reference points of his theorizing, namely its individualization and naturalism – themes which resonated (and still resonate)
with much psychological theory. As Pollock has noted (1988: 385),
Selye suggested that it is up to individuals to avoid the damaging
extremes of either too much or too little stress, by learning to
control the foe within ourselves:

> We are on our guard against external intoxicants, but hormones are part
> of our bodies; it takes wisdom to recognise and overcome the foe who
> fights from *within*. In all our actions throughout the day we must
> consciously look for signs of being keyed up too much – and we must
> learn to stop in time. (1956: 265, my italics; quoted in Pollock, 1988: 388)

Such arguments strongly echo those of Cannon with the same
depiction of the continual struggle between ourselves and our
(outdated) biology. They reinforce the naturalist account of stress
wherein social life is seen as predicated upon the biological, with the
consequence that an understanding of stress can 'guide our actions
in conformity with natural laws' (Selye, 1956: 4).

Given that Selye combined this emphasis upon individualism and naturalism, it does not appear surprising that his invited address to the 1955 American Psychological Association was well received. Meanwhile, Selye provided one final element to raise the significance of stress, through arguing that stress can cause ill-health and disease (Pollock, 1988). As propaganda this argument can be seen as replacing the kind of eugenicist concerns witnessed in Cannon and Wallas with a more modern concern with the promotion of life and health (Foucault, 1981). Selye can be seen as making a claim for the 'bio-power' of stress based on its ability to promote 'normal' psychophysiological health (see chapter 3), a claim which still forms a central component of its legitimation (for example, one principal defence of the need for occupational stress research is that workplace stress causes ill-health). The stress–health relationship remains however far from clear (Kasl, 1983; Karasek et al., 1987; Kessler, 1987; Cohen and Williamson, 1991), and as Pollock (1988) and Briner and Reynolds (1993) argue, the link between stress and illness remains a highly questionable assumption. As Mason (1975) has noted, Selye was himself not even successful in finding the 'first mediators' of stress, namely the agents which are responsible for the same non-specific response to a diversity of stimuli.

Creating Psychological Stress: Laboratory Research

Work on 'psychological stress' is more difficult to neatly define than the biological and physiological emphasis of Cannon and Selye because of the diversity of discursive influences. Commenting in 1964, Cofer and Appley noted that: 'stress has been used as a synonym for anxiety, conflict, ego-involvement, frustration, threat, and emotionality, generally, depending on a given writer's particular predilections' (1964: 449).

The aim here is to differentiate between some of these varying definitions of psychological stress, and to examine their level of impact on subsequent discourse development. During the 1950s there were two important developments: laboratory research and psychodynamic work. Laboratory research on stress will be examined in this section, but discussion of psychodynamic work will be deferred to later in the chapter because it stands in marked contrast to other developments in stress research.

In a discursive sense, the development of laboratory research of stress can be seen as conditioned by the rise of *non*-physiological experimental psychology. As Danziger has noted, the first psychological laboratory created by Wilhelm Wundt in the late 1870s drew directly on experimental physiology to the extent that 'the term "physiological psychology" often functioned as a synonym for experimental psychology' (1990: 24). By the mid twentieth century, however, non-physiological experimental psychology was well established in areas such as motivation, learning, perception and human performance.[10]

To the extent that non-physiological experimental psychology appeared increasingly dominant within post-war psychology, it is not surprising that research on stress should be undertaken within this discursive framework. By itself, however, this doesn't explain the post-war interest in stress, an explanation for which lies more in the war itself. As Rose (1990) noted, psychology and psychiatry made a major impact during the war, especially in the USA. Rose quotes Eisenhower's comments on the wartime application of psychology and psychiatry:

> In this war, which was Total in every sense of the word, we have seen many great changes in military science. It seems to me that not the least of these was the development of psychological warfare as a specific and effective weapon . . . Without doubt psychological warfare has proved its right to a place of dignity in our military arsenal. (Dwight D. Eisenhower, cited in Rose, 1990: 33)

Aside from the propaganda effort, considerable attention was paid to the selection of army personnel, to the influence of group psychology on combat units, and to the maintenance of morale amongst the Allies (Newton, 1994a). At the same time, there was attention to the 'psychoneuroses' associated with war amongst both soldiers and civilians (Gillespie, 1942; Ellery, 1945; Air Ministry, 1947), restimulating the interest in psychiatry and psychotherapy occasioned by the First World War (Ahrenfeldt, 1958; Stone, 1985). In part, this reascendance of psychiatry and psychology was aided by fears that the (then) new aerial bombing of the Second World War would produce large-scale mental breakdown and neuroses in the civilian population, a fear that was subsequently found to be largely unwarranted. And within this wartime psychoneuroses literature there was also a concern with stress. For example, Ellery attempted to document 'psychiatric reactions to stress' (1945: 61). Similarly a consultant neuropsychiatrist and British Air Vice-Marshal, Sir Charles Symonds, gave a lecture on 'The human response to flying stress' at Harvard University in March 1943, and at the Royal College of Physicians, London, in May 1943 (Symonds, 1947). Commissioned by the RAND corporation, Irving Janis assessed the intense emotional stresses thought to be occasioned by air raids (though noting that, barring the atomic bomb attacks on Hiroshima and Nagasaki, there were few large-scale psychiatric disorders associated with air bombardment: 1951: 72–83).

Whilst a concern with stress appeared in this psychoneuroses literature, there was very little development of anything resembling a stress theory. To a large extent, stress was synonymous with combat fear, and the concern of psychiatrists was chiefly with what they saw as neurotic or psychopathic predispositions to such stress.[11] Nevertheless some stress technology did develop during the war. In the US, psychologists at the Office of Strategic Services (OSS) developed a series of stress tests in order to 'select men who would be most effective in intelligence operation in enemy territory during World War II' (Lazarus et al., 1952: 308–9). The OSS was set up by Congress in 1942 and, as well as maintaining 'an elaborate network of [intelligence] agents', its aim was to plan 'destructive operations behind enemy lines, to aid and train resistance groups, and by radio, pamphlets and other means, to disintegrate the morale of enemy troops and encourage the forces of the underground' (OSS Assessment Staff, 1948: 10). The OSS Assessment Staff devised an elaborate series of selection exercises with the aim of selecting agents who would be able to cope with the stresses of maintaining cover, and possibly being interrogated by enemy forces overseas. This need is shown in an anonymous excerpt illustrating the 'task information' that was supplied to OSS Assessment Staff relating to recruits who would be deployed in China:

> We simply must have men who can shoulder responsibility and use initiative with common sense. Simply because a man has intelligence does not qualify him for this type of work. In some instances we also have had men who fall into the class of the high-strung or emotional type. We simply cannot use men of that type in the field when they have to live with Chinese, eat Chinese food, and be under pressure at times. In most cases these men have suffered nervous breakdowns and other nervous ailments. Whether men are recruited in the States or here in the field they must be checked by a doctor and a psychiatrist before being pronounced fit for the field. The check by a psychiatrist is especially desirable. (1948: 13)

This quote illustrates part of the military rationale that was supportive of psychiatry and the investigation of psychoneuroses during the war (see above). But the OSS Assessment Staff did not respond to such demands by simply instituting a 'check by a psychiatrist'. In part, this may have been because whilst they were composed of psychologists and psychiatrists, they were slightly dominated by the former (1948: v–vii). Included in the OSS Assessment Staff were such psychology notables as Robert Chin,[12] Donald Fiske, Edward Tolman and Theodore Newcomb, whilst Kurt Lewin counted amongst the consultants to the OSS.[13] In part it was also because the OSS had a 'particular debt to the band of imaginative and progressive psychiatrists and psychologists who devised and conducted the War Office Selection Board (WOSB) program for testing officer candidates for the British Army' (1948: 3) – most of whom were associated with the Tavistock (see Miller and Rose, 1988; Newton, 1994a). The OSS Assessment Staff both used WOSB procedures, but also devised many additional exercises including the stress interview and the post-stress interview. These latter exercises were particularly concerned to address the 'emotional stability under strain' (OSS Assessment Staff, 1948: 137) of would-be agents, factors such as their 'ability to govern disturbing emotions, steadiness and endurance under pressure, snafu tolerance [i.e. tolerance of chaotic conditions], freedom from neurotic tendencies' (1948: 30). The stress interview and post-stress interview assessed this ability by what, in effect, was a job simulation, asking candidates to maintain a cover story (as real-life intelligence agents might be expected to do), and then subjecting them to a gruelling and cunning series of interrogations to assess both how they coped (and hence their 'emotional stability'), and whether they would 'break cover'.

Whilst the work of the OSS Assessment Staff did not lead to well-developed stress theory, the attention to stress provided by the OSS work was further reinforced by the development of similar 'stress tests' in the US Army Air Forces Psychology Program in order to help select effective pilots (Melton, 1947). However this work appears far less conditioned by WOSB than OSS work, and far more influenced by experimental psychology. The emphasis was on the selection of pilots through testing their task performance in a laboratory environment when subject to stressors such as loud sounds, verbal threats or distracting tasks (e.g. 1947: 502).

It was this laboratory variant of wartime stress research that was promoted after the war. In particular, the US Air Force funded a major research programme by Richard Lazarus and his psychologist colleagues into the effects of stress upon laboratory task performance (Lazarus et al., 1952; Lazarus and Eriksen, 1952). From the outset, this was a research programme with a clear military connection, as exampled by the way in which Lazarus et al. opened their influential stress review article:

An understanding of the effect of psychological stress upon skilled performance is of great theoretical and practical importance. People are often faced with the necessity of performing skilled work under conditions which are highly stressful. Such is obviously the case in military combat. The effectiveness of a pilot, gunner, or radar observer must be maintained even when he is threatened by physical injury or harassed by the need to hurry the performance of a complicated task. The obvious fact that human beings are required to work under stress does not call for further elaboration. (1952: 293)

This quotation illustrates both the post-war confidence in the belief in stress as an important area of study, and how that confidence was related to the recent experience of war, wherein the assumed importance of stress to the performance of pilots, gunners and others means that there is no need for further elaboration of its relevance.

In a manner reminiscent of Selye, the post-war research programme of Lazarus and his colleagues made a determined attempt at discursive colonization, wherein the concept of stress was well and truly spread over the surface of pre-existing experimental psychology discourse. For example, Lazarus et al. (1952) referred to a number of studies which, they alleged, illustrated performance under stress, even though the original articles don't even mention the word 'stress' at all. Where the original research did refer to stress, its chief concern was generally with some more traditional interest of experimental psychology such as perception, and the use of the word 'stress' merely referred to the experimentally induced performance difficulties hypothesized to affect, say, perception (e.g. Postman and Bruner, 1948; cf. Selye, 1946). The rationalization of this interest in stress therefore appears not as dependent on some pre-existing body of work, which might have suggested interesting theoretical questions, but rather as primarily occasioned by the military concerns generated by the war. Similarly the research designs of Lazarus and his colleagues also appeared to reflect military demands through their focus on the relationship between stress and task performance. Conventionally within psychology the fact that the primary concern of Lazarus et al. was with task performance would probably be seen as reflecting arguments to use clear outcome measures. However, it is also conveniently in keeping with the primary concern of the military *vis-à-vis* stress, namely the ability of the combatant to maintain effective task performance *whilst* subject to the stresses of war. In sum, the beginnings of post-war laboratory research interest in stress appear more likely to reflect military concerns during the war (and post-war military funding) than a discursive development of pre-existing theoretical traditions within experimental psychology.[14]

Creating Work Stress: Role Stress Theory

By the end of the 1950s, stress as a legitimate subject of academic study had arrived. To take just one reflection of this, in the UK, the

Mental Health Research Fund hosted a four-day conference on stress and psychiatric disorder at Lincoln College, Oxford in July 1958 (Tanner, 1960). The reference to psychiatry in the title appears as a reflection of the dominance of psychiatry in the wartime creation of stress in the UK (see above), and within the mental health and mental hygiene movement (Rose, 1985; 1990). Yet the conference was also attended by physiologists (including Hans Selye), animal experimenters and psychologists. In the early 1960s, research into work stress began to appear, and given that this is the primary concern of this book, the remainder of the chapter will focus on it. As we shall see, the emerging work stress literature embodied many of the images of the stressed subject that were *already* written into stress discourse; this subject was very largely apolitical, ahistorical and individualistic rather than collectivized.

Centred around the University of Michigan, there developed a theoretical approach to stress which came to define and dominate work stress research over the next two decades, focused on the idea of 'role stress'. At the same time, an alternative, yet largely ignored, approach to psychological stress developed amongst Scandinavian researchers. Since this latter work stands in marked contrast to mainstream accounts, it will be considered later along with socio-psychoanalytic research on work stress.

The definitive study of role stress was that of Kahn et al. (1964), entitled *Organizational Stress: Studies in Role Conflict and Ambi-guity*, a study that was to spawn a minor industry in work stress research. For example, just focusing on the period between 1970 and 1983, Jackson and Schuler located *200* articles relating to role stress (1985: 18). Given the prominence of role stress within the occupational stress literature, it is worth giving some detailed attention to it, and the way in which it has been both developed *and* constrained.

If one wants to pursue a (broken) line of development, role stress research is perhaps best understood as discursively situated within what Michael Rose calls the psychological wing of the US human relations movement (1988: 175), and particularly within the work of the Survey Research Center (SRC) of the Institute of Social Research at the University of Michigan. As Rose notes, the SRC, founded in 1947, had similar aims to the Tavistock Institute of Human Relations, with a particular focus on human relations within organizations. Rensis Likert headed a programme of research in this area from 1947 onwards (Katz and Kahn, 1966: vii) which was 'concerned with the relationship of leadership and organization structure to the productivity of functioning organizations and to the satisfactions and dissatisfactions experienced by their members'

(Likert and Campbell, 1951; Likert was then director of the Institute for Social Research, and Campbell was director of the Survey Research Center). This quote neatly illustrated the unitary harmony that their work aspired to, an alliance of economic efficiency and the morale and welfare of workers, well expressed in classic neo-human-relations texts such as Likert's (1961) *New Patterns of Management* and McGregor's (1960) *The Human Side of Enterprise*.

The first study of the SRC was an investigation of group productivity and morale at the Prudential Insurance Company, a study which directly credited the Hawthorne studies, and the 'pioneer work . . . carried on by Mayo and Roethlisberger', but sought a more scientific approach which attended to the psychology of 'employee feelings, attitudes and values' through a particular concern with 'relationships between *measures* of the psychological factors and *measures* of group performance' (Katz et al., 1950: 2– 3).[15] This and later studies indicated that high-performance groups were led by supervisors who were employee oriented rather than production oriented and who avoided overly close supervision. As well as being the discursive forerunner of a major neo-human-relations industry on leadership (e.g. the work of McGregor, Likert and Argyris), these studies also stimulated theoretical debate within the SRC. And in the first special issue of the *Journal of Social Issues* to report on the work of the SRC, Jacobsen et al. drew on role theory to explain the findings of the early SRC studies, arguing that issues surrounding role expectations could explain a 'supervisor's behaviour . . . and . . . the attitudes of those who work with supervisors' (1951: 18). Jacobsen et al. paid particular attention to the problem of 'role conflict', as well as outlining a methodology of role analysis.

The ideas for role stress theory were first put forward in a special issue of the *Journal of Social Issues* published in 1962, published by the Society for the Psychological Study of Social Issues, a society long associated with the promotion of human relations ideas *within* a social psychological framework influenced by the work of Kurt Lewin (there was a close association between the SRC and Lewin's Research Center for Group Dynamics which moved to the University of Michigan[16]). Much of the later theorizing on role stress is laid out in a paper by French and Kahn (1962) published in this special issue. This paper particularly emphasized Lewin's social psychology and the importance of mental health,[17] drawing directly on post-war studies into the mental health of the industrial worker (e.g. Fraser, 1947; Walker and Guest, 1952), particularly the social psychological variant of this work (e.g. Jahoda, 1955; 1958; Kornhauser, 1960).[18] The 1962 French and Kahn paper also particularly emphasized the relevance of role theory, in part because the role concept appeared to provide a route through the complexity of organizations and individuals. As Katz and Kahn were to argue:

> To the extent that choice of concepts can contribute to so complex a synthesis, the concept of role is singularly promising. It is at once the building block of social systems and the summation of the requirements with which the system confronts the individual member. Indeed, it has been touted for a generation as the example of a concept uniquely fitted to social-psychological investigations and theory. (Katz and Kahn, 1966: 171)

With arguments like this, how could Kahn et al. have looked at anything else in their subsequent 'definitive' study of role stress? However, they picked a very particular Lewinian concept of role, which can be seen as having particular consequences for how the stressed subject was subsequently articulated within much of stress theory and research. Their role concept was very different to that applied within earlier SRC studies. For example, for SRC researchers such as Jacobsen et al., 'role conflict refers to cultural discrepancies and does *not* imply that the subject of the discrepant expectations necessarily perceives them or experiences psychological conflict as a result of them' (1951: 22–3, my italics). In contrast, for Kahn et al. (1964) role stress is defined in exactly the kind of subjective/perceptual terms that Jacobsen et al. denied: namely, it is what the subject perceives and experiences that now matters. This emphasis in their theory can be seen as a consequence of their reassertion of Lewinian theory in interpreting role expectations, a shift which was highly significant in furthering the individualization of the stress discourse. For example, for most writers on role theory, the concept of role provided a means of looking at the way social relations were structured, on the basis of the social status that someone occupied: 'the statuses of physician, husband, father, professor, church elder, Conservative Party member' (Merton, 1957: 111). Within this kind of role concept, social behaviour remains 'part of a predefined social context' (Burrell and Morgan, 1979: 91), wherein key aspects of social relations (such as roles) can be predicted from the social position an individual occupies. Yet such a social structuralist notion stands in stark contrast to the approach of role stress researchers, where the main emphasis was *not* on the structural features of any particular role, but on the individual's *perception* of them. Thus Kahn et al. stated: 'We are concerned with role conflict as a fact in the environment of the person and as a fact in his *internal, psychological life*' (1964: 19, my italics), a notion which draws directly from the Lewinian concept of life space wherein behaviour is seen as occurring through the interaction of the individual and her *psychological* environment (Lewin, 1952).[19] One way of illustrating the theoretical consequences of this Lewinian emphasis is to examine some of the possible avenues for discourse development which were *not* followed by stress researchers in the 1960s, 1970s and 1980s. What is interesting here is that research had already been published which emphasized social structure rather than individual perception. One such example is found in the work of Dohrenwend (1961) who drew on Selye's distinction between stressors and strains, yet argued that the stressor–strain relationship was mediated by inner *and* external constraints.[20] By inner constraints Dohrenwend denoted an area to some extent covered elsewhere in occupational stress theorizing: the individual's drives, desires and internalized rules. In contrast, external constraints referred to a concern that is still largely overlooked, the effect of social stratification, especially social class and race.

Dohrenwend became interested in the idea of external constraints as a result of a study he undertook looking at the stress experienced by '1800 New York City families who found themselves [living] in the path of improvements being made in the approach to a major bridge' (1961: 297), and as a consequence had to relocate. He observed that the families' ability to cope with this stressor was dependent not just on their individual needs and abilities but on external constraints that derived from their position in the class structure and their ethnic background. Put simply, those were white and from wealthier backgrounds found less difficulty in relocating than those who were poor, or were black or hispanic.[21] Such external constraints seriously affected coping ability, and Dohrenwend noted that it seemed likely that these were not the only forms of constraint, suggesting other factors such as gender and age (1961: 299). He concluded that external constraint depended on the norms of others in the individual's relational system (cf. role theory), but that it also 'varies inversely with status as defined by the wider society, and directly with the relative deprivation experienced by the individual as he compares his position to that of others in the situation' (1961: 297).[22]

In comparison with the work of Kahn et al., Dohrenwend thus presented an analysis of stress which was attentive both to social structure and to political inequalities related to race, gender, age and income. Kahn et al. conveniently avoided such issues by using a rather idiosyncratic version of role theory, whose primary concern was the psychological environment as perceived by the individual rather than social structure. And although there has been some re-examination of their work (Newton and Keenan, 1987), there has been little serious questioning of their highly apolitical role concept (in spite of the vast number of studies which have applied it). The question that remains is why stress researchers have been so faithful to this concept, particularly given the alternatives already on offer in the early 1960s, and given the subsequent criticism of role theory. On the one hand, there have been refinements in role theorizing (e.g. Dahrendorf, 1968). On the other hand, there have been criticisms of the underlying determinism of role theory, and arguments that roles involve creativity as much as conformity. Salaman (1980) cites John Urry as an example of one proponent of the argument that people are 'interpretative and purposive agents within their social world, [so that] role-taking is not only the result of pre-existing social norms' (Salaman, 1980: 139). As Crozier and Friedberg (1980) later argued, 'the ability to depart from the expectations and norms associated with one's "role" is an advantage and a source of power "opening" the possibility for bargaining'. They continue:

> everyone seems capable of profiting from the ambiguities, incoherences, and contradictions inherent in his role.
> The best exponents of the structuro-functionalist approach, such as Robert Kahn and his colleagues [1964], are prevented by their theory from recognizing this fact. As faithful adherents of the clarity and coherence of roles, they diagnose situations of role conflict as 'abnormal', if not pathological. For them, role conflicts and ambiguities are instances of *stress* and hence appear as important sources of modern anxieties. They fail to notice that the pathological cases who experience these ambiguities and contradictions are always persons who are in an inferior position, as distinct from the winners or stronger opponents. (1980: 49)

In a similar vein, Salaman noted that:

> The idea of organizational roles frequently carries the implication of the organization as an integrated, or emergent, production with all members (actors) contributing their bit. This conception is probably particularly attractive to managers . . . It is far less applicable to those members or organizations whose work experience leads them to conceptualize the enterprise in terms of conflict rather than cooperation. (1980: 140)

Given that the initial aim of the SRC was to harmoniously marry productivity and morale (see above), we should perhaps not be altogether surprised that subsequent SRC researchers should apply an individualized concept of role within a new welfare language of stress. That the concept subsequently spawned a minor research industry is in part due to the way in which this individualism and apoliticism resonated with the central assumptions of both organizational psychology and much of personnel management practice (see chapter 3). It may also be because of the ease with which role stress research could be undertaken, with articles mass produced off a seemingly never-ending production line. Within this quickly serviceable modernist machine, all that was needed was a questionnaire in order to publish, with attention to empirical requirements sometimes remaining pretty lax (for example, measurements of work stressors and psychological strain were often poorly differentiated, from the seminal work of Kahn et al., 1964 onwards: see Kasl, 1978; Newton, 1989). It is not of course that all stress research has been so programmatic, and a small amount of qualitative research has been undertaken (e.g. Dewe et al., 1979; Newton and Keenan, 1985). Nevertheless this machine research is an identifiable feature of both stress and other organizational psychology research. Regrettably the articles rolling off the stress production line exhibited very little theoretical scrutiny of role theory, and almost no questioning of the individualism and apoliticism which so defines this work.

Socio-psychodynamic Research

As noted above, there have been two discursive developments that represent alternatives to mainstream stress research, namely the psychodynamic work of the 1950s, and the Scandinavian research that developed from the 1960s onward. Both of these alternative discourses will be briefly considered in order to explore further the theoretical avenues which have been sidelined within mainstream stress discourse. This section considers socio-psychodynamic research.

The psychodynamic work on stress is particularly associated with the Tavistock Institute of Human Relations (Miller and Rose, 1988). This work has been almost entirely ignored by mainstream stress researchers. This is not however because those of a more socio-psychoanalytic persuasion have not attempted to capture stress, and rewrite it in their own terms. For example, at the 1958 Oxford conference on stress and psychiatric disorder (see above), Jock Sutherland, then Director of the Tavistock Clinic, attempted to demonstrate the relevance of the Tavistock's work to an understanding of stress, with particular reference to psychoanalysis and the use of applied analytic methods (Sutherland, 1960). At the same conference, Eric Trist, of the Tavistock Institute of Human Relations, attempted to show the relevance of the socio-technical systems approach developed in their classic series of studies of the British coal-mining industry (Trist and Bamforth, 1951). Trist argued that their research showed 'how the response of the human to stress is affected by a specifically social factor, the form of group organization or social structure' (Sutherland, 1960: 115). As this quote suggests, this approach employed a very different conception of the stressed subject, one which was less individualized and more dependent upon organization and social structure. And the work of the Tavistock researchers is worth exploring further in order to illustrate just how different this subject appears.

Like the laboratory work on stress, the military demands of World War II were central to the focus of the earlier Tavistock Clinic (which split in 1947, with the clinic incorporated into the National Health Service, and the Social Department becoming the independent Tavistock Institute of Social Relations: see Miller and Rose, 1988; Trist and Murray, 1990). Menzies Lyth's (1988) classic study will be used here as an illustration as it is particularly pertinent to work stress.

Her study was based on an analysis of work stress in a London teaching hospital. It arose out of a request to the Tavistock Institute of Human Relations to undertake consultancy in order to solve problems relating to the system of allocating student nurses to hospital wards. In contrast to the quantitative emphasis of nearly all stress research, Menzies Lyth's analysis was based very largely on qualitative data, utilizing group interviews, individual interviews and observation. Treating the problem of student allocation as the 'presenting problem', Menzies Lyth argued that much of the work organization within the hospital was based on primitive modes of coping with the strain of nursing. This work organization was inefficient and, Menzies Lyth argued, led to a high wastage of student nurses, because the most competent found difficulty in accepting the primitive coping which the work organization enshrined. Over time, nurses had regressed to primitive modes because of the essential nature of nursing work – dealing with death and dying patients, having intimate physical contact with patients, and so on (Parkes, 1985). Coping was characterized by 'social defence' techniques, such as minimizing decision-making by reducing nursing tasks to the most simple level, and then performing the tasks in a ritual manner: 'Precise instructions are given about the way each task must be performed, the order of the tasks, and the time for their performance, although such precise instructions are not objectively necessary, or even wholly desirable' (Menzies Lyth, 1988: 55).

Psychological strain in Menzies Lyth's analysis derives then principally from the effect that collective *coping* has had, over time, on the organization of work. Her analysis provides a marked point of contrast to mainstream occupational stress research. For example, had Menzies Lyth been operating within role stress theory, it is likely that she would have reported that the main stressor facing the nurses was a high level of qualitative role underload – that is to say, doing work which is below the skill level and ability of the employee. As she noted, 'Many student nurses complain bitterly that, while ostensibly in a very responsible job, they have less responsibility than they had as senior schoolgirls' (1988: 69). She would also have probably reported that nurses experienced high quantitative role underload (having little to do), though had her mainstream research looked at acute stress (Newton and Keenan, 1985), she might also have observed that there were peak times when the nurses were quantitatively overloaded (see Menzies Lyth, 1988: 65). Operating from within a mainstream occupational stress framework, Menzies Lyth might have gone on to report correlations between these 'job stressors' and 'strains', such as anxiety and job dissatisfaction.

However, if we apply any validity to Menzies Lyth's analysis, then a mainstream model can be seen as largely obscuring the relationship between work organization, coping and job stressors. Reporting that there were high levels of qualitative and quantitative role underload would hint at the form of work organization, but would (a) not detail salient characteristics of the work organization (for example, ritual task performance), and (b) portray role underload as though it were a permanent 'external' feature of the 'work environment'. Instead in Menzies Lyth's analysis, underload is seen to reflect the *form of work organization* that had evolved in order to *cope* with the underlying anxieties. It does not therefore have some external reality as the concept of job stressor implies, but rather is seen as continually *socially* created and reproduced. For example, underload as reflected in routines such as doing tasks in a ritual manner can be seen as enabling nurses to collectively reproduce their work organization in a manner which enabled them to go on in the face of strong anxieties (see chapter 5). More generally, coping is depicted as being based on a largely unconscious *collusive* interaction between nurses, whereby it becomes 'an aspect of external reality [reflected in existing work organization] with which old and new members of the institution must come to terms' (Jaques, 1955).

The work of Tavistock writers like Menzies Lyth thus presents a rather different image of the stressed subject as someone whose stress cannot be understood outside collective experience. Coping with stress is dependent on social defence and shared experience within particular kinds of context (e.g. that of nursing). The stressed subject thus becomes both collectivized and contextualized. In spite of the interesting variant which this represents, psychodynamic work is still almost totally ignored by stress researchers (even though the psychodynamic tradition is still active in this and related areas – for example, see Hirschhorn, 1989).

Scandinavian Research

The Scandinavian research is particularly interesting because of the way in which it combines elements of mainstream stress discourse with a concern with work reform and societal change. On the one hand, Scandinavian researchers drew on the work of Selye and laboratory stress research, whilst in their later work there is some overlap with the approaches of role stress researchers. On the other hand, the Norwegian work is strongly related to the work reform movement (Kelly, 1982; Rose, 1985), as well as to socio-technical systems thinking (and the work of the Tavistock Institute of Human Relations).

The early work was principally undertaken in Sweden, and is particularly associated with Levi and Frankenhaeuser, the former based at the Laboratory for Clinical Stress Research in Stockholm (which became a World Health Organization centre in 1973: Levi and Kagan, 1980: 124), and the latter at the Psychological Laboratories at the University of Stockholm. Both writers drew heavily on the naturalism promoted by Selye and Cannon, wherein social problems like stress are seen as a consequence of our limited and outmoded biology. Ill-health can arise because 'bodily responses may, of course, be totally inappropriate for coping with the pressures of life today [owing to] the mismatch between our old biology and the demands of the new sociotechnical world' (Frankenhaeuser, 1989: 748).[23] Both Levi and Frankenhaeuser investigated the supposed link between our outmoded biology and ill-health through analysing the relationship between stress, catecholamine output (e.g. adrenalin) and illness indicators. They had difficulty however in establishing such a relationship with, for example, Levi admitting that 'the causation of disease by such [psychosocial] stimuli is not proven' (1974: 43). Researchers associated with the Swedish schools, such as Karasek and Gardell (see below), have continued to pursue this hypothesis, though with less than conclusive success. Thus Karasek et al. (1987) noted that they 'failed to find a clear linkage between particular stressors and particular physical illnesses', and other researchers have observed relations between stress and psychophysiological measures opposite to those which might be expected (for example, stress associated with *lower* rather than higher blood pressure: e.g. Fletcher and Jones, 1993).

Except for the fact that there is some emphasis on social structures in the work of Levi and Frankenhaeuser, their work is not seriously at variance with the heavy naturalism of mainstream stress discourse. However, in the early 1970s Swedish research began to emerge which was less in keeping with research in the USA and the UK. Within this work, the research of Bertil Gardell at the Psychological Laboratories of the University of Stockholm is often proclaimed as being definitive in outlining an alternative agenda. For example, Karasek has argued that: 'future research . . . will require integrative thinking combining social research and its political implications – the legacy of Bertil Gardell's work' (1989: 506). Gardell, though 'a long standing collaborator and friend' of Frankenhaeuser (Johnson and Johannson, 1989: 722), nevertheless pursued rather different research interests to those of Frankenhaeuser and Levi. On the one hand his work had similarities to the work of researchers such as Goldthorpe et al. (1968) in the UK, and Kornhauser (1965) in the US. Like Kornhauser, Gardell noted that 'jobs with low degrees of autonomy and skill generally have low "needs-satisfying value" for the individual' and that this was related to 'lower self-confidence, lower general life satisfaction, and more symptoms of low mental health' (1971: 893). In this respect, Gardell's work appears similar to that of role stress researchers, relating job demands to satisfaction and strain, but staying closer to the traditional concerns of mental and occupational health. On the other hand, Gardell was keen to argue for the need to attend to social structure and stratification:

> Ever since the emergence of industrialism, Western societies have been mainly stratified on a work basis according to the education and income that have been tied to a particular task. By and large, status in the organization determined status in the surrounding society. The situation of manual workers has been characterized by low pay, heavy, dangerous and dull work, and slight or no influence over job design and working conditions. (1976: 886)

These kinds of argument need to be seen both against the background of Gardell's work in Stockholm, and within the context of the work reform movement and its application in Scandinavia. The former will briefly be described before we turn to Scandinavian research on work reform.

Gardell's work, particularly that undertaken in the 1970s, can be seen as a less individualistic variant of role stress research. Within Gardell's work, there is less of an emphasis on the 'subjective life space' of the individual (after Lewin), and far greater concern with the 'work environment' and occupational health. An example of the 1970s work is a project jointly undertaken with Frankenhaeuser, and sponsored by the Swedish National Board of Occupational Safety and Health. This project investigated working conditions within the sawmill and woodworking industries (Ager, 1975; Frankenhaeuser and Gardell, 1976; Johansson et al., 1978). A project survey indicated that there was a high-risk group of sawmill workers, mainly sawyers, edgers and graders in the larger mechanized sawmills, who reported job monotony, high attention demands and psychological strain, as well as higher catecholamine output than a control group, and higher levels of psychosomatic illness and absenteeism (Johansson et al., 1978: 583). The project subsequently continued by investigating psychophysiological responses to working with computers, couched jointly within the 'psychobiological' framework deriving from Frankenhaeuser, and Gardell's more social psychological framework (Johansson, 1979; Johansson and Aronsson, 1984). Their work underlined the importance of the degree of job discretion and control allowed to workers, an emphasis popularized by Karasek (1979) with his simple two-axis model of job strain relating job demands to job discretion (Karasek's model was developed from research that he undertook whilst partly based at the Institute for Social Research at the University of Stockholm: Karasek, 1978).

Gardell's work might have remained within this broadly social psychological and mental health framework, had he not interpreted it within the context of the Scandinavian work reform research.[24] Given the contrast which work reform concerns provide to mainstream stress, it's worth examining the development of this work in more detail.[25]

Scandinavian Work Reform Research

The Scandinavian work reform research arose in the context of 1970s academic and political discourse, and found its most notable expression in Norwegian research institutes (for example, the Work Research Institute of the University of Oslo). The Norwegian research drew on human relations and socio-technical systems (STS) theory, but interpreted them within a more politicized framework. For example, in the early 1960s Lysgaard (1961) coined the term 'workers' collectivity' to reflect the informal relationships that had been observed in the Hawthorne studies, but also to point to the need for a 'political workers' collectivity at the workplace' which would draw 'not only upon concrete experiences in the workplace but also upon general political ideas, as found in socialism' (Gardell, 1983: 354).

At around the same time, a programme of research on the problems of industrial democracy was commenced at the newly created Institute for Industrial Social Research at Trondheim. This programme was sponsored by the Norwegian Trades Union Congress and the Confederation of Employers, as well as being promoted by the Norwegian Minister of Social Affairs, Olav

Bruvik. It was also conducted jointly with, and was strongly influenced by, the Tavistock Institute of Human Relations in London, with the direct involvement of Eric Trist and Fred Emery (Emery and Thorsrud, 1969: vii–viii; Trist, 1981: 25). The research led to a number of experiments in industrial democracy which drew on STS research undertaken at the Tavistock of the 1950s, utilizing semi-autonomous work groups to provide a joint optimization of the social and technical systems (Emery and Trist, 1969: 132). The work was influenced by the promotion of 'new values' by neo-human-relations writers such as McGregor (Emery and Trist, 1969: 254; Emery and Thorsrud, 1976: 158), though it also exhibited a concern for socio-political influences on developments in industrial democracy. Emery and Thorsrud implied that this interest in industrial democracy reflected Norwegian cultural considerations (the 'autonomous, self-reliant traditions of Norwegian society': 1976: 9), as well as political pressures occasioned by 'the growing restlessness of the left wing of the then ruling [i.e. early 1960s Norwegian] Labour Party' (1976: 9).

Based on these experiments, there was something of an expectation that job redesign practices would not only spread, but also lead to more general social changes (Herbst, 1976). Such a diffusion was however slow to occur. Bolveg (1976) has argued that in part the problem lay with the lack of attention within STS theory to the conflicting interests of unions and management, because whilst the former were interested in industrial democracy, management's main concern was with productivity (cf. Blackler and Brown, 1978). Yet though there was a limited diffusion from the STS experiments, the impetus for work reform did not disappear. As Blackler (1982) notes, by the mid 1970s a further opportunity had arisen to influence work reform arising from the development of health and safety at work as a political issue. Reflecting this political concern, a new Act was drafted for the Norwegian parliament. And Bjorn Gustavsen of the Work Research Institute at Oslo (later at the Swedish Center for Working Life, Stockholm) was given the 'opportunity to influence the legislative process through participating in a work group that developed the first proposal for a new Work Environment Act' (Gustavsen, 1988: 683). Gustavsen argues that part of this Act was directly influenced by Scandinavian researchers such as himself and Gardell:

> As indicated above – a point that was particularly well covered in the research of Bertil Gardell – work must be organized so that it allows for the development of competence, social contacts, and ability to make decisions. Against this background the Norwegian Act came to include the following article [Article 12 of the Act]. (1988: 684)

Article 12 was the main article of the Act referring to work organization, and it does bear some correspondence with the work of stress researchers such as Gardell. In addition to stating that employees should be 'given reasonable opportunities for professional and personal developments through their work', the Act also states that 'effort shall be made to avoid undiversified, repetitive work and work that is governed by machine or assembly line'.[26]

Gustavsen argued that Article 12 of the Act did have some impact in Norway in the 1980s. Based on surveys conducted by the Oslo Work Research Institute, Gustavsen estimated in 1988 that '20 per cent of the work force in Norway is involved in, or at least touched by, efforts to make work provide possibilities for developing competence, social contacts, and the ability to make decisions' (1988: 687). He further argued that:

> Even though 'the 20 per cent level' is limited compared with working life as a whole, it nevertheless far exceeds that in earlier periods when the issue or organization of work was hardly dealt with beyond a few field experiments or some 'star cases' such as the Volvo Kalmar plant in Sweden. (1988: 687)

The problem however with Gustavsen's 20 per cent argument is that, regardless of its accuracy, it is very difficult to determine to what extent it might represent a consequence of litigation.

In part the belief in the consequences of litigation may have reflected the strong faith which Gardell and Gustavsen had in legal-administrative strategies. For example, in 1980 Gardell and Gustavsen suggested that:

> Many social scientists tend to outrightly refute legal-administrative strategies as having no relevance at all to social development in working life; what such efforts might contribute to is usually thought to be bureaucracy rather than progress. This is a view the authors of this article do not share. We accept that legal-administrative strategies may lead to bureaucratization and phoney 'solutions' – they do not, however, *a priori* have to function like that. We do, in fact, believe that if any major progress is to be made within such enormous fields as work reform, the ordinary resources of society – including those of organized labour – must be brought to bear on these issues.

Yet Gardell later acknowledged that, at least in Sweden, legislation (the Swedish Act of Co-Determination, 1977) had limited impact on work reform, and the significance of legislation does remain open to debate.

In spite of these questions over the efficacy of legislation, the Scandinavian work reform movement still remains interesting because of its very attempts to link legislative, social and organizational concerns, and the way in which these relate to social science discourse, such as socio-technical systems theory and Scandinavian work stress research.

Work Reform and Stress Research

Gardell provides one study which directly links work reform with stress research. The study examined autonomous group working at AB ALMEX, a company specializing in the manufacture of portable mechanical ticket machines for use on buses and other forms of public transport. The ALMEX case represented 'an example of a union-based strategy for the development of a democratic work organization, where co-determination in representative forms and autonomous production groups have been united' (Gardell, 1983: 360).[27] The co-determination worked through union representation, with the union influencing policy decisions on matters such as investment abroad, as well as personnel issues such as selection, training and development. It also influenced work organization, and Gardell (1983) describes how autonomous work groups set up by the company were central to this influence, inputting into production planning and purchasing, as well as the organization and distribution of work.

Through the establishment of autonomous work groups, Gardell argued that the workers' self-confidence had risen, and their self-identity had changed in that they saw themselves as more competent and more influential. He based his arguments on comparisons between departments which had autonomous work groups and those that did not. From the perspective of work stress, his most interesting observation is that, where autonomous work groups were established, workers reported lower levels of psychological strain.

There are a number of criticisms though which can be made of Gardell's (1983) work reform research. Firstly, he presents limited data relating to the 'outcomes' of co-determination or to the interaction between co-determination and autonomous group working. Secondly, the supposed reductions in stress appear rather limited in nature. For example, his argument that the autonomous work groups experienced less stress was based on the finding that '18 per cent of those in the non-autonomous departments say they experience stress very often or quite often, compared to 7 per cent in the autonomous departments' (1983: 377). It is difficult to assess the significance of such results beyond saying that they suggest that *few* employees experienced very much stress. It is also impossible to determine from Gardell's analysis whether the lack of stress related to the introduction of co-determination and autonomous group working. Finally, AB ALMEX does appear to have represented a particular case; as Gardell noted, the 'low level of mechanization and the manual "craftmanship" involved in much of the work has made it impossible up to now to impose a detailed control system in accordance with the traditional methods of scientific management' (1983: 370). Given this background, it may have been that the management interest in worker participation was chiefly occasioned by the nature of the work organization, and the limitations it imposed on improving productivity through more traditional methods. In this context, reducing stress may just represent one component of a predominant concern with productivity, but veiled in the language of welfarism and democracy. Yet, to be fair to Gardell, this was an issue of which he was aware:

> the experiments now going on in different western countries – including Sweden – with sociotechnical changes and increased worker participation seem to focus too narrowly on economic concerns. Corporate managements are interested in them because they offer a method which seeks to adapt *job-world factors to new challenges, but with the terms governing conventional productivity thinking left intact.* There is considerabe risk that the firms will lose interest if productivity declines even in cases where positive social effects can be demonstrated. (1976: 897, my italics)

Although Gardell was aware of such issues, the Scandinavian work reform and stress research can still be subject to much of the same criticism that has been applied to other attempts at employee participation and work reform (Kelly, 1982). From a labour process perspective (e.g. Friedman, 1977; Ramsay, 1983; Thompson, 1992), it can be seen as a convenient means for managerial groups to maximize the surplus value of labour and accommodate to the vagaries of capital and labour markets, whilst presenting a welfarist/democratic front (see chapter 3).

Notwithstanding such criticisms (or those relating to legislative efficacy), the Scandinavian work remains of interest because it presents a quite different view of the stressed subject: one that, like that of psychodynamic work, is more collectivized and contextualized, and not quite so ahistorical. Stress is portrayed as being primarily not about the individual's subjective appraisal of environmental stressors, but about the politics of work organization. As a result, stress is also about workers' sense of their 'collectivity', and the ability to organize collectively, since this is central to their ability to reform work, and to exercise discretion and (following Scandinavian theory) reduce stress. Attempts at work reform are themselves seen as constrained by the traditional concern of managerial groups with productivity and minimizing labour costs, and the need to gain a return on capital. And partly in consequence, the aims of reform are not seen as solely dependent on *voluntary* change by corporate managers, but must be aided by legislative requirements, in terms of both providing workers with the right of discretion and autonomy, and legitimizing the representation of organized labour.

The lack of attention to such arguments from mainstream stress research is hardly surprising given that they stand in marked contrast to the latter's assumptions. To the extent that Scandinavian stress discourse has been adopted elsewhere, it has tended to be where it fits in with individualistic apolitical assumptions of mainstream stress discourse. Thus Karasek's popularization of elements of Scandinavian stress discourse in his job discretion model has been subject to a fair amount of attention, but the concern has very largely been with its ability to predict psychophysiological strain, rather than with its implications for work reform etc. In effect, attention has been focused on the naturalist aspect of Scandinavian research which has a clear correspondence with mainstream UK/US research (and the same discursive legacy drawing on the work of Cannon and Selye). As noted, Karasek's model has also been applied to test supposed stress–illness links, and again, this is a project well in keeping with the naturalistic underpinning of mainstream stress discourse. Work in the Scandinavian tradition does however continue (most notably the edited volume of Johnson and Johannson, 1991), but this work is largely published outwith stress journals (e.g. the *International Journal of Health Services*).

A postscript should be added to this discussion of Scandinavian work. This is that within the current ascendancy of neo-liberalism (see chapter 3), the Scandinavian discourse is in danger of appearing rather jaded and *passé*, particularly given recent changes in the governments of some Scandinavian countries. For example, Theorell has recently described 'the end of the Swedish system' (1993: 201). Occupational health budgets have been drastically cut ('approximately one third of the personnel in occupational health care teams have been fired': 1993: 201); principles of collective bargaining, employment insecurity and work compensation are increasingly questioned, and there are concerns that 'the government is throwing out systems that have been built over decades' (1993: 202). Such observations, though depressing, do have the one virtue that they again question the argument that we can understand stress in some context-less, apolitical, ahistorical vacuum. They also illustrate how discourses of subjectivity such as that of stress do not exist independently of economic discourse and practice (e.g. neo-liberal versus Keynesian versus socialist), even though this is a view actively promoted by the scientism of much psychology, and its pretence to objective apoliticism (a theme which we will explore further in chapter 3).

At the same time, the differences between Scandinavian and US/UK stress research imply that it may be helpful to think beyond discourse, and to consider issues of time and geographical space (Giddens, 1984). For example, Scandinavian stress discourse needs to be seen in the context of the kind of democratic socialist movement that was particularly identified with post-war Sweden and Norway. Given the kind of interventionist thinking that went with this movement, it becomes much easier to both conceptualize stress in a more politicized form, and conceive of reformist workplace changes that are dependent upon state support and legislation. In short, it seems no accident that a more reformist approach to stress developed in post-war Scandinavia, and one which enshrined a generally more collectivist view of stress.

Conclusion

Within US/UK universities, the stress discourse has allowed for a relatively straightforward and easy mass production of books, articles and PhDs, and has gained legitimacy within *and* beyond academe on the basis of a seemingly objective and scientific method. Alternative approaches such as psychodynamic and Scandinavian work research have not made very much impact. In general, the socio-political context has remained peripheral because (a) the social is reduced to the biological, witnessed in the prior work of Cannon and Selye, and (b) even where the social does enter into consideration, it is reduced to the narrow questions of the 'psychological environment' following Lewin, or 'job control' following Karasek. The idea that, say, people might collusively reproduce social structures which they found distressing would appear pretty strange to researchers imbued with the assumptions of the mainstream stress discourse. Equally, entertaining the notion that such reproduction might also be related to political (e.g. gender, class) inequalities within and without the workplace seems impossible within most mainstream stress models (Pearlin, 1989). And finally, the idea that the stress discourse itself contained effects of power appears almost inconceivable.

The stress discourse has been very successful in its promotion through academic research, stress management practice and the media. At the same time it has progressively narrowed in on a decontextualized and apolitical account of stress. This view has gone hand in hand with the individualization and naturalization of stress, where the central question is that of how the *individual* appraises and copes with stress within the limits of her phylogenetically outmoded behaviour patterns. The workplace is reduced to being just a source of stressors, and requires little further analysis since stress is chiefly about the individual. Notions of workplace reform or societal change are also therefore largely peripheral. It may be recalled from chapter 1 that these assumptions are almost exactly those witnessed in the popular media depiction of stress. Though somewhat stripped of scientific rhetoric and its academic pretence, the journalese of the media accounts do present a reasonably faithful translation of the central tenets of the academic stress discourse (see chapter 1). In both we see a stressed subject who is naturalized, individualized, decontextualized and so on.

The history of stress that has been presented in this chapter has notable similarities with Foucauldian genealogies of social science discourse. For example, the influence of social Darwinism and eugenics appears as far from unique to the stress discourse (see chapter 3; and see Hollway, 1989; Rose, 1985, 1990). The emphasis on naturalism is common to other areas of psychology and organizational psychology (Rose, 1990; Hollway, 1991). Equally, the Second World War represented a critical period in the development of much social science discourse and practice (Miller and Rose, 1988; Rose, 1990). In consequence, analysis of the stress discourse can be seen to provide a focused example of developments witnessed elsewhere in psychology and other social and medical sciences (see chapters 3 and 7).

In the next chapter, I shall attempt to place this history of stress in a theoretical context, through viewing stress discourse and practice from the varying perspectives provided by labour process theory, Foucault and Elias. The concern in the chapter will be to explain why the stressed subject currently looks like she does, and to further examine the socio-political conditions surrounding the post-war emergence and acceleration of the stress discourse. At the same time, the chapter will try to explore some of the difficulties in theorizing about agency, discourse and subjectivity.

Notes

1 There have been some limited attempts at a historical analysis of the derivation of the 'stress' term. Implicit in most of this work is the argument that the present-day usage of the term 'stress' is of very recent origin, and has been shaped very largely by medical and social science researchers. For example, Hinkle (1973) suggested that the development of the concept of stress resulted from the theoretical difficulties experienced by medical and social researchers in explaining apparent connections

between medical phenomena (for example, a heart attack) and social events (for example, being made redundant). The stress concept filled the vacuum between the two by providing an intervening linking variable. In her anthropological analysis, Pollock made explicit what was implicit in Hinkle's research by stating that the present concept of stress was 'originally a product of social and behavioural science research' (1988: 390), with 'the emergence of stress and its rapid diffusion throughout society' directly paralleling 'its discovery and elaboration as a theoretical concept' (1988: 388).

Though Pollock (1988) presents a well-argued case, it is difficult to reliably establish that the present usage of the 'stress' term has only recently emerged through the actions of social scientists. Hinkle's evidence of the social science development of the concept of stress relies on analysis of literary sources provided by the *Shorter Oxford English Dictionary* (*OED*). He thus argues that the seventeenth century definition of stress as 'hardship, straits, adversity, affliction' was replaced by an eighteenth and nineteenth century meaning of 'force, pressure, strain or strong effort' (1973: 32), and it is this latter sense of stress which has been developed and promoted by medical and social science. However, it is difficult to come to anything but tentative conclusions about the date at which our present sense of stress developed. In my own analysis of the longer or complete *OED*, I found sixteenth century definitions that were very close to present usage in the social and medical sciences. For example, one sixteenth century source quoted in the complete *OED* defines stress as 'the overpowering pressure of some adverse force or influence', a definition very similar to contemporary ones, such as that of Lazarus and Launier: 'Stress is any event in which environmental or internal demands (or both) exceed or tax the adaptive resources of an individual, social system, or tissue system' (1978: 296). With both definitions, there is reference to a demand or pressure, and in both there is an emphasis on stress being defined by situations where demands are excessive, taxing or overpowering. Where there is a difference though is in how the term 'stress' is applied. For example, the above *OED* sixteenth century definition derives from literary sources where the recipient of stress has a tendency to be an inanimate object (often a ship), and the stressor is generally environmental and uncontrollable (generally the weather), as in 'Which shipp had beene at sea three monthes and bett back by stress of weather' (Douglas in 1665). It is possible that it is this definition that was applied in the use of the term in physics and engineering where stress is seen as the physical distortion of a material when subject to a physical load. What contemporary social science stress researchers may have done is to utilize this physical definition of stress, applying it against humans rather than inanimate objects. However this usage is hardly new, since there are *OED* variants from the late seventeenth century onwards (e.g. Locke's 1698 application: 'Though the faculties of the mind are improved by exercise, yet they must not be put to a stress beyond their strength').

In sum, it can be argued that there has been a fair degree of consistency in the use of the 'stress' term from at least the sixteenth century onward, in that throughout there is an emphasis on adversity, and by the seventeenth century the recipients of this adversity can clearly be human beings. This suggests that there can be no simple privileged position of social scientists in inventing our contemporary understanding of stress, but rather it seems more appropriate to conceive of a 'double hermeneutic' (Giddens, 1984), wherein social scientists feed off and feed into the existing social landscape, drawing on existing meanings of stress, and discursively developing and promoting them.

2 Wallas provides an example of early twentieth century arguments about the need to attach social psychology to the eugenicist endeavour. He suggested that: 'social psychology can never lead men to wise practical conclusions unless it keeps in view its relation to that science of human breeding which Sir Francis Galton named Eugenics' (1914: 55). At the same time, he emphasized how eugenics needed social psychology because the 'eugenic motives and methods [cannot] be effective in a society unhygienic, uneducated, and unorganised.'

3 Cannon appears to be influenced by ideas current at the time of his research. Thus in his later work the naturalistic explanations survive, but the implicit reference to eugenics and racial welfare is to some extent supplanted by a seeming adherence to a kind of welfare capitalism, where the natural mechanisms of the body provided not just a metaphor, but a practical model for societal control:

> In a functional sense the nearest equivalent to the fluid matrix of animal organisms that is found in a state or a nation is the system of distribution in all its aspects – canals, rivers, roads, and railroads, with boats, trucks and trains, serving, like the blood and lymph, as common carriers. (1932: 296)

Such distribution systems formed a 'vast and intricate stream', where 'the products of farm and factory, of mine and forest, are borne to and fro' (1932: 296). Just as the animal organism maintains a homoeostasis, so must the social organism through 'intelligently regulating the processes of production and distribution' (1932: 304–5). Just as lack of stability threatens the animal organism, so does it endanger the social organism, and therefore social homoeostasis has to be the main goal of society. Towards this goal, Cannon suggested homoeostatic devices such as the 'accumulation of wage reserves which could be used at times of temporary unemployment', or 'training for new types of labour skill' (1932: 300). In his later work, Cannon thus presents a vision of a social homoeostasis somewhat akin to welfare capitalism, which achieves its rationale from science, and from the argument that the body is wise, that the biological (still) forms the basis for the social.

4 Cannon elsewhere directly acknowledged that his arguments about fight/flight were directly derived from McDougall (see Cannon, 1939: 195).

5 The Stone Age argument also neatly ignores subsequent developments in psychology, which, though it can still be highly naturalistic in its explanations of human behaviour, has nevertheless now become highly critical of instinct theories. The concept of instincts was already subject to considerable criticism in the 1920s such that, as Baritz notes, 'by the end of the decade [the 1920s], social psychology was shorn of instincts and left without any theoretical base' (1960: 26). While instinct theory has survived, it has arguably never regained its former position in mainstream psychology. Current stress writers have both totally ignored the near obliteration of instinct theory, and accepted the fight/flight instincts in a remarkably uncritical fashion (furthermore there is no consideration of developments in the concept of instinct that do exist, such as that of Bowlby, 1969).

6 For example, Ryan, an occupational psychologist, notes how the 1941 report of the US National Research Council (Committee on Work in Industry) 'devoted the greatest portion of [it] to a discussion of the Western Electric Company studies'. He then goes on to severely criticize the Hawthorne methods which are 'vague, qualitative, and inconclusive' (1947: 193), before arguing that:

> What we find objectionable in some current personnel literature is the implication that studies of the effects of work methods or the like are of very little value in comparison to studies of the attitudes of workers toward management and

supervision [as made salient in the Hawthorne studies]. The question to be considered boils down to this: What is the value of knowledge of the effect of the work itself in studying the efficiency of the worker under normal circumstances? We believe that this knowledge should have greater importance than is attributed to it in current dispositions, particularly those which are based upon the Western Electric Company findings. (1947: 194)

In sum, Ryan presents an attempt to defend the interest (and research funding) of occupational psychologists researching fatigue studies.

One interesting aspect of fatigue studies is that they appear in part to have originally represented a reaction to eugenics and to concerns of the hygienic movement (Rose, 1985). As Viteles notes, 'Increased infant mortality, lowered birth rate, degeneration of the race itself have been ascribed by early investigators to the effects of industrial fatigue' (1932: 440; Viteles provides a number of examples). At the same time, fatigue studies also represented a marrying of the kind of humanistic and economic concern that appears central to the project of pre-war industrial psychology, helping to mark its differentiation from scientific management. Thus Viteles speaks of the 'revision by the industrial psychologist of Taylor's plans in such a way that industrial inefficiency may be achieved without the sacrifice of individual welfare' (1932: 18).

7 Whilst this may have led Selye to abandon the use of the label 'stress' in lectures, in print there was little to abandon. The only reference to stress that I could discover in Selye's publications before the war was in an article written together with Tom McKeown where they refer to the 'severe stress' that may have been experienced by their experimental rats (Selye and McKeown, 1935: 15). But this usage has no theoretical reference point whatsoever, and appears entirely tangential to the physiological concerns of their paper.

8 Mason has argued for the specificity rather than non-specificity of physiological responses to stressors (for example, coldness may produce a different physiological pattern to heat: Mason, 1975). Where there is a non-specific response to stress, Mason argued that it was due to the commonality of *emotional arousal* that occurs across a diverse range of situations.

9 Mason notes that it remains questionable whether 'there may be logical continuity or compatibility of concepts developed in the psychological stress field with Selye's concept of stress as a non-specific physiological response pattern' (1975: 12). The answer perhaps is that Selye's research has *some* bearing but remains tangential even as a physiological account of what is now seen as psychological stress. That Selye is credited as a father of stress may have as much to do with his post-war promotion of the psychological sense of stress as with his physiology of the GAS.

10 Indeed some commentators argued for a lesser emphasis on physiological psychology within experimental psychology. For example, Lanier, commenting on the then recently published *Handbook of Experimental Psychology* (Stevens, 1951), complained that 'the inclusion of the physiological chapters . . . is . . . questionable' and argued that 'a poll would be necessary to determine whether such material is believed to be more useful to psychologists than equivalent space devoted to an expanded treatment of such topics as motivation and perception' (1952: 157).

11 Whilst psychiatrists acknowledged that extreme stress may produce pathological reactions in the 'normal' individual, the main emphasis was on the neurotic or pathological predisposition to stress. To this extent, they had not adopted the arguments of some psychologists concerning the normality of reactions to stress (arguments which were later to become the common position of psychological stress

research). For example, Stone (1985) quotes one prominent psychologist, Sir Cyril Burt, who argued in 1935 that:

> It was perhaps the First World War that most effectively brought home the artificiality of the distinction between the normal mind on the one hand and its abnormal condition on the other. In the military hospitals the study of so-called shellshock revealed that symptoms quite as serious as the well-defined psychoses might arise through simple stress and strain and yet prove quickly curable by psychotherapeutic means. And thus it gradually became apparent that much of what had been considered abnormal might be discovered in the mind of the average man. (Burt, 1977: 5)

12 It's interesting to note that Chin was editor of the *Journal of Social Issues* when the first reports of the SRC research programme on mental health were published (including the French and Kahn, 1962 paper that set out much of the theorizing on role stress): see the title page of the issue in which the French and Kahn paper appears.

13 One striking aspect of the OSS Assessment Staff is how enjoyable their work appeared. For most of them, not only did they operate well away from the front line, but they were also often based in pleasant country retreats, locations justified by the argument that they constituted an important determinant in lifting the morale of would-be recruits, and increasing 'their capacity to endure the ordeal and humiliations which they experienced along the way [i.e. the OSS assessment exercises]' (OSS Assessment Staff, 1948: 24). Such settings were also 'great sources of satisfaction to the [OSS Assessment] staff members' (1948: 24) who, in addition, found that: 'the whole experience was an exceedingly happy and rewarding one. Besides the essential feeling that we were forwarding the success of OSS activities and in this way contributing to the defeat of Fascism, there were countless satisfactions to be derived from working as members of a congenial, stimulating, dedicated group' (1948: 6).

14 Laboratory research investigating psychological stress continued through the 1950s and 1960s, although criticism of its assumptions appeared at an early stage, even amongst laboratory researchers themselves. Even Lazarus et al. admitted that experimental subjects may not accept the experimental situation as genuine, since 'subjects' reactions to the experiment vary from skepticism to severe ego-involvement' (1952: 207). To some extent, these comments anticipate growing doubts about the validity of experimental psychology in assessing 'applied' subjects such as stress (Lazarus was later to largely dismiss the relevance of laboratory research: e.g. Lazarus and Launier, 1978). Dohrenwend provided an early summary of the limitations of laboratory stress research:

> The laboratory situations for human subjects must, of necessity, be relatively benign and short-lived. They cannot have, as their aim, the creation of mental disorder. These contrived situations add to a certain artificiality a large degree of impotence compared to stress situations manufactured in social and cultural environments outside the laboratory. Further the laboratory stress conditions tend to lack even theoretical relevance to the very social conditions designated as the major sources of stress. (1961: 294)

Aside from anything else, laboratory research could appear both somewhat unethical and somewhat painful for the subject. For example, Pronko and Leith (1956) created 'experimental stress' by applying electrode jelly to the wrists of their unfortunate students, attaching electrodes, and then telling them: 'Now let me adjust the shock to as great an intensity as you can bear' (1956: 212).

One other feature of laboratory research is worth noting. This is that from an early stage in laboratory research, there was a focus on differences between individuals (for example, in need for cognition or tolerance of ambiguity) which might moderate the stressor/performance relationship. In their review paper Lazarus et al. stated that, 'In studies of psychological stress individual differences tend to be one of the main findings' (1952: 295). As Appley and Trumbull (1986) note, a focus on individual differences represented the essential tools of their trade which psychologists brought to the study of stress, with their central argument being that, 'Individual differences had to be recognized even in studies using the criteria employed by Selye and others of a greater medical orientation' (1986: 7). Once again, this tradition in laboratory research can be seen to have resonated well with the promotion of individualism already apparent in the work of Cannon, Wallas and Selye.

15 A critical difference that separated the Michigan researchers from most writers on, say, fatigue was that the former group, as social psychologists, naturally accepted the legitimacy of the social psychological issues raised by Hawthorne, but argued that they had not been researched with proper psychological research rigour.

16 The directors of the role stress research programme were French, Kahn and Mann. French was based at the Research Center for Group Dynamics, whilst Kahn and Mann were employed by the (closely related) Survey Research Center, which was also located at Michigan (French et al., 1962: preface).

17 The mental health discourse drew on wartime concerns about mental health and neuroses that helped to establish institutions such as the Tavistock (Miller and Rose) and the Survey Research Center (which was originally largely funded by the US Office of Naval Research). The concerns expressed within this discourse have notable parallels with the still earlier mental hygiene movement of the early twentieth century, which was itself related to the new psychology of writers such as McDougal and Burt (Rose, 1985). As Rose notes, within this developing psychology:

the conduct of the worker was to be explained through the relationship between the personality . . . and the industrial surroundings in which work took place . . . social and industrial inefficiency and unhappiness were the outcome of failures of adjustment of the internal life of the individual to the external reality in which he or she lived and worked. (1990: 68)

Such a concern still appears central within the stress discourse, particularly in its role stress guise, and variants thereof such as person–environment fit theory. There is the same concern with adjustment, though labelled as role congruence or degree of person–environment fit – and the same perceived problems of individual maladaptation (stress) and industrial inefficiency (e.g. poor job performance).

The US social psychological variant of the mental health movement shares much of the language of the earlier hygiene movement (Rose, 1990), though the goals of healthy adjustment and correct habits are less aligned to the eugenicist language of population degeneration, and more firmly focused on the notion of normality (see chapter 3). Though Jahoda (1958) noted the dangers of over-reliance on the concept of normality, she did note how it could rather conveniently be used as a 'statistical frequency concept and . . . as a synonym for the elusive concept of mental health' (1955: 300).

The notion of normality can be seen as providing an appealing combination of theoretical definition and methodological procedure. And such practical endeavour was needed if the post-war missionary zeal of the mental health movement was to be realized. Tufts noted its 'function' as being to 'enlighten individuals' and 'to build a citizenry that is not only informed but responsible in regard to mental health' (1955: 41); this is the ideal of the autonomous self-governing citizen, not only enlightened about the desirability of normal, adjusted mental health, but responsible for its maintenance in themselves and those around them (Rose, 1990; Rose and Miller, 1992). In sum, the post-war mental health movement fits remarkably well into Foucauldian ideas about normality and governmentality (see chapter 3).

This is further illustrated by Jahoda's (1955) paper on the social psychology of mental health which was 'originally prepared for a special meeting called by the [Josiah Macy, Jr] Foundation's Conference on Infancy and Childhood to discuss certain questions posed by the Fact Finding Committee of the Midcentury White House Conference [on Children and Youth]' (Kotinsky and Witmer, 1955: vii). The spirit of the Midcentury White House Conference is summed up by Jahoda in noting how her research on mental health was guided by the Conference's aim 'to consider how we can develop in children the mental, emotional and spiritual qualities essential to individual happiness and *responsible citizenship*, and what physical, economic and social conditions are deemed necessary to this development' (Jahoda, 1955: 297, my italics). The concern of the US government thus appears to have been written in a mental hygienist language, but one sensitive to the need for responsible autonomous citizenship.

18 French and Kahn were particularly concerned not to equate mental health with the absence of mental 'abnormality', and in consequence they stated that 'we will borrow criteria of mental health from sources which emphasize positive criteria (e.g. Jahoda, 1958), as well as from sources which concentrate on pathology' (1962: 35). The centrality of mental health in this early paper was conditioned by the US post-war mental health movement, and also by its more practical expression in terms of the four grants which the SRC had received from the US National Institute of Mental Health (French et al., 1962: preface).

19 Lewin stated that 'objectivity in psychology demands representing the field correctly as it exists for the individual in question at that particular time' (1952: 240). What determines an individual's behaviour is thus the way she perceives the environment, her psychological environment.

20 There are one or two other examples which illustrate the directions that were not taken. One such is the work of Goode (1960) who extended Merton's (1957) notion of the 'mechanisms' which articulate role sets (see above). Goode presents a list of coping strategies but, unlike much current occupational stress theory, these strategies are determined chiefly not by the individual's internal resources (e.g. their approach–avoidance tendencies) but by the external resources afforded within the social structure of the work environment. Although Goode's research predates that of Karasek by almost two decades, there are a lot of similarities between their approaches. For example, what Karasek (1979) refers to as job decision latitude, Goode refers to as role strain reducing mechanisms. The focus is the same: a functionalist explanation of stress based on the structural constraints of the work environment. Both give greater consideration to the environmental configuration than is usually the case in occupational stress research, albeit that neither analyses the political or discursive context of stress in any depth (though this is rectified in Karasek's later work). Given the similarities between their work it is interesting that (1) Goode's ideas have been totally ignored by subsequent stress researchers, and (2) Karasek's work developed through his contact with the Scandinavian, not the US, stress research tradition.

21 As Pearlin has argued, 'All too often, people's background and circumstantial

attributes are either overlooked in [stress] analyses or receive only scant attention' (1989: 243). Pearlin's recent work also echoes that of Dohrenwend's early research, emphasizing the importance of the structural context of stress, as well as 'the various systems of stratification that cut across societies, such as those based on social and economic class, race and ethnicity, gender, and age' (1989: 242). He argues that stress researchers should attend to such stratification issues since 'the structural contexts of people's lives are not extraneous to the stress process but are fundamental to that process. They are the sources of hardship and privilege, threat and security, conflict and harmony' (1989: 242). This argument has received support from the work of E.M. Hall (1989), whose research suggests that those most liable to stress are working class women, while those least liable are upper and middle class men.

22 It is interesting that such arguments have more recently received some attention outwith the occupational stress field. For example, Lennon (1989) attempted to relate power and dependency to the experience of stress.

23 Frankenhaeuser stated that:

> The mismatch between people and their environment that we experience today should be viewed in an evolutionary perspective . . . While today's demands are generally psychological rather than physical in nature, they trigger the same bodily stress responses that served our ancestors by making them 'fit for fight' [cf. Cannon]. These bodily responses may, of course, be totally inappropriate for coping with the pressures of life today . . . It is this mismatch between our old biology and the demands of the new sociotechnical world that . . . [ensures] we pay a price in terms of coronary heart disease, hypertension, psychosomatic disturbances, and distress. (1989: 748–9)

Levi used similar naturalistic language, drawing directly on the work of Cannon and Selye:

> The term 'stress' is used as Selye has used it: that is, the *non-specific response of the body to any demand made upon it* (Selye, 1971). The intensity and duration of this stereotyped, phylogenetically old adaptation pattern which prepares the organism for flight or fight is assumed to be closely related to the rate of wear and tear in the organism. (1974: 31, author's emphasis)

24 The concern with work reform can be seen in Gardell's earlier papers (see above) and his book published in Swedish on *Job Content and the Quality of Working Life* (1976). It appears to have been reinforced by collaboration with other researchers, particularly with Gustavsen who was based at the Institute of Work Psychology at the Work Research Institute in Oslo, Norway (Gardell and Gustavsen, 1980). As Gustavsen (1988) has recently noted, though they shared a common interest in work reform, the Scandinavian collaborators came from different backgrounds:

> One effort was made when four researchers with different backgrounds – Bertil Gardell with his background in empirical, originally fairly 'positivist' research; Sverre Lysgaard, with a background in hermeneutic, or interpretative, sociology; Ragnavald Kalleberg, with a background in critical theory; and myself, with a background in action theory – formed a group to start working on these [work reform] issues.

25 For a more detailed analysis of the socio-political context surrounding the development of Scandinavian work reform research, see Gustavsen and Hunnius (1981) on the Norwegian experience.

26 Although some writers have argued that Article 12 represented a direct translation of STS thinking (Elden, 1986: 240), Gustavsen consistently cites Gardell and other stress researchers (e.g. Karasek) in explaining the research background to Article 12, though he does note that their emphasis on job discretion and skill is 'parallel to the industrial democracy argument as put forward by, for example, Emery and Thorsrud (1976)' (Gustavsen, 1983: 547).

27 Gardell had previously emphasized that trade unions had a central role in making work reform work. As representatives of the 'workers' collectivity' (Lysgaard, 1961), unions could make working conditions a political issue through the process of worker participation, an argument Gardell presented to the Swedish Confederation of Trade Unions at their 1976 Congress (Gardell, 1983: 359).

Retheorizing Stress and Emotion: Labour Process Theory, Foucault and Elias

The aim of this chapter is to construct a theoretical analysis capable of relating the stress discourse to wider issues concerning power and subjectivity. The emotions which we label 'stress' are, like other emotions, not some stable natural or biological fact about the way human beings respond to the environment. Rather it will be argued that distressful emotions are culturally and discursively constrained, and that they are tied to broader power relations, such as capital/labour relations, family relations and gender relations. This argument will be explored through reference to labour process theory, and the work of Foucault and Elias. I shall start with labour process theory because it provides a very clear point of contrast to the image of the subject created in current stress discourse.

Reference to the work of Foucault and of Elias is helpful in placing stress discourse within a historical and genealogical context. They point to the way in which discourses of subjectivity like that of stress do not accidentally produce subjects who are depoliticized, decontextualized and so on. Yet the work of Foucault shares a limitation with that of labour process theory in its relative neglect of issues relating to human agency. This is not as true however with Elias whose writing can be used to show that the stress discourse works from and through human agency, challenging some tacit social rules of emotional expression (e.g. emotions are not a taboo), whilst reinforcing others (e.g. emotions are private, the individual's responsibility: 'own your own stuff').

These contrasting theories will inform but not rigidly define our subsequent discussions. With all of the theoretical treatments considered in this chapter, a brief account of pertinent aspects of the theories will firstly be presented (expanded on in the notes). These accounts will then be related to the stress discourse and stress management practice.

Labour Process Theory

Operating within a neo-Marxist framework, labour process theory posits a fundamental tension between the needs of capital and labour within capitalist economies. Within the diversity of labour process writing, there is a shared emphasis on the Marxist concept of valorization, or the process by which the capitalist usurps value beyond the amount paid to labour, so-called surplus value. Through valorization the relation of capital to labour is always repressive since the worker is seen as being robbed of part of the value of the labour. As Burawoy put it, 'In reality they [workers] are paid only the equivalent in monetary terms of the value they produce in part of the working day, say five out of eight hours' (1979: 23). In addition to this economic exploitation, workers are also alienated from the products of their labour through the wage–labour relationship. Since 'the worker no longer owns or controls the products of labour, individual needs and capacities are subordinated to the requirement of capital accumulation, with the psychological consequence that the worker feels a stranger in his or her work' (Thompson and McHugh, 1990: 309).

Maximizing surplus value depends on the form of the labour process, since there is no simple relationship between buying and utilizing labour. Labour is a variable capital which cannot be turned on like a switch; rather the capitalist must 'strive to extract actual labour from the labour power he now legally owns' (Edwards, 1979: 12). Labour process writers agree that control is problematic for the capitalist since 'workers retain their power to resist being treated like a commodity' (1979: 12). As a result, the focus of labour process writers has been on the forms of capitalist control, and management strategy. Labour process theory has developed from the universalistic single-track stance of Braverman (1974) that deskilling and labour degradation (such as through Taylorism) constitute the basic and inexorable form of capitalist control to the recognition of the need to distinguish both different forms and differing cycles of control (Ramsay, 1983; Thompson, 1983; 1992). In addition, there has been a questioning of whether management should be seen as having any systematic coherent strategies aimed at the domination of labour. As Thompson argues, there is 'no specific requirement for a single type of [control] trend' (1990: 105). Yet while simple notions of a clear over-rationalistic strategy are out, and while it's acknowledged that there may be considerable inter-professional competition between management functions (i.e. a struggle for control within capital), the core argument remains that of the conflict and contradictions arising from capital's need to control labour towards the extraction of surplus value (Thompson, 1992).[1]

The above provides only a very cursory account of labour process theory, since my main concern here is to explore its implications for the analysis of stress discourse and practice. The essential implication is that the stress discourse and stress management practices are generally consistent with manufacturing employee consent. The stress discourse can be seen to neatly smooth over the contradiction between the control and commitment of labour, since the ideal it fosters is that of an individual who defines her psychological and physical well-being in terms of her ability to be a good coper – someone who can do her job well, who is a good little worker. Stress management practices are designed towards this end through creating the stress-fit individual. At the same time, the stress discourse tells us how the person who is not stress-fit and cannot cope is likely to suffer mental and physical ill-health. Since the stress-fit worker is also the productive worker, the stress discourse conveniently conjoins individual and organizational health. As Thompson and McHugh suggest with regard to stress-fitness in managers, 'The ability to deal with and to some extent actually relish a high-pressure working environment is seen as a valued characteristic in managers' (1990: 325). From a labour process perspective, the subject in stress discourse begins to look rather like a Marxist caricature: an individual who is desperately concerned to remain stress-fit, a good coper who can, whatever the pressures, deliver the last drop of her labour to her employer.

The stress discourse is not original in its seeming potential to manufacture consent. Labour process writers have long argued that worker commitment may be aided through encouraging workers to identify with the competitive logic of the enterprise. Thus Friedman (1977) introduced the concept of responsible autonomy in order to differentiate employee control strategies which rely on employee autonomy and responsibility, rather than on direct control and discipline. From a labour process perspective, stress management practices are in keeping with the fostering of such employee commitment and involvement through encouraging individual employees to own responsibility for individual and (implicitly) corporate performance.

Stress management practices such as meditation, stress inoculation or counselling appear then as an oil which can help to keep the human machine functioning efficiently. Yet the promotion of the stress discourse also needs to be seen in the context of the development of human factors and human relations ideas more generally (Baritz, 1960; Rose, 1988; Hollway, 1991). Compared with earlier human relations ideas, the emphasis in stress is on self-preservation rather than the kind of self-growth promoted by writers such as Maslow and McGregor. It is a matter not of the humanistic imperative to self-actualize but rather of the injunction to survive through at least being adequate, being normal, to avoid being castigated as the inadequate coper and poor performer. It is therefore an injunction to maintain good standards of work behaviour rather than an appeal to the rather nebulous neo-human-relations ideals of growth, autonomy and self-actualization. As a play on the work ethic, it links work performance not only to self-esteem (Dubin, 1956) but also to intimate concerns about personal well-being. And fortunately for stress consultants, the promotion of the stress discourse is not reliant solely on company health promotion but is reinforced weekly by the mass media's exposure of the 'dangers' of stress (see chapter 1). It is easy to say therefore that stress management is good for the company and good for the employee, and though not necessarily rationalized as such, its emphasis on kind control may be seen (from a labour process perspective) as providing one of the best twists yet in containing the contradiction between employee control and employee commitment.

Labour process theory thus raises some interesting questions with regard to the stress discourse, since it draws attention to the way that the discourse appears to contain ideological elements which are supportive of the alignment of labour to the needs of capital. In itself however this does not explain why the discourse rose to prominence in the 1970s, and especially the 1980s. Nevertheless there are some suggestions from labour process writing which are of relevance here. For example, Friedman (1977) and Ramsay (1983; 1985) have provided examples of how discourses relating to employee involvement and participation have been variably deployed in relation to labour market conditions. Ramsay's detailed analysis of the period from 1860 to the 1970s illustrates how deployment of participatory practices was most common when labour supply was tight. More generally, his work might be read to suggest that most neo-human-relations practices – including those of stress management – will be more popular (i.e. more widely deployed) when labour is in short supply. Potentially then we have an explanation for the rise of stress discourse and practice. Yet observation of stress management practice does not tally with such an argument. For example, given the significant blue *and* white collar unemployment of the 1980s, it might be expected that stress management investment would be curtailed. After all, why not just sack the poor coper? Yet commentators noted a sharp increase in stress management company investment through the 1980s (see chapter 5). It was also in the 1980s that the mass production of stress academic articles really took off, along with the relentless pursuit of the subject by the general media (see chapter 1). It could be argued that companies were reserving neo-human-relations privileges for the permanent core of their workforce, except for the lack of evidence that firms do employ any core/periphery distinctions (Pollert, 1981; 1991). In sum, explanations of the rise of the stress discourse and other prominent discourses of the 1980s (e.g. organizational culture, new HRM) are not easily reducible to variability in the labour market.

The limited ability of the labour process theory to explain the rise of discourses of subjectivity like that of the stress discourse may result in part from its relative failure to attend to subjectivity (in spite of pleas to do so: Willmott, 1989; Thompson, 1990; 1992). As Thompson noted, 'The construction of a full theory of the *missing subject* is probably the greatest task facing labour process theory' (1990: 114; he has more recently reiterated this point in 1992: 249–50).[2] An example of this limitation comes from a labour process analysis of Hochschild's (1983) work investigating the work stresses of air stewardesses suffering the emotional labour associated with the need to continually please airline passengers and maintain a permanent smile (see chapters 4 and 6). Such stresses relate in part to the semi-institutionalized flirting expected between (generally) female air stewardesses and male airline passengers, reflected in airline advertising, such as the Continental Airlines slogan, 'We really move our tails for you to make your every wish come true', or the National Airlines imploration, 'Fly me, you'll like it' (Hochschild, 1983: 93). In an interesting application of labour process theory, Tancred-Sheriff (1989) provides an analysis of the way in which this promotion of certain images of women and women's sexuality is convenient within the full circuit of capital. Yet there is little consideration within Tancred-Sheriff's analysis of how such sexuality is constructed, and instead it is treated almost as a theoretical given. In consequence there is a limited analysis of human agency. But if we are to understand how work stress and gender relations operate within capitalism we also need to analyse how processes of subjectivity develop so that they appear inevitable and taken for granted – for example, why airline cabin staff or office secretaries are seen as more naturally women. If a labour process account is to explain sexuality or stress within organizations, it needs to attend to such questions and more fully develop theories of subjectivity. Filby (1992) has provided one example of a study which does move significantly in this direction. In a study of largely female cashiers in the betting industry, Filby not only illustrates the way in which selling sexuality is central to the labour process, but also analyses the way in which sexuality is part of gendered power relations within betting shops, and how this interrelates with the subjectivity of male managers, male clients and female cashiers.

In sum, labour process theory presents a sharp contrast to the image of the subject found in academic stress discourse. As we saw in chapter 2, this subject is individualized, naturalized, decontextualized and depoliticized (like its popular media counterpart – see chapter 1). In marked contrast, applying labour process theory emphasizes how the stress-fit subject is one which is very convenient in ameliorating any tensions between gaining control of and securing the commitment of employees. Since stress-fitness is defined by the ability to cope and do a job well in spite of high pressure, the stress-fit subject is one who has done more than give her consent to her position within the labour process. She is one who will potentially give her all, whatever the pressure, and engage in stress management practices in order to heighten her ability to do so. Yet whilst this kind of analysis provides a strong corrective to the apoliticism of the current academic stress discourse, labour process theory still remains in need of development in order to account both for the processes of agency and subjectivity (for example, how we know ourselves as stressed subjects), and for how and why the stress discourse rose to prominence at a particular historical period.[3] In trying to address these issues, I shall now turn to ideas which are more successful in terms of the latter, if not the former, project: the work of Michel Foucault.

Foucault, Power and Discourse

As with labour process theory, the attempt here will be to outline central elements of Foucault's theorizing prior to applying it to the stress discourse.[4] The first thing to note is that Foucault presents a rather different view of power to that contained in labour process theory. For Foucault, power was seen as intimately related to knowledge such that 'power and knowledge directly imply one another' (1979: 27). It is not that knowledge is some separately produced thing which is then controlled and used by a more dominant power. Rather knowledge is both produced in relation to power and influential of power. Particularly in his later work, Foucault explored this reciprocality between power and knowledge by examining the work of 'practitioners of the soul', such as psychologists, psychiatrists, teachers and social workers. He argued that the discourses associated with their disciplines have produced a panoply of scientific techniques, of methods for charting the psyche, producing a sophisticated 'technology of power over the body'

(1979: 29). Examples are the personality test, the psychiatric assessment, the teacher's report and the social worker's report.

Foucault drew out the importance of such techniques of observation and surveillance through reference to Bentham's panopticon (Foucault, 1979). The panopticon was a design of a model prison produced by Bentham which aimed to provide a perfect 'inspection house', where all prisoners could be surveyed at any time. The design placed prison warders in a central observation tower, from where they could gaze into each and every prison cell. At the same time, the prisoners could see neither the warders nor their fellow prisoners. They therefore knew that they were seen, but they could not themselves see.[5]

In *The History of Sexuality*, Volume 1, Foucault further developed the relationship between such discursive practices and power through an exploration of the pleasures of analysis from the Christian confessional to the psychiatric couch. He argued that the link between these different forms of human analysis was 'the task of telling everything concerning . . . sex'. For example, Foucault argued that within catholicism the flesh came to be seen as the root of all evil, so that telling of the sins of the flesh was vital to the maintenance of the pure soul. Like the prisoner in Bentham's panopticon, the sinner must lay bare her soul and be open to God's gaze. This problematization of sex became secularized in the Victorian era when medicine and psychiatry increasingly focused on the sexuality of children and the dangers of 'youth's universal sin'. In the more general academic analysis of sex there arose a vast multiplicity of 'distinct discursivities which took form in demography, biology, medicine, psychiatry, psychology, ethics, pedagogy, and political criticism' (1981: 33). Rather than the generally assumed Victorian censorship of sex, this detailed discursive attention to it meant that there was an incitement to 'speaking of it *ad infinitum*, while exploiting it as *the* secret' (1981: 35). And whilst still drawing on the Christian pastoral methodology, the secular discourse transformed the debate by locating it in terms of scientific notions of normality, a concept which was operationally defined with respect to its opposite, the new secular sin of abnormality (for which social and medical science proffered therapeutic 'cures').[6]

Foucault also argued that the emerging sexuality discourse marked a shift in the focus of power from controlling death to controlling life, a consequence of a historical shift away from the exercise of power by right, symbolized by royal monarchs who imposed their will (ultimately) through their right to terminate the life of disobedient subjects (what Foucault calls 'the shadow of the [queen's/king's] sword'). In the modern era, Foucault argues that such monarchic and juridical power has increasingly lost sway in favour of an operation of power through observation and discipline, using mechanisms by which it can 'qualify, measure, appraise, and hierarchize, rather than display itself in its murderous splendour' (1981: 144). Once again, medicine, education, psychology, psychiatry, social work and so on provide examples of discursive practices which employ a host of such observational mechanisms. And their aim is not to threaten death, but rather to control life through the promotion of 'normal' and (therefore) healthy psychological and physical well-being.

Foucault's *History of Sexuality* presents an interesting account of discursive development, but one that also appears particularly pertinent to the stress discourse. For example, as with sexuality, stress can be seen as reflecting a concern with controlling life, with health, vigour and longevity. Survival depends on overcoming the modern-day evil of stress, and ensuring that one's progeny are stress-fit, since otherwise they will be unable to meet the challenges of modernity. In addition, the stress discourse also illustrates the Foucauldian sense of problematization via a vision of normality that is operationally defined through reference to abnormality (for example the type A behaviour pattern, and the General Health Questionnaire 'case'). Just as the individual in Victorian society was impelled to guard against the possibility of perverse sexuality, so the individual in the stress discourse must guard against the dangers of abnormal strain, and the possibility of burnout. Like sexuality, stress has been spread across the surface of things, being everywhere a potential problem in need of attention (see chapter 1). Just as Foucault noted the contradiction between the seeming Victorian aim of repressing sexuality and the exhaustive attention to it, so there appears a conflict between the stated aims of stress practitioners to control stress, and a discourse which emphasizes the prevalence of stress to the extent that it takes on the form of an unavoidable and natural feature of life (see chapter 2).

The stress discourse also furthers a panoptic vision of the workplace, particularly with the technology of employee counselling. From a Foucauldian perspective, Hawthorne marked the point of entry of the great requirement of confession into the workplace, wherein counsellors could observe and probe the most intimate thoughts of the (potentially) sinful employee. What also differentiates counselling from other observational methods employed in the workplace is the extent of observation which it allows. For example, Zuboff (1988) and Sewell and Wilkinson (1992) have illustrated the panoptic power of recent innovations in information technology which potentially can enable the chief executive to gaze upon the bahaviour of the lowliest employee. But, whilst enabling considerable surveillance, such technology is limited by its inability to reveal the thoughts of the employees. It can show whether they have completed a particular task on time, and determine that they have not cheated the system. However, unlike counselling, it cannot reveal how they felt whilst doing the task, and whether, for example, they thought about cheating the system. In contrast, as Wilensky and Wilensky (1951) long ago noted, stress management practices such as employee counselling give employers' representatives a direct line to the soul of their employees, wherein they can truly play the kind of celestial power game implied in Foucault's reference to the panopticon, to play at being the God who sees and knows and guides. And while the confidentiality of this employee confessional must be assured, aggregate data can nevertheless be shared with line managers and executives within the organization.

The work stress discourse thus appears to conform to Foucauldian arguments about the modern prerogative to attain a healthy life via an emphasis on normalization and observation. A major question that remains though is that of why the stress discourse rose to prominence in the 1970s and 1980s. There are however a number of suggestions which can be made, following Foucault, as to how a discursive space opened up to which the stress discourse could respond. Firstly, some space was created by the inability of the medical discourse to adequately explain the major plagues of the West, namely coronary heart disease (CHD) and cancer. As Pollock's (1988) anthropological work illustrated, stress has become a common device for explaining the inexplicable in health (see chapter 1). This ability of the stress discourse to fill the discursive space left inadequately occupied by medical accounts in part derives from the mystery of stress, and from the tantalizing difficulty of forcing its secret. Researchers have continually emphasized how stress cannot be observed in the way that a body cell can. Stress is only knowable indirectly through the subjective eyes of the stressed, using error-prone analyses of their 'psychological space' (see chapter 2). It is true that some psychophysiological assessment can be made through neuro-endocrine activity, but such measures are subject to error, and are still merely indicators of a (stress) experience which can only be truly known subjectively. In consequence, whilst stress may not have the secrecy of sexuality, it does have the power of being never totally knowable. Like sexuality, because it cannot be clearly seen, it is always potentially everywhere; just as someone might always be sexually perverse, so it is always possible that they are highly stressed (they may be denying it, covering it up). So, for example, if people die from a heart attack, there is always the possibility to reconstruct their illness with stress at its base ('they never looked stressed, but then that was their problem, they never let it out'). As with any account founded on subjectivity, its unknowingness (to the outside observer) makes it highly appropriate for filling discursive spaces left by the unknown (such as CHD, cancer). By providing scientific dressing to legitimize this problematic unknown, researchers have participated in the development of a discourse with a very wide application. It may not have the pervasiveness of some of Foucault's great unknowns (e.g. sin, sexuality), but it does have a mystery which enables a particular kind of discursive strength.

Allied to the inadequacy of medical accounts of major illnesses is the rate of technological and market change since the war. That the stress discourse was particularly promoted in the 1980s may be related to discourses of modernity, particularly what might be termed discourses of change. For example, managers are told that an effective leader must embrace change, and must judge their own performance by their ability to continually change and adapt (Peters, 1988). Though people may influence its direction (for example, they may have choice over information technology), change itself is promoted as inevitable and desirable (see chapter 1). This promotion of change can be seen as complemented by that of stress in two ways. Firstly, the stress discourse reinforces the normality of environmental change because it portrays an image of people being able to cope with any kind of change provided they are stress-fit. Secondly, it emphasizes how the problem lies not with the rate of environmental change itself, but rather with the phylogenetically outmoded patterns of individual human behaviour (see chapter 2). The problem is our need to move beyond the straitjacket of caveman fight/flight patterns, and develop flexibility by turning the 'threats' of change into 'opportunities'. Stress management techniques provide one tool in the process of encouraging such flexibility. In this manner, the stress discourse reinvigorates individualism by emphasizing how the individual can overcome the increasing dangers of modernity, the fallout that may result in a rapidly changing world.[7]

And generally in the 1980s, the individualistic logic of the stress discourse was notably in keeping with anti-collectivist politics, epitomized by the neo-liberalism of Reaganism and Thatcherism and the revolution in Eastern Europe (Burrows, 1991). Part of the currency of the stress discourse in the 1980s may therefore have derived from the way in which it interlocked with discourses of individualism, enterprise and change, where 'citizenship is manifested through the free exercise of choice amongst a variety of options' (Miller and Rose, 1990: 24). Foucauldians like Miller and Rose illustrate the alignment between the individual, the organization and the state through an individualistic definition of citizenship epitomized by the language of enterprise (Miller and Rose, 1990; Rose and Miller, 1992). They argue that this language promotes the notion of maximizing one's quality of life through the careful assembly of a self-regulating lifestyle.[8] Rose has also noted how psychotherapy is consonant with the language of enterprise since its 'espousal of the morality of freedom, autonomy, and fulfilment provides for the mutual translatability of the language of psychic health and individual liberty' (1990: 256; see also Rose, 1991). Similar comments might be made with respect to the stress discourse. Though drawing on varying discursive roots, both stress research theory and stress management practice emphasize the responsibility of the individual, reliant on a vision of an autonomous stress-fit self who is guided by the expertise of the stress discourse.[9]

A broadly Foucauldian framework can thus be seen to give us a vehicle to analyse stress discourse and practice, and to think about why the discourse blossomed so well in the 1970s and 1980s. Yet there are some difficulties with Foucault's work. One is the question marks surrounding Foucault's emphasis on power as potentially positive and productive, particularly given the difficulty in hanging on to it when considering power in the workplace. For example, the stress discourse can be seen as a celebration of the healthy life, guiding individuals to know themselves and experience good psychophysiological health. Yet the stress discourse and practice are deployed within a work setting which appears to be less than entirely concerned with the promotion of health. Since the employment setting contains the effect of the law, contrary to Foucault, monarchic and juridical power does not appear to be entirely on the wane. Employers do still have the quasi-monarchic power to dismiss employees, to 'terminate' their economic life, and employees are in consequence still subject to a potential coercion which may require them ultimately, following Foucault, to lie naked beneath the shadow of the employer's 'sword' (see above). And this power strongly relates to the conflicts and contradictions between capital and labour so well depicted in labour process theory. On the one hand, the subject is freely invited to enter into the stress discourse, a major therapy of freedom which spreads well beyond the counselling room, and invites us all to better our physical and psychological health (cf. Miller and Rose, 1990). On the other hand, like other neo-human-relations constructions of subjectivity (Hollway, 1991), the deployment of stress discourse and its techniques takes place within workplaces characterized by good old-fashioned coercive possibilities. Whilst we are not simply dominated, we do nevertheless implicitly acknowledge the need to placate and please our superiors if we are to receive their favours, and we may well put up with very unhealthy and 'stressful' conditions in order to do so.[10]

Another problem with applying Foucault's work comes from his lack of attention to questions of human agency. Human action is portrayed as the outcome of the identity of subjects being constituted within particular discourses. Whilst discourses are formed through the actions of people, Foucault's writing portrays an image of subjects as somewhat passive followers of the dictates of discourse. Benhabib sums up the problem with this argument:

> If the subject who produces discourse is but a product of the discourse it has created . . . then the responsibility for this discourse cannot be attributed to the author but must be attributable to some fictive 'authorial position', constituted by the intersection of 'discursive planes'. (1992: 216)

As she adds, such an emphasis on discursive constitution starts to look like 'a kind of Lockean *tabula rasa* in latter-day Foucaultian garb!' (1992: 217). To be fair to Foucault, it is true that he attempted to negate this image. For example, he argued that subjects will be constituted in a discourse as much by their resistance to it as by their acceptance of it. He also stressed that 'power is only exercised over free subjects . . . who are faced with a field of possibilities in which several ways of behaving . . . may be realized' (1982: 221). Attempting to apply this point at the level of human agency, Knights and Morgan argued that 'individuals and groups exercise power to elaborate some and resist other elements of the discourse' (1991: 35). But there is no explanation in Foucault's work of *why* or *how* people may elaborate, resist or manipulate the discourse, with only a partial account of the process by which people exercise power. If discourses provide a basis upon which 'subjectivity itself is constructed' (1991: 5), then we have a theory of subjectivity which, to a very large extent, leaves out the subject. Though Foucault noted how people 'agonize' within the 'permanent provocation' of a 'field of possibilities' (1982: 221–2), this remains merely an acknowledgement of some freedom of action; it does not explain how or why subjects may act given such freedom.[11]

In spite of these limitations, the work of Foucault remains particularly interesting because of the focus it provides on the relation between stress discourse, power and subjectivity. It gives a more interesting framework than labour process theory when it comes to explaining why discourses of subjectivity, like that of stress, rise to prominence at certain times. Whilst it is limited in accounting for human agency, Foucault's work does nevertheless provide a basis for considering images of the stressed subject, and to that extent gives us some idea of how this subject comes to know herself.

In the last section of this chapter, I shall turn to the ideas of Norbert Elias, who provides a theoretical framework which affords some measure of reconciliation between the different views of power contained in labour process theory and the work of Foucault. Elias also provides some further basis for considering human agency, in particular how individuals learn the stress discourse, and how it can be seen to rearticulate tacit social codes relating to the public and private expression of emotion. Some brief attention will also be paid to the work of Wouters who has applied and extended some of the ideas of Elias.

Elias

Wetherell and Potter (1992) provide a bridge between the work of Foucault and Elias in distinguishing between what they call constitutive discourse and established discourse.[12] The former refers to the general Foucauldian account of the way in which subjects are constituted within discourse (see above). The latter expresses an acknowledgement that discourse is developed or established through human agency under particular kinds of social conditions, and that it does not emerge out of a vacuum:

> Discourse does take place in history, it feeds off the social landscape, the social groups, the material interests already constituted. In analyzing *establishment* it is possible to talk of directions of domination, of past campaigns which author present campaigns, of interests which are served, of power which is located and possessed, and to invoke some of the functional apparatus and articulations of practices, so well described in Marxist theory. (1992: 86, my italics)

The work of Elias provides one way of examining how discourse is established through a historical framework which relates social structures to subjectivity. Central elements of his theorizing will be firstly described, and their significance for the stress discourse will then be examined.

Elias attempted to relate our current sense of emotion and of emotional self-control to the changes in power structures that were consequent upon the establishment of a stable monarchy. Drawing on a wide range of historical sources, he argued that new forms of subjectivity arose as the result of the concentration of power within the hands of one monarch, rather than being geographically dispersed amongst rival chieftains. For example, he suggested that in the Middle Ages, individuals could take open pleasure in acts of violence that would be greeted with general repugnance today: 'The warrior of the Middle Ages not only loved battle, he lived it' (1978: 195). But with the monopoly of violence that occurred with monarchy, Elias argued that the new servants of a centralized power had to show a far greater civility than before. The emotional displays of this new civility are symbolized by court society, wherein courtiers beg favour to the king or queen, whilst others beg access to the court. Violence and aggression are replaced by politeness and the careful display of emotions as a tacit understanding of political process. Our present civility can appear then as the consequence of an earlier denial of pleasure in violence and aggression, and their replacement with the tacit requirement to maintain appropriate civil emotions.[13]

As further illustration of this 'formalization' of behaviour and affect, Elias analysed the way in which manners became increasingly prescribed as we moved from the Middle Ages to the courtly aristocracy and the increasing monopolization of power. Through the examination of manners such as those of table manners or bedroom manners, Elias showed how the embarrassment threshold became increasingly constrained. More significantly he showed how these affective and behavioural constraints were intimately associated with the courtly aristocracy, and the need of courtiers to show appropriate restraint to their betters (reflected in current words such as 'courtly', 'civility', 'delicacy'). He argued that such control was gradually diffused from the courtly aristocracy through lower levels of society: 'the feelings and affects are first transformed in the upper class, and the structure of society as a whole permits the changed affect standard to spread slowly throughout society' (1978: 115).

Elias also emphasized how the development of affect constraints was associated with an increasing privatization of emotion, wherein there was a 'pressure placed on adults to privatize all their impulses (particularly sexual ones)' (1978: 182). For example, although the 'bedroom has become one of the most "private" and "intimate" areas of human life' (1978: 163), Elias notes how this was not the case in medieval society, when it 'was quite normal to receive visitors in rooms with beds' and where 'it was very common for many people to spend the night in one room' (1978: 163). Increasing emotional control was associated with sharper distinctions between the private and the public, with the intimacy of emotional expression confined largely to the former.

In the twentieth century this increasing formalization of affective and behavioural norms can be seen as going into something of a reversal, epitomized by the supposedly swinging sixties and seemingly greater permissiveness of social codes. Yet Elias and his followers argue that this informalization should be seen as reflecting not the negation of emotional and behavioural restraint (let it all hang out), but a 'controlled decontrolling of emotional controls' (Elias, University of Amsterdam lectures, 1970–1: quoted in Wouters, 1987: 426). Wouters (1977; 1986; 1987) has particularly developed this argument in suggesting that the apparent informalization witnessed in the twentieth century masks increasing needs for self-restraint. Wouters links informalization to a lessening of power inequalities as between men and women, or parents and children. Yet greater equality brings greater demands for self-restraint; so, for example, while children may experience less authoritarian control from parents, they learn to bring behavioural codes under their own control, and in this way exhibit greater self-restraint. Women may be less beholden to men, and children to parents, and most Western people to external rules, yet at the same time there is a need for the use of personal behavioural codes which are both subtle and flexible.[14]

In sum, the work of Elias and his followers such as Wouters suggest that our emotional control is not just about social customs and the sensibilities of particular cultures, but is closely related to changing power relations. As Burkitt emphasizes, Elias both provides us with a historical account of emotions and reinforces the argument that emotion is 'socially created and historically variable' (Burkitt, 1991: 200). Though the focus of Elias and his followers is not generally on social science discourse, their work presents interesting implications for our understanding of stress theory and practice. Firstly, stress discourse can be read as an example of formalization and the further articulation of pre-existing tacit codes of emotional control. Stress rhetoric appears as one further tactic in the demand for greater emotional control. For example, instead of, say, venting our aggression on our desired target, we are instructed to 'relieve the tension' through relaxation, meditation and 'stress inoculation' (see chapter 5). If we are stress-fit we are expected not just to ride but to relish pressure and our ability to deal with it. This ability is seen in the fact that we remain 'cool' and 'own our own stuff'. We certainly don't ventilate our feelings or express open aggression because that would show that we are not coping, and at worst might indicate that we were 'cracking up' (see chapter 6).

Much of the mainstream stress discourse also appears in keeping with the privatization of emotion, with employees expected to maintain emotional control at work, especially when operating front-stage (Goffman, 1971), relegating any emotional difficulties to back-stage or off-stage arenas (see Hochschild, 1983; and Wouters's 1989 critique of Hochschild). Stress management practices are also very largely the province of off-stage arenas, either through creating confidential arenas at work (such as in counselling), or through special 'supportive' training environments (e.g. learning progressive muscle relaxation), or through private practice (e.g. practising meditation in private).

Analysing the stress discourse draws our attention to the way in which formalization varies between the public and the private. On the one hand, in the realm of the home the tacit rule of the stiff upper lip, and the need to continually hide emotions, appear to have been gradually replaced by a growing norm of the need, however difficult, to 'let out' how you feel (an inversion perhaps particularly witnessed in Western middle class homes). For example, whereas parents and children were once encouraged to minimize emotionality (e.g. not in front of the children), such parental behaviour has been increasingly problematized because denial of emotion is seen as harmful to both children *and* their parents (Newton, 1994c). Indeed the healthy family is encouraged to get together two or three times a week for regular family therapy.[15] There can be seen to be a number of discursive influences on this kind of thinking, but perhaps pre-eminent is that of the psychoanalytical injunction to release psychic energy, and let out how you feel (as Foucault noted, the problem with sex in psychoanalysis became not its expression, but its *repression*). It is not just that (as Wouters argues) along with informalization comes a requirement for individual self-restraint, but that the private has been increasingly constituted within discourses which problematize earlier codes of behaviour (the stiff upper lip etc.) and proclaim new healthy norms of emotional expression. Yet this discursive rewriting of the tacit, of what Giddens calls our practical consciousness, does not seem to have extended so much to the public sphere, and certainly not to the workplace. Whilst there may be a slightly greater informality at work than, say, in Victorian times, there is still a fair degree of emotional and behavioural restraint, with employees generally expected to keep their cool and so on. Rather than challenging such tacit codes, the stress discourse promotes them by effectively arguing that the relief of work pressure should not be done in public, and that distressful emotions should generally be contained (if not hermetically sealed), aided by the private use of relaxation, meditation, counselling and the rest. In sum, stress discourse and practice appear to actively support both pre-existing codes of formalization and emotional restraint in the workplace, and the privatization of emotion.

The question that arises from these observations is why there is such a difference between the constraints of the workplace and those of the home. If we follow Foucault, we might expect there to be little difference between the two arenas since discursive practices should extend as much into the workplace as into the home. In (Foucauldian) theory, there is no reason why, say, the gaze of psychoanalytic legacy should be any less penetrative of the workplace than of the home – and why in consequence we should experience any less of a psychoanalytical injunction towards, say, the open expression of emotions. A Foucauldian account thus appears to be limited in its ability to explain differences in affective constraint between the home and the workplace. In contrast, by emphasizing the social relations of power, Elias provides a means of examining the political context within which discursive practices are *established*. As a result, he can be read so as to provide an explanation of home/workplace differences. For example, it can be argued that norms of emotional restraint at work (that are supported by the stress discourse) are in part a consequence of the dependency of employees on the favours of their superiors. Although employers do not simply rule by right, dictating exactly what their employees will do, it can nevertheless be argued that the employer's right to punish and reward does still create a lot of coercive possibilities. Though this monarchic power of right is rarely nakedly displayed, it does still seem relevant to the way in which people generally toe the line, how they try to please and placate their superiors so that they may one day be granted favours, just as kings and queens once rewarded their courtiers for their civility and emotional restraint (Newton and Findlay, 1994 provide an example of applying this kind of Eliasian analysis in a reinterpretation of Grey's 1994 Foucauldian study of the performance appraisal of trainee and chartered accountants). Elias's theorizing underlines how the display codes surrounding our emotions and subjectivity in the workplace are likely to be related to the power relations of employment.

It can be argued of course that emotional and behavioural restraint does *not* just depend on the power relations implicit in the employment contract. For example, we may often show such restraint in settings other than those related to employment. Yet, Elias's point is that emotional and behavioural control needs to be seen in the historical context of changing social structures and power relations, such as the monopoly of power consequent upon stable monarchies. Our customs and cultural habits cannot be divorced from such social relations because they have been historically formed within them. Extending this argument, emotional restraint is not dependent solely upon employment relations since such restraint has been conditioned within the changing power relations of past centuries (such as the monopolization of power consequent upon courtly aristocracy). At the same time, it can be argued that the metaphor of the royal court still has relevance to employment settings, since though there are far greater interdependencies in the modern age, employees are still expected to exhibit tact and emotional restraint if they are to be in the good books of their superiors, and receive their favours. The greater formalization in the workplace can be seen then to be in part a consequence of the power relations that surround it.[16]

The monarchic power of employers also seems relevant to the way that discourse and practice are framed. For example, is it just a coincidence that stress management and discourse are framed in managerialist terms (see chapter 5)? Certainly stress discourse and practice appear as useful aids in ensuring that employees show appropriate civility and keep their cool. And stress writers rarely make any serious attempt to challenge emotional codes. For example, they do not tend to suggest that part of the problem of stress is that individuals are expected to maintain a tight emotional control at work. Whilst they may argue that stress should not be a taboo, they do not generally argue for any radical alternatives – for example, that people should ventilate their feelings at work, that employees should be encouraged to share their feelings openly, or (worst of all perhaps) that they should organize and express their grievances collectively (see chapters 4 and 6). Part of the problem is that challenging tacit emotional codes also means thinking about power relations (see chapters 6 and 7), a subject that (as we saw in chapter 2) the stress discourse rather studiously denies. Instead the stress discourse and its practitioners appear both as supportive of the power relations of the workplace, and as helping to further sharpen the divide between the expression of emotion in the home and that in the workplace.

In sum, reading Elias provides a framework by which to understand the stress discourse in relation to both subjectivity and power. In terms of the former, the stress discourse can be seen to rearticulate tacit codes of emotional restraint that still apply in public and (perhaps especially) workplace settings. In relation to the latter, the managerialist form of the discourse and its practices can also be seen as being influenced by the power relations surrounding the workplace. To this extent, the work of Elias goes some way towards correcting the omissions of labour process theory and of Foucault: it both directly addresses subjectivity, and stresses that power relations must be considered in relation to human agency. Yet as with Foucault and labour process theory, it is possible to point to certain limitations in Elias's theorizing. For example, his analysis of contemporary capitalism lacks the depth witnessed in his investigation of courtly aristocracy. As Bogner notes, the analyses contained in his most influential text, *The Civilizing Process*, 'are mainly concerned with the courtly aristocracy' (1987: 256). In addition, though the work of Elias and his followers is attentive to the effects of gender (e.g. Wouters, 1987), its implications do appear to be less than fully analysed. For example, it is possible to argue that many tacit codes of emotional control are *solely* a reflection of a highly androcentric society. As Hearn argues, 'men "at work" are generally not expected to display certain categories of emotion, especially those associated with women' (1993: 143). Since men also typically have the positions of power and authority in organizations, they may define what is appropriate emotional display not only in themselves, but also in others. Whilst it may appear overly reductionistic to argue that emotional restraint in the workplace is solely a function of male patriarchy, it is arguable that Elias's detailed historical account would benefit from a greater historical analysis of gender issues. And though Elias is attentive to gender issues (e.g. Elias, 1978; 1982; 1987), it still remains the case that the gendered nature of emotional expression and subjectivity is only partly explored in his work.

In spite of these limitations, however, the work of Elias is interesting if only because of the way in which it begins to address some of the lacunae witnessed in the application of Foucault and labour process theory to the stress discourse. For example, applying Elias suggests that the discourse did not just emerge out of a vacuum; rather, its establishment can be seen to rearticulate pre-existing codes of emotion and emotional control. Additionally, its deployment occurs within work settings which, though they involve complex interdependencies, nevertheless still bear some similarity to the monarchic power relations analysed by Elias. At the level of human agency, responsibility for discourse is not just a consequence of the 'intersection of "discursive planes" ' (Benhabib, 1992: 216; see above); rather, discourse is the product of emerging social and power relations. In this light, the stress discourse can be seen as (1) a product of current socio-political relations of the workplace (e.g. it is largely defined in management terms), and (2) a product of pre-existing socio-political relations (e.g. monarchy, capitalism), and in consequence of pre-existing codes of emotion.

Conclusion

The aim of this chapter has been to challenge the way in which we think about stress, and provide an alternative to its current theoretical representation. In its present form, the discourse is individualistic, naturalistic, decontextual and apolitical both in its media presentation (see chapter 1) and in its academic treatment (see chapter 2). The work of labour process theory, Foucault and Elias provide alternative critical analyses of this image of stress, whilst at the same time providing some clues to the question raised in chapter 1 concerning why the stress discourse is so appealing. Labour process theory provided a clear initial alternative to the representation of the stressed subject contained in mainstream stress discourse, illustrating how stress discourse and practice can help employers to move beyond the need to obtain employee consent, and towards the maximizing of employee commitment. Through the promotion of effective coping, the stress discourse encourages employees to define themselves in terms of their ability to successfully handle job pressures, and links this definition to personal anxieties about mental and physical health (with ultimate failure occurring when the individual reaches the dreaded stress 'burnout'). The work of Foucault, with its emphasis upon knowledge and power, gave a means by which to examine in more detail the kind of stressed subject that the stress discourse creates, and to analyse why the stress discourse took off in the 1970s and 1980s. A Foucauldian emphasis alerts us to stress as a technology of the self and of government, and to the way in which we know stress through its promulgation in a host of stress management practices, through a variety of media such as magazines, newspapers, academic journals and conferences, and through a number of institutions such as universities, hospitals and surgeries. Stress can be seen to incorporate central aspects of the Foucauldian litany: panopticism, normality, the promotion of health and bio-power, the contradiction between containment (of stress) and its celebration as a universal feature of life. A broadly Foucauldian perspective also helps us to consider the way in which the stress discourse articulates with other discourses of excellence, enterprise and culture through its promotion of an autonomous entrepreneurial stress-fit self, a self which appears particularly in keeping with the espoused aims of neoliberal government. Yet a Foucauldian treatment does appear open to the accusation that it represses consideration of social relations (Burkitt, 1993) so that, at worst, subjects appear almost like the proverbial *tabula rasa* waiting to be inscribed (Benhabib, 1992). In contrast the work of Elias promotes one link between social relations, power and subjectivity, and therefore provides a platform to think about the role of human agency. The ways in which individuals learn to go on (Giddens, 1984), our tacit understandings and codes of behaviour, are seen to be intimately related with the changing power relations as the West moved from the contestation of power witnessed in the Middle Ages, to the subsequent monopolization of power associated with courtly aristocracy, and to an expression through more impersonal mechanisms with the arrival of bourgeois capitalism (e.g. labour and product markets). Emotion and subjectivity are portrayed as closely associated with such power relations, and the stress discourse can be seen in a similar light, both in the present and in a historical sense; its representation can be seen as influenced by the power relations of current employment settings, whilst its establishment can be seen, in part, as rearticulating and reinforcing much earlier codes of emotional display and behaviour.

The three theories considered in this chapter pose different answers to the question raised in chapter 1 as to why and how the stress discourse speaks to us. From a labour process perspective, we cannot consider how the discourse speaks to us without considering the power relations of the workplace. It is only in this context that the stress discourse makes sense (e.g. its managerialist phraseology). Applying Foucault, the stress discourse speaks to us through a wide array of discursive practices promulgated by academics, practitioners and journalists, and through its articulation with other discourses which promote bio-power, normality, health, human growth and enterprise. With the work of Elias, the discourse speaks to us by rearticulating our pre-existing codes of emotion, and through complementing the privatization of emotion. As with labour process theory, there also implicitly remains a need to consider the power relations of the workplace.

In the rest of this book, there is no simple mapping of our analyses on to the above theoretical schema. As noted at the start of this chapter, the main aim in presenting these varying theoretical perspectives was to broaden what we see as the currently very narrow consideration of stress and work stress. However, in so doing the concern has not been to arrive at some new, all-encompassing meta-theoretical account which we would then use to strait-jacket our theoretical explorations through the rest of the book. Though the remaining chapters may emphasize varying aspects of the three theoretical perspectives, they will rarely conform exclusively to them. Thus the historical analysis of the stress discourse presented in chapter 2 was clearly influenced by Foucauldian work, but the aim was not to present a Foucauldian genealogy. Similarly, to the extent that chapters 4 and 5 emphasize the relevance of the stress discourse and practice to employee control and consent, they echo aspects of labour process theory. Nevertheless they are not simply labour process accounts, but also draw on other influences such as radical-structural critique. Finally, though the examination of explicit and implicit feeling rules in chapter 6 has some parallel with the work of Elias, its focus is far more on present rather than historical analysis. In sum, the present chapter gives a backdrop to the remainder of the book, but our concern from here on is to work around this theoretical 'stage' rather than to remain entirely bound by it.

In the next chapter, Jocelyn Handy will provide a radically different view of stress and distress through being attentive to issues of power and structural context. The chapter will relate dominant models of work stress to Burrell and Morgan's (1979) paradigmatic distinctions. It will then particularly develop the emphasis on the *collective* experience of stress that we have seen exampled in the Tavistock and Scandinavian work, illustrating the collective human agency that is involved in the reproduction of stressful social structures (see chapter 2). In chapter 5 I will then explore the correspondence between the individualism of stress theory and stress management, through examining the deployment in organizations of stress management practices such as relaxation, meditation and counselling.

Notes

1 Nevertheless, there has for some time been acknowledgement of the need to look beyond the labour process to the full 'circuit of capital' (Kelly, 1985), and the need to examine other factors such as the recruitment of labour and the realization of surplus value in product markets. To 'put it in plainer business language, management is more likely to be concerned with the *outcomes* of the labour process in terms of sales, marketing or cash flow' (Thompson, 1992: 231). Analysis of factors relating to labour and product markets are therefore potentially as important as those focusing on the production process.

2 Labour process writers have long argued for the need for a Marxist psychology which could examine the social psychological processes by which employee consent is obtained in the workplace (Burawoy, 1979). Thompson argues that a psychology informed by a Marxist interpretation is inevitably limited because the Marxist analysis of capitalism does not address issues of individual identity. He suggests that there is a fundamental need to examine how the labour process and class formation are related to individual identity by exploring the 'subjective factor' in the workplace. In reviewing the contributions of labour process writers to an analysis of subjectivity, Thompson argues that there has been very little attention to the relationship between identity and the existence or lack of worker resistance. He emphasizes that it is insufficient to have 'every confidence in the working class'

(Thompson, 1990 quoting Braverman, 1974: 116), or other variations on some leap of faith in order to present a glimmer of revolutionary change.

3 Labour process theory has also been subject to the criticism that it overemphasizes the significance of the workplace as a site of social change. Though Braverman's thesis placed serious doubts on the proposition that the workplace constituted the primary site of struggle, subsequent major labour process texts have tended to end their deliberations by outlining some vision of a revolution of consciousness, wherein it is up to workers to become aware of their 'real' interests, and their oppression within capitalism (e.g. Edwards's argument that workers will 'see the common content of their struggles' when they 'raise a challenge to the existing system of control in the firm': 1979: 215). Though more recent labour process thinking has rejected such false consciousness determinism, as well as moving toward a piecemeal rather than revolutionary account of change (e.g. Thompson, 1990), it remains the case that the workplace is still often assumed to represent the primary site of struggle, the essential means of a change in people's political consciousness and identity. But as Tanner et al. (1992) have recently argued, there is very little research evidence to support this view. Rather they demonstrate how there has been a 'failure to document a strong connection between objective work experiences and working class social imagery', and that in any case 'most research indicates that work-centred factors exert less influence upon worker consciousness and action than other social experiences' (1992: 447). They do note that not all labour process theorists support the centrality of the workplace in social change, and that Thompson in particular has argued that 'there is no necessary theoretical or empirical link between conflict and exploitation at work and those wider social transformations' (1992: 448, quoting Thompson, 1990: 448). Yet as Tanner et al. further argue, once this point is ceded, labour process theory looks in danger of losing its main theoretical energy. For if the workplace is not significant, and if the prospect of revolutionary change looks 'far from the case' (Thompson, 1990: 445), the question remains as to what then distinguishes labour process theory from any pluralistic account of organizations. Tanner et al. argue that Thompson's reformulation expressed in his core theory 'renders the (shifting) paradigm virtually indistinguishable from more mainstream formulations' (1992: 448).

The work of Tanner et al. presents a strong critique hitting at the heartland of labour process theory. Yet to be fair here, it could still be argued that labour process theory remains distinctive because of its very emphasis both on the workplace and on processes of workplace control. It is true that it is hardly unique in this respect, but it has served to highlight control processes within a radical framework that is continually attentive to the negative and repressive possibilities of power.

4 A very brief account of Foucault is presented here, focusing on his later work because of its relevance to the consideration of subjectivity. It should be noted however that, while there are a number of similarities between the earlier and later work of Foucault, there are also a number of differences (e.g. between the emphasis given in his archaeological and genealogical periods of analysis, and with the focus on ethics in the later volumes of *The History of Sexuality*; see Rabinow, 1984).

5 For Foucault, this perfect architecture of surveillance represented 'the diagram of a mechanism of power reduced to its ideal form' (1979: 205). He utilized the symbol of the panopticon to illustrate how modernity is characterized by fine webs of surveillance, centred around the ability to make normalizing judgements through observational techniques such as psychiatric, psychological and educational examinations and tests. The panopticon 'does the work of the naturalist' since it is possible

to 'map attitudes, to assess characters, to draw up rigorous classifications' (1979: 203).

6 Social science and medical discourse had to uncover the sexual deviancy underlying 'cases' such as 'the nervous woman, the frigid wife, the indifferent mother – or worse, the mother beset by murderous obsessions – the impotent, sadistic, perverse husband, the hysterical or neurasthenic girl, the precocious and already exhausted child, and the young homosexual who rejects marriage and neglects his wife' (Foucault, 1981: 110). Such cases appear as the secular equivalent of the sinner, and discourses such as medicine, psychiatry and psychology proffered solutions to these perversions of the normal and the healthy. The power of such discourses was strengthened by eugenic arguments that sexual abnormalities would be genetically passed on to future generations, wherein perversions would be cumulative and eventually lead to a total degeneration of the population. Foucault concluded: 'The series composed of perversion–heredity–degenerescence formed the solid nucleus of the new technologies of sex' (1981: 118).

Foucault further suggested that the significance of sex was heightened by the development of psychoanalysis. For Freud, sex still appears as the dangerous secret, but now its danger lay not so much in its celebration as in its repression. The discourse of psychoanalysis provided a technology to alleviate this repression, and further aid individuals to find themselves through discovering the truth which sex conceals, 'to the endless task of forcing its secret' (1981: 159). The irony of this supposed liberation is that we are trapped inside psychoanalytical discourse, and the discourses which have flowed from it (e.g. self-growth and psychotherapeutic discourse). Such discourses suggest that we must free ourselves through overcoming the dangers of any kind of repression. Foucault conjectured that in future centuries people may wonder at the power of such discourse, and its ability to convince us that 'our "liberation" is in the balance' (1981: 159). Sexuality 'has become more important than our soul' (1981: 156), and yet to medieval minds, concupiscence was a madness, a wound upon the body. It is not difficult to find present-day illustrations of the supposed significance of sexuality (and repression more generally), and the liberatory potential that derives from learning the truth about ourselves. To take just one example, an article on sexual 'chemistry' in *Cosmopolitan* concludes: 'Sex is really just a mirror for us, a mirror that reflects the state of our mind, our heart and our soul. Knowing this, you can actually transform your sex life from being something mysterious and confusing into something that is both enlightening and magical' (January 1993: 143). Forcing the secret of sex will be enlightening and magical because sex is just a mirror to our hearts, minds and soul.

7 The stress discourse can also be seen as a more subtle deployment of a consensus, unitary or industrial harmony image associated with other 1980s discourses such as that of the flexible firm model. At the level of personnel employment strategy, the latter model can be seen as celebrating the image of the worker as a flexible resource, and in consequence may legitimize 'an array of management practices ranging from job enlargement to labour intensification, casualization, and de-unionization' (Pollert, 1991: 27). The stress discourse has the advantage in that it is less politically transparent than the flexible firm model, yet the worker subject it creates is certainly in keeping with the image of flexibility, being that of a finely honed and toned stress-fit resource who is ready to do almost anything an employer wants, and keen to do it well.

8 Though utilizing a quite different framework, Giddens (1991) makes a similar point in his discussion of self-reflexivity.

9 The goal of stress management in developing the enterprising coper also complements another 1980s discursive development, namely the interest in culture and in developing cultures of excellence (Peters and Waterman, 1982; Deal and Kennedy, 1982), since turning a culture around means having stress-fit employees who will be able to cope with rapid change. Thus stress and culture provide complementary discourses which interlock with ideals of enterprise associated with 1980s developments in the government of both state and organization.

10 Nevertheless, one can argue that the stress discourse reveals how people are *produced* as stress-fit subjects in a manner which cannot be viewed as simply repressive, and indeed may be positive since people may learn insights and practices that they find valuable and helpful in making sense of their lives, and they may be better able to cope with both their work and their domestic lives. Following this argument, one might be receptive to the generally neutral stance taken by Foucault, what Dews has called his 'standard fall-back position' (1987: 162).

11 While the second and third volumes of *The History of Sexuality* pay greater attention to the ethics of the self, and though elsewhere Foucault (1988) explores the implication of discourse for subjectivity, there is still no detailed account of how subjects manoeuvre in and around discourse and practice.

One final point about Foucault's work is that his arguments are not always as novel and uniquely inspired as they are sometimes made to appear. For example, though operating in a quite different theoretical framework, Sennett has made some similar comments on the modern meaning of sexuality to those of Foucault, arguing that 'sex is a revelation of the self' whereby 'we unendingly and frustratingly go in search of ourselves through our genitals' (1977: 7). Similarly Lasch argued that the 'new mode of social control' operates through a 'diffusion of discipline' (1977: 185). As illustration, he quotes a study of US high-school students who were asked how they thought unruly students should be disciplined. They suggested that such students should be neither beaten nor publicly humiliated; rather the 'students voted overwhelmingly that the offender should be sent to the school psychiatrist' (1977: 185). Following Lasch, discipline occurs through discourse, rather than a simple punishment of the body, a theme very similar to that espoused in Foucault's *Discipline and Punish*.

12 Another bridge between Foucault and Elias is provided by Burkitt's (1993) critique of Foucault. Burkitt argues that there is a denial of the social within Foucault's explanation of the relation between discourse and practice. Ultimately the motor for the development of particular practices, whether those relating to the school, the asylum or the office, lies with Nietzschean notions of the inevitability of conflict because of 'the clash between disparate individuals each struggling for its own survival and the satisfaction of its instincts' (Burkitt, 1993: 60). Because conflict is seen as arising out of *essential* instincts, such an account effectively denies the social. Though Foucault does not adopt Nietzschean neo-Darwinism wholesale, Burkitt argues that he still relies on a fundamentally asocial view, promoting essentialist notions of the inevitability of conflict.

13 There are notable parallels between the work of Elias and the attention of Giddens to tacit 'rules'. For example, Giddens argues that 'most of the rules implicated in the production and reproduction of social practices are only tacitly grasped by actors: they know how to "go on" ' (1984: 22). An example of this knowledgeability about how to go on is provided by Goffman's notion of framing, or the clusters of rules which define social activities, so that we know that 'a fight can be "play", and apparently serious comment, a joke' (Giddens, 1984: 88). Because

Giddens sees rules as often only tacitly grasped by individuals, they are also closely related to another central concept of Giddens's theorizing, namely that of practical consciousness, or the 'recall to which the agent has access in the *durée* of action without being able to express what he or she knows' (1984: 49). Practical consciousness is distinguished from discursive consciousness, that which the individual can express verbally. For Giddens, the knowledgeability about how to go on and, in consequence, to reproduce social structures and systems is 'founded less upon discursive than practical consciousness' (1984: 26). Following this argument, the codes of practical consciousness and the influences upon them, become central to understanding human behaviour. The work of Elias can be seen as providing a historical analysis of the way in which power relations are relevant to the forming of significant aspects of our practical consciousness.

14 Wouters also argues that 'academic, artistic and social care centres' (1987: 424) acted as promoters of the most recent period of informalization (which he dates as 1966–79). In the period since 1979, he sees a temporary move back towards greater formalization, as ideals of equality faded under anxieties over *economic* security and unemployment. Such insecurities meant that 'many people once again felt much more dependent on their immediate superiors and on the elites in the commercial and managerial centres' (1987: 425). In consequence the 1980s saw a promotion of the mores of such elites, of yuppie values, which themselves incorporated more traditional notions of inequality (e.g. that men should provide for women). Yet in spite of the 1980s, Wouters (1987) argues that the trajectory is towards greater informalization (for example, he notes that Dutch etiquette books of the 1980s tend to stress that social rules are now far less clear, and that it is up to the individual to respond flexibly to particular social situations). It's interesting that Wouters here implies a relation between discourse (e.g. on equality), its institutionalization (e.g. 'academic, artistic, social care centres'), and tacit behavioural/affective codes.

15 It is not difficult to find examples in the general media of discourse which argues that healthy families are those which are emotionally open. One such example is provided by an article in *The Independent on Sunday* (27 December 1992: 37), the messages of which are far from atypical. Published close to Christmas, it deals with the then topical subject of coping with families, or 'War and peace in the home'. The author, Angela Neustatter, tried to explain 'why rows can be good for you' since 'family battles inflict injuries but also release tensions'. As with the articles on stress which I examined in chapter 1, the article proceeds via a problematization of emotional expression in the family to prescriptions for fitness practice through the calling up of a host of experts. For example, the article cites an illustration from Hugh Jenkins, the Director of the Institute of Family Therapy, which shows how 'furies that are never expressed can create tensions and an atmosphere of hostility':

> He [Jenkins] points to a family where the husband had learnt as a child to control his emotions, particularly anger. He would go to great lengths to avoid conflict, while his wife was emotionally eruptive; she was used to getting things out, dealing with them and leaving them behind. She became convinced he didn't care about her because he didn't respond to her. Tensions mounted until one day she hit him with a saucepan. He responded by grabbing her throat. At this point, they realized they had a crisis and went for help.

Clearly the too tight control of emotional expression is now a problem area: the stiff upper lip would appear to be in danger of resulting in something resembling attempted homicide (and of course, we 'know' that murder often is committed by lovers and relatives). In the modern age, though, people can go for help and learn to become 'family-fit'. For example, quoting Jenkins again, the article suggests that 'the family gets together two or three times a week for about 15 minutes, during which each member can have their say'. This seems a far cry from now outmoded imperatives to minimize emotionality, since the family is now encouraged to let it all out through creating its own regular group therapy. It also ironically implies that the new tacit rule is precisely that family life can no longer be taken for granted. The discourse thus directly addresses our practical consciousness, how people normally go on in families, through the kind of problematization observed by Foucault, and through the elaboration of new discursive practices which both observe and speak to the problem.

16 It might however also be argued that there are factors other than power relations which support emotional restraint in the workplace. One such is the physical containment that most employees experience. For example, because people cannot easily escape the workplace, they may be wary of having an argument with a colleague on Friday since they will still be there on Monday – and in consequence, restraint makes sense. Yet the same is true of domestic settings which may be far harder to escape from, but where there is far less emotional constraint. There is though a significant difference between the domestic and the employment setting in that the former is generally associated with greater intimacy, which in itself might be expected to encourage greater emotional expression. Yet whilst this may often be the case, it doesn't explain the question of why there are barriers to either intimacy or emotional expression in the workplace. Elias however does provide us with an answer in pointing to how power relations relate to affective and behavioural constraint. Within a post-monarchic history of civility and deference to our betters, it is not entirely surprising that we show emotional tact and diplomacy rather than letting it all hang out.

4

Rethinking Stress: Seeing the Collective

Jocelyn Handy

Chapter 2 charted the discursive development of stress research. In order to illustrate further the theoretical narrowness of this discourse, this chapter will relate it to the paradigm analysis provided by Burrell and Morgan (1979). It will then attempt to explore alternative ways in which the discourse might have been written through the examination of four empirical studies which each bear out different aspects of the complex relationship between the collective experiences of the workers and the conditions in which they labour.

Current Models

In their seminal work on organizational analysis, Burrell and Morgan (1979) suggested that the core assumptions governing different theories can often be clarified by utilizing a heuristic centring on the two key dimensions of social regulation versus social change, and subjectivity versus objectivity. They argue that if these two issues are regarded as orthogonal dimensions, four relatively self-contained paradigms emerge (see figure 4.1). Each paradigm has internally self-consistent assumptions concerning the individual, society, evidence and intervention, but each neglects, or opposes, the insights provided by other perspectives. Thus, if research in a given field is dominated by a particular set of meta-theoretical assumptions it will tend to supply a view of social reality which is superficially plausible but which may, on re-examination, prove to have a number of rather questionable assumptions lying unexamined at its core. Such can be seen to be the case with stress research where the dominance of an ostensibly apolitical and highly individualistic approach located firmly within Burrell and Morgan's functionalist paradigm has ensured that alternative viewpoints, such as the more socially aware studies which have characterized Scandinavian research on work stress, remain marginalized (see chapter 2).

Change

	Radical humanist	*Radical structuralist*
	Core view of society: social institutions such as the state, multinational corporations and the professions dominate the production of knowledge.	*Core view of society*: fundamental and unresolvable conflicts originate in capitalist economic structures which give disparate wealth, power and opportunity to different classes.
	Sources of stress: the social and organizational structures promulgated by these institutions produce alienation, individualism and the breakdown of communities.	*Sources of stress*: the demands of a capitalist economy which creates economic exploitation, inequalities in education and health care, and marginalization of economically irrelevant groups.
	Typical solutions: mutual self-aid and consciousness leading to economic and structural changes.	*Typical solutions*: radical restructuring of economic bases of society.

Subjective ————————————————————————— **Objective**

	Interpretative	*Functionalist*
	Core view of society: society is maintained through shared meanings and subjective interpretations.	*Core view of society*: social structures are based on a broadly shared value system which benefits all and is both enduring and adaptable.
	Sources of stress: the meanings people give to their actions or to the actions of others.	*Sources of stress*: personal misfortune or pathology, inappropriate adaptation by specific subcultures or communities, minor structural dysfunctions.
	Typical solutions: therapy aimed at facilitating the reframing of events.	*Typical solutions*: individual counselling or treatment, promotion of dominant value system, fine tuning of existing structures.

Regulation

Figure 4.1 *Paradigmatic views of occupational stress (adapted from Burrell and Morgan, 1979; Whittingham and Holland, 1985)*

The traditional work stress literature contains numerous competing models (see chapter 2). For the sake of brevity, I shall apply Burrell and Morgan's heuristic to one model which exhibits many of the common characteristics of recent stress models, namely that provided by Cooper (1986). His model adopts the transactional perspective found in many 1980s models of stress (e.g. Fletcher and Payne, 1980), wherein stress is seen as the product of an interaction between individual needs and resources and the various demands, constraints and facilitators within the individual's immediate environment. The model is illustrated in figure 4.2.

Cooper's model initially appears to offer an informative and comprehensive overview of both the causes of work stress and the organizational and individual problems which may arise when the individual worker experiences those stressors. He locates the individual worker centre-stage within his model and then analyses the causes of stress in terms of a series of discrete low-level stressors located firmly within the boundaries of the organization or the nuclear family. At first glance this seems the logical, and perhaps the only, starting place for models of work stress, as stress is undeniably a subjective psychological experience. However, by placing the individual centre-stage, Cooper presents his reader with an explanation which implies that stress is primarily about character defects of the individual worker (evinced by personality traits, 'type A', neuroticism etc.), and her inability to cope with the vagaries of organizational life. And implicit in this kind of analysis is a symbiotic relationship between its individualism and the focus in stress management practice on 'remedial' work on individuals designed to make them stress-fit and productive (chapter 5 will provide a more detailed analysis of the way in which this symbiosis evokes images of social control and regulation).

Cooper thus presents his reader with a model which starts from a theoretical position emphasizing the differences between workers rather than the ways in which the collective experiences of particular groups of workers generate common forms of perception and action. As noted with the stress models examined in chapter 2, the effect of this is to depoliticize the entire problem of work stress by denying the primacy of shared experiences and reducing organizational issues affecting the collective to a question of individual differences in stress appraisal and coping ability.

The medical terminology adopted by Cooper also facilitates the task of sanitizing organizational life by implying that both the individual and the organizational outcomes of stress are self-evidently pathological and thus in need of treatment rather than illumination. By extending the medical analogy from the physical

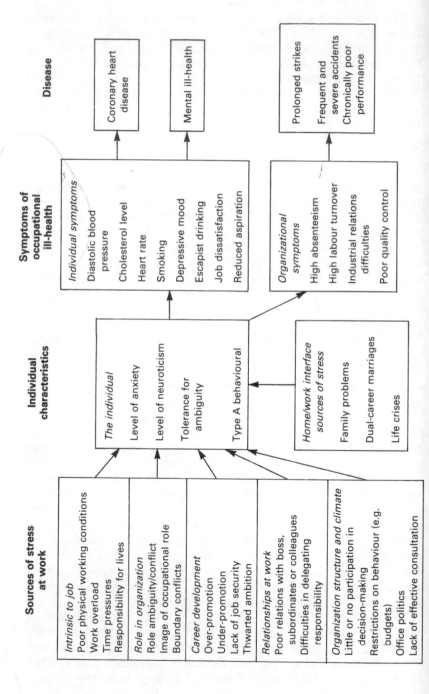

problems of the worker to organizational problems as defined by management, Cooper effectively creates the illusion that the organization itself is an organic entity which shows 'symptoms' such as absenteeism and suffers from 'diseases' ranging from strikes to chronically poor performance. Reifying the organization in this way has two main effects. Firstly, this strategy diverts attention from the effects of human agency in the creation of organizational life and by so doing helps to obscure the differing political allegiances, goals and power bases of competing groups within the organization. Secondly, this metaphor helps to justify the use of individualistic and medicalized solutions such as stress management training (see chapter 5). A consensus model of society which tacitly assumes that organizations are specialized subsystems of the wider social system, geared to the rational achievement of various socially agreed goals, is thus legitimized by using quasi-medical terminology to obtain a veneer of political neutrality and scientific authority.

This kind of analytic framework is clearly not the only perspective on organizational life which could be adopted. Rather, the dominance of this view within the British and American stress literature reflects the essential conservatism within this field. It is true that there have been a number of calls for change within the last decade (e.g. Kasl, 1978; Payne, 1978; Parkes, 1982; Brief and Atieh, 1987), but the issues raised have generally either concerned intra-paradigmatic issues such as definitions, measurement techniques and experimental design or involved pleas for a move from a functionalist perspective to a theoretical position which Burrell and Morgan would probably characterize as falling within an interpretative but still essentially regulatory paradigm. This type of approach is revealed most clearly in the work of someone like Firth-Cozens (Firth, 1985; Firth and Shapiro, 1986; Firth-Cozens, 1992) who adopts a fairly conventional psychoanalytic framework and argues that problems which initially appear to be work related can be reinterpreted as intrapsychic dilemmas which have their roots in childhood and are amenable to therapeutic intervention using an individually oriented psychoanalytic theoretical framework. Whilst this approach may reveal the complexities of the individual psyche more clearly than the traditional nomothetic approach to work stress, it remains highly conservative in its political implications since it emphasizes the primacy of past and private traumas, and fails to address the relationship between the current social environment and the individual's subjective experience in any depth.

Rethinking the subjectivity of distress means moving beyond simplistic models which isolate the individual worker from the rest of the workforce and towards more complex analyses which acknowledge both the collective nature of people's adaptation to the work environment and the centrality of power and conflict within organizational life. This does not imply that the analysis of individual differences is irrelevant since the character of different individuals will probably vary to some degree as a result of different genetic inheritances and life experiences. However, as noted in chapter 2, it does suggest that the current preoccupation with individual processes of appraisal and coping inevitably obscures the manifold commonalities between members of a given social group. In consequence, research investigating stress and subjectivity needs to recognize that the process of collective adaptation to the work environment involves the dynamic unfolding of collective coping strategies which may help to reproduce environments which many employees already experience as stressful.

In sum, discourses of subjectivity such as that of stress are currently limited by their de-emphasizing of the collective work experiences of particular occupational groups. The second section of this chapter will now attempt to explore alternative ways in which the discourse might have been written by describing four research studies which, though they are not traditionally classified as stress research, are of relevance to employees' collective experience of stress and distress.

Four Exemplars

The four studies described in this section all fall broadly within the radical humanist/structuralist perspective as defined by Burrell and Morgan (1979), and share several common features. Firstly, they all take the relationship between interlinked social groups as the key unit of study and use the insights provided by this focus to derive an enhanced appreciation of individual experiences. Secondly, they all emphasize that subjective experiences of stress cannot be fully understood either through a theoretical stance which isolates individual experience from its context, or through an approach which regards people as mere puppets of inexorable structural forces operating without their involvement. Thirdly, they all argue that contradictions within society and organizations are reflected in people's fragmentary and ambiguous understanding of their situation, with the result that actions often take place within unacknowledged conditions and have unintended consequences (Giddens, 1984). Fourthly, they all suggest that these unintended outcomes tend to undermine the efficacy of people's coping strategies, thus increasing their subjective experiences of stress. Finally, they all utilize in-depth qualitative data to demonstrate the complex unfolding of these processes over time.

The first example is Pollert's (1981) study of women workers' responses to the impending closure of the tobacco factory where they were employed. While this study has received considerable attention within sociological literature, its relevance to an understanding of distress has been totally ignored by mainstream stress researchers. In contrast to many studies within the stress literature, which have relied on workers' subjective accounts of their job conditions, Pollert draws upon her industrial relations background to develop a clear analysis of the company structure and the women's actual working conditions. These factors are then related to the women's subjective experiences and to the process of adaptation to the plant closure. The strength of Pollert's book thus lies not only in the wealth of ethnographic data which she presents to substantiate her arguments, but also in her careful interweaving of the social structural and subjective elements of social reality. Pollert's analysis of the conditions facing the workforce reveals that the women formed the majority of a relatively uneducated labour force within a company structure where both management and union activities were dominated by males. In consequence, the women's involvement in the labour process was trivialized by those in positions of power, the skill and difficulty of their jobs was underestimated in company job evaluation schemes, and the economic necessity driving most of them to work was discounted.

Pollert's clear descriptions of the stresses created by this work environment and the dual burdens of work and family responsibilities are compatible with much research within the traditional stress literature. However, she advances beyond this approach with her analysis of the complex web of resistance and collusion which characterized the women's habitual responses to the dominant ideology of factory life. On the one hand, the women recognized and resented the devaluation of their labour, but on the other hand, they concurred with the male view that their primary identities resided in their roles as sex objects, wives and mothers. In consequence, they generally attempted to come to terms with their conditions of work either by conceptualizing work as a stopgap between school and marriage or by emphasizing the importance of their other traditional roles in their interactions with male colleagues and management. This response pattern reinforced union and management stereotypes concerning female workers and thus helped deny the women the limited control exercised by male workers (cf. E.M. Hall, 1989). This lack of control was then interpreted as their own fault by the women while the objective constraints limiting their involvement in the union went unrecognized. As a result, they conceptualized their passivity in terms of personal or gender-related failings, an attribution which reinforced their feelings of inferiority and helped to perpetuate a fatalistic and acquiescent attitude towards the factory closure. Thus, as Pollert shows, social structures within the women's environment acted both as stressors in their own right and as factors which shaped the women's perceptions and actions in ways which caused them to contribute to the maintenance of many of the stress-producing features of the factory environment.

The second example is Hochschild's (1983) study of emotional labour which examines the ways in which the contractual obligation to 'manufacture' emotion as a saleable commodity damages workers within the growing service sector. Hochschild concentrates primarily on the experiences of female workers, using airline hostesses in one of the larger American companies as her exemplar. However, like Pollert before her, she locates the experiences of her focal group within a network of gendered relationships with customers and other staff, and ties her analysis into a wider examination of changing economic circumstances facing the airline industry during the late 1970s and early 1980s.

Hochschild suggests that there is a fundamental contradiction in paying people to offer emotional care which ultimately degrades both the purveyors and the recipients of such ersatz experiences by blurring the divide between authenticity and sham within human relationships. As she shows, cabin crew at Delta Airlines were socialized during their initial training into believing not only that they had to make customers feel cosseted and valued but that they had to genuinely experience positive regard for them and suppress both negative behaviour and negative emotions towards the airline's clientele. In Hochschild's terms, staff were indoctrinated into believing that they had a contractual obligation to engage in 'deep' rather than 'surface' acting and draw upon their emotional resources to offer a genuine welcome which would enhance the reputation, profit and market share of the company. Customers, in contrast, had no obligation to repay staff emotion through reciprocal displays of concern, having paid for the staff's care in the ticket price. They did, however, have a problem in deciding whether the friendliness demonstrated by staff was simply a routine response, in which case its emotional value could be discounted, or whether staff were giving something additional to them as particular individuals. These two factors often combined to influence customers' behaviour, making them demand additional services from staff as proof of some personal involvement. These problems were worse for female cabin staff, partly because of social stereotypes concerning the quasi-sexual and maternal role of air-hostesses, and partly because the majority of the airline's customers were males, a proportion of whom acted as though both their gender and their economic relationship with staff entitled them to enter into a relationship of token intimacy with female staff. These problems were exacerbated by the advent of mass travel in the 1970s, when the number of passengers needing to be serviced ensured that staff had to work to tight schedules in order to complete their allocated tasks, and were therefore unable to give customers the individual care which the airline's advertising continued to promise. This created a backlash from disgruntled customers which staff were expected to cope with through emotional labour which gave priority to customers' needs. Faced with these stresses, staff tended to react in one of two ways, each with its own emotional risks. Some workers tended to move from a position of being genuinely emotionally involved in their work to a position of emotional detachment in both their work and their personal lives. Thus having initially responded to the company's exhortations to identify themselves with their jobs, these workers were unable to conceptualize the hostile behaviour of customers as a response to their occupational roles rather than their 'true' selves and were forced to deal with the emotional pain of their jobs through a global deadening of the capacity to feel. Other staff initially dealt with their work problems by developing a healthy estrangement from the job which enabled them to recognize when, and to what extent, they were acting. This solution worked adequately whilst staff maintained some control over the pacing of their work, although it often created an uneasy sense of their own emotional shallowness in staff, but it failed when the rate of work increased and obviated the time available for emotional acting. Since one of the basic prerequisites of satisfactory job performance was the capacity to act in a friendly and caring manner at all times, the increasing detachment of such staff meant that they were often perceived as performing their jobs badly and were reacted to negatively by customers, occasioning further emotional withdrawal by staff. Thus, as Hochschild illustrates, the stresses involved in performing emotional labour under conditions which militate against successful performance can create a situation in which staff became alienated from both the job and their own personal identities as feeling human beings.

The third example is Satyamurti's (1981) study of social workers. Both the theoretical perspective and the methodology employed within this research distinguish it from the numerous studies of social work stress which have appeared in the mainstream literature. Such studies often identify issues of particular concern to social workers in their daily lives, but rarely analyse the ways in which these issues are influenced by the superordinate functions and structure of social work as an institution. In contrast, Satyamurti's study locates individual jobs within a wider framework and emphasizes the interrelationships between the inherent contradictions of the institution and the subjective experiences and actions of field social workers.

The central argument developed by Satyamurti is that the stresses experienced by social workers have their roots in the imbalance between the demands which the state places on social workers and the resources that it places at their disposal. Satyamurti argued that most of the practical and emotional problems experienced by the clients of the social workers could be traced back to the chronic material deprivation in which they lived. Unfortunately, the social workers had limited access to the material resources necessary to alleviate the root causes of their clients' problems. In consequence, they were forced to try and tackle these problems through individually focused strategies aimed at changing their clients' behaviours or providing them with emotional support. Satyamurti further argued that, not surprisingly, such strategies often failed, leaving the social workers feeling inadequate and frustrated. The individual focus of the social workers' daily interactions with their clients often caused them to blame the clients both for the negative outcomes of their helping strategies and also for their resultant feelings of professional inadequacy and dissatisfaction. These attributions often led, in their turn, to altered work patterns in which the social workers tried to cope with their stress by withdrawing their emotional labour and routinizing their relationships with clients. Regrettably, this often had the paradoxical effect of reducing the social workers' already limited ability to help their clients and exacerbating the tensions in their relationship with clients. Thus, as a result of personal feelings of stress generated by the contradictions of their work, many social workers ended up blaming the very people they originally intended to help. Interestingly, Satyamurti also found that social workers who had a clear understanding of these contradictions were less inclined to feel personally incompetent when their helping strategies failed and were therefore better equipped to cope with the vagaries of their work without withdrawing from clients.

The final example is Handy's (1990) study of stress in psychiatric nurses. Like the authors of the other studies described in this section, Handy eschews the traditional preoccupation with one group of players, arguing instead that the stresses which staff face cannot be fully understood without interpreting the various ways in which people participate in the psychiatric system. The main theme of Handy's study is that psychiatry's dual mandate to control and care for the 'mentally ill' creates fundamental contradictions which find concrete expression in the daily interactions between staff and patients. As a result their relationships frequently have a variety of unintended and equivocal consequences which are highly distressing for all concerned and which contribute to the reproduction of many of the more pernicious characteristics of organizational life within psychiatric institutions.

One of the clearest findings of the study was that the nurses' daily activities centred on social control. Such activities were frequently incompatible with strategies which might have helped patients to understand, alter or come to terms with the personal circumstances of their lives and also with the nurses' self-image as professional carers. The nurses frequently tried to resolve this conflict by conceptualizing the problem patients as either 'bad' or 'mad'. The first group were regarded as abusers of the system who not only were undeserving of help but also prevented other patients from receiving the help they deserved. The second group tended to be conceptualized as lacking control as a result of their illness, which enabled control-oriented activities such as the administration of tranquilizing medication to disruptive patients to be reinterpreted as therapeutic activities. This interpretation neatly integrated with the social control and treatment concerns of the staff in a manner which helped maintain the psychiatric ideology of uncoercive care but often had the unintended consequence of heightening patients' hostility towards the nurses and increasing the necessity for further control-oriented activities. While their routine interpretations of patients' behaviour helped the nurses integrate their daily actions with their self-image as helpers, the interview data revealed that many of the younger nurses were aware of, and troubled by, discrepancies between their daily actions and their therapeutic ideals. This awareness sometimes led to piecemeal attempts to develop more therapeutically oriented relationships with individual patients. Unfortunately, such innovations often failed because of both the nurses' inexperience and the control-oriented structure of the hospital environment. The repeated failure of their attempts to help often triggered feelings of intense insecurity in staff and frequently led to defensive reactions in which they blamed patients for being unmotivated to change. One solution to these feelings of rejection and incompetence was to adopt a more instrumental and routine-oriented attitude towards work. This strategy was encouraged by more experienced staff, partly because it facilitated the smooth maintenance of ward routines, and partly because they saw it as a way of helping younger staff avoid the disappointments of close patient contact. The potential for change which was inherent in the younger nurses' dissatisfaction with their working conditions was thus becoming channelled into the maintenance of existing patterns and facilitated the re-creation of the very system many nurses found unsatisfactory and stress producing.

Conclusion

This chapter has argued that the theoretical and methodological individualism underpinning most current models of work stress places such research firmly within a functionalist paradigm. The exemplars provided above show however that this is far from the only way in which the stress discourse might have been written. Rather the current text of the discourse appears as a consequence of its elevation of the individual, and the denial of the ways in which employees may collectively reproduce work conditions which they already experience as stressful. At the same time, it downplays (a) the economic, organizational and occupational context of stress, (b) the relevance of social stratification, as in the relationship between gender and stress, and (c) the regulatory implications of an individualistic and functionalist discourse.

The implications of this individualism will be further explored in the next chapter, which provides a detailed analysis of organizational practices associated with the stress discourse, the techniques of so-called stress management.

5

Becoming 'Stress-Fit'

'But I am not guilty,' said K., 'it's a misunderstanding. And if it comes to that, how can any man be called guilty? We are all simply men here, one as much as the other.'

'That is true,' said the priest, 'but that's how all guilty men talk.'

(Franz Kafka, *The Trial*)

In this chapter we shall move on from consideration of the work stress discourse, and alternatives to it, to examining the kinds of organizational practice that are associated with it; that is to say, what organizations are doing in managing stress amongst their employees. I will use the label that the stress discourse generally employs to describe these practices, namely 'stress management', and attempt to analyse these practices within the socio-political context of the organization in which they are employed.

As we shall see, there is no direct correspondence between work stress research and theory, and stress management (SM) practice. Rather SM practice draws on psychodynamic and psychotherapeutic work that (see chapter 2) has been largely bypassed by the mainstream 'scientific' work stress theory. Nevertheless, as noted in chapter 4, there is a symbiotic relationship between stress theory, research and practice in that they legitimate one another (e.g. evidence of the 'medically damaging symptoms' of work stress necessitates applying the 'treatment' of stress management practice to the 'ill' organization), and they both rely on a highly individualized and apolitical account of stress.

The Practice of Stress Management

Currently most writers on work stress management refer to one of three forms of SM practice: employee assistance programmes (EAPs); stress management training (SMT); and stress reduction or intervention (SI) (Murphy, 1988). The first of these forms, EAPs, generally refers to the provision of employee counselling services by an organization. The second, SMT, refers to training courses designed to provide employees with improved coping (with stress) skills, including training in techniques such as meditation, bio-feedback, muscle relaxation and stress inoculation (Newton, 1992). The third, SI, denotes interventions designed to change the level or form of job stressors experienced by employees, usually through job redesign or work reform. The first two, EAPs and SMT, appear to be increasingly common. Macleod (1985) estimated that in the USA there are at least 8000 companies offering EAPs, whilst their use seems to be increasing in the UK, with organizations such as the Post Office, Whitbread Brewers and the TSB Bank recently introducing counselling services. With SMT, Murphy noted that it has grown in popularity and 'dramatically so in recent years' (1987: 217); whilst in the UK, Arroba and James have argued that the demand for SMT has 'increased noticeably' in the last ten years (1987: xiii). The last form, SI, however, appears only as a prescription by a small number of researchers, and has received very little application as an SM practice (Murphy, 1988).

Survey evidence relating to SM practice is limited, although some data were provided by a study conducted by Neale et al. (1982) for the US National Institute for Occupational Safety and Health (NIOSH). Neale et al. compared the perspectives of US management and union groups towards SM, utilizing a telephone survey of 217 organizations (including union bodies and private and public sector organizations), followed by questionnaire surveys to smaller samples of business and union representatives. They asked questions about SMT and EAPs as well as about work reform. Of the 57 per cent of companies who replied to the questionnaire, 80 per cent said they had 'stress education offerings including litera-ture, classes, and workshops' (1982: 34). With specific regard to SMT, 'interventions, such as relaxation training or meditation, were utilized by 50% to 60% of the companies responding' (1982: 34). They found that both stress education and stress management were more likely to be offered to professional staff. SM programmes were administered by a variety of company departments, including 'Human resources, Personnel, Employee advisory services, Medical department, Educational training, Employee service organization, Psychological services, and Office of stress management' (1982: 32). Those providing the SM included psychologists, health educators, exercise physiologists, training and development staff and legal staff. This research therefore suggests that, as with other social science discourses, the stress discourse summons a wide variety of experts who at the same time draw in a complex range of different discursivities such as psychology, medicine, physiology, manage-ment and law.

A similar discursive input appears when we look beyond the

currently defined confines of work stress management to writers concerned with health promotion. Within the latter literature, the forms of SM noted above appear as part of more general health promotion programmes, composed of 'education, screening or intervention designed to change employees' behavior in a health-ward direction and reduce the associated health risks' (Conrad, 1986). Thus health promotion includes practices such as hypertension screening, smoking cessation, nutrition education, exercise and fitness programmes, as well as EAPs and SMT. Usually however there is also some distinction in this literature between health promotion programmes (HPPs) and EAPs. Thus Roman and Blum define HPPs as being concerned with minimizing health risks in a proactive fashion, whereas EAPs are designed to deal with 'symptoms that have already emerged' (1988: 504). The position of SMT within such a categorization is unclear, but it appears to be treated by health promotion writers as part of HPPs (e.g. Conrad, 1988; Kronenfeld et al., 1988), perhaps because SMT often forms part of proactive training programmes, and is not just applied where employees are perceived to 'have problems'.

Whichever SM area is examined, the primary concern appears to be with labour costs, with the programmes invariably being sold on the basis of improved job performance, reduced absenteeism and so on. For example, in describing the stress counselling service introduced into the UK Post Office in September 1986, Allinson et al. are clear about its rationale:

> Apart from basic humanitarian ideals, there is only one major interest for an organisation in providing counselling facilities for its staff: its success in contributing to enhanced performance levels and decreases in employee costs indicators (e.g. sickness absence, unacceptable levels of labour turnover). (1989: 385)

Similarly in reviewing 'The how, what and why of stress management training', Matteson and Ivancevich noted that, aside from humanitarian concern, the issue of labour costs was a 'compelling' reason for SMT, 'viewed from virtually any perspective' (1982: 770). And finally for an example with HPPs, Bertera argues that 'comprehensive workplace health promotion programs can reduce disability days among blue collar workers and provide a good return on investment' (1990: 1101).

Our primary concern here is with those forms of SM practice which are currently in use, namely EAPs and SMT. I will focus in the main though on EAPs, because they have a longer history of use and, in consequence, can be subject to more detailed critical analysis. The content of EAPs is therefore looked at in some detail below. However, for the benefit of readers unfamiliar with SMT, I

will firstly briefly outline some SMT examples, in order to differentiate and compare it with the subsequent analysis of EAPs.

As noted above, SMT includes training in practices such as
meditation, bio-feedback, progressive muscle relaxation and cognitive training. One can distinguish between those practices which
primarily focus on training people to be able to control the
symptoms of stress, and those which try to provide skills to tackle
job stressors. Meditation, bio-feedback and muscle relaxation are
examples of the former. Meditation is generally advanced in the SM
literature because of its supposed ability to induce a state of
consciousness experienced as deeply relaxing, and characterized by
lowered states of physiological arousal and altered brainwave
activity (particularly increased alpha wave activity). Bio-feedback
attempts to achieve similar ends, but using external means: for
example, electronic sensors can be placed on the body to feed back
information pertinent to the achievement of a relaxed state, such as
the level of alpha brainwave activity. Progressive muscle relaxation
trains individuals to contract and then relax body muscles in order
that they can learn to recognize and relieve bodily tension. In
contrast to these symptom-focused techniques, approaches such as
stress inoculation (Meichenbaum, 1975) focus on the development
of skills to enable individuals to deal with and 'diffuse' stressful
situations at work. Thus stress inoculation gives people a conceptual
framework by which to 'understand' stress, introduces them to
cognitive and behavioural skills which are meant to be effective in
dealing with stress, and then provides practice of such skills whilst
exposed to simulations of real-life job stressors.

With this brief outline of SMT, we can proceed to an analysis of
the development of stress management practice. As noted above, I
will focus here on EAPs, and then examine the implications of this
analysis for SMTs.

The Development of Employee Assistance Programmes

The forerunner of EAPs was the counselling programme undertaken at the Hawthorne works of the Western Electric Company in
Chicago (Levinson, 1961; Murphy, 1988). Although the Hawthorne
counselling programme has been subject to some critical analysis
(Baritz, 1960; Rose, 1988; Hollway, 1991), it is worth re-examining
because (a) it was the forerunner of all other EAPs, (b) it was
applied on a massive scale and (c) it illustrates issues that recur in
subsequent EAPs as well as in SMT.

Western Electric supplied American Telegraph with telephones and other communication equipment (Baritz, 1960). The works themselves constituted a large, yet attractive, industrial complex:

> The Hawthorne Works at first glance resembles a small city. Toward the end of 1950 nearly 20,000 people worked there; in the spring of 1947 it employed over 35,000. Its ivy-covered buildings surround what is known as 'The Campus' – a beautifully landscaped park with gardens, pools, a marble dance floor, and a bandshell. (Wilensky and Wilensky, 1951: 266)

The counselling programme evolved out of the long-term Hawthorne research programme into industrial attitudes and behaviour which commenced in the mid 1920s (Rose, 1988). The counselling programme started in 1936 with a single counsellor, but grew rapidly thereafter. There were five counsellors by the end of 1956, ten by 1938, 29 by 1941, 40 by 1945, 55 by 1948, and finally 64 full-time counsellors by 1954 (Dickson, 1945; Baritz, 1960; Dickson and Roethlisberger, 1966). In 1956, the programme was put under review and subsequently ended for reasons not disclosed by the company. Between 1936 and 1955, about 550,000 counselling interviews were undertaken; the large majority (73 per cent) of these interviews were initiated by the counsellors with the consent of the worker involved (Baritz, 1960: 104). According to Dickson, the head of Hawthorne counselling, each counsellor was assigned about 300 employees 'to whom his entire time is devoted' (1945: 343). Dickson and his colleagues developed a non-directive style of counselling designed to provide 'an emotional release and a relief from tensions' (1945: 347). As Dickson summarized the process:

> The counsellor never interrupts, he never argues, he never gives advice. His function is that of a skilled listener and the attitude he displays encourages the employee to talk about anything which may be of importance to him. The counsellor, while he listens, is seriously trying to understand what *the person is revealing about himself.* (1945: 346, my italics)

As this quotation illustrates, the focus was on analysing individuals and what they might reveal about themselves, not the particularities of the work that they did. However, the problems the workers reported do appear to be directly related to their job and their work experience. The five main categories of 'employee concern' were: keeping and losing a job; unsatisfactory work relations; felt injustices; unsatisfactory relations with authority; and job development. These are issues which do appear to be the stuff of traditional grievance complaints. However, rather than accepting such grievances at face value, the Hawthorne counsellors adopted the psychoanalytical distinction between the manifest problem and the latent or underlying issue: 'frequently the complaint as stated was not the real source of the individual's trouble. Consequently, action based upon the manifest content of the complaint did not assure us that the difficulty would be eliminated' (Dickson, 1945: 244). Thus problems such as felt injustices, or unsatisfactory relations with authority, were not accepted as legitimate grievances. Rather they were treated as the presenting problem and were analysed for what they revealed about the individual, and the latent difficulties she experienced. The counselling interview would allow the employee to explore her underlying feelings, and the possible problems with the ideas and fantasies which she may have (incorrectly) built up:

> the interview . . . stimulates the employee to re-examine the ideas, beliefs and fantasies which have been built up in his mind. Frequently this process brings about a modification of the interpretations the individual makes of his experiences. It is not unusual, for example, for an employee to start out making extreme accusations of unfairness against a particular individual and at the end of the interview to remark, 'Well, I guess he's got his problems and it's not so bad after all.' (Dickson, 1945: 347)

Thus the individual worker could be helped to realize that what she at first might have felt to be a legitimate complaint relating to extreme unfairness was really 'not so bad after all'. As Dickson argued, 'the counselor relationship with the employee is an important stabilizing force' (1945: 347). There is of course an obvious question here: for whom was it stabilizing, the employee or her employer? As Dickson concluded: 'the maladjusted person [i.e. the two-thirds of the workforce who were counselled] can be dealt with without disrupting his normal routines of living' (1945: 347). In this way, counselling might have been valued for its stabilizing potential by some of the Hawthorne management since it promised to minimize any downturn in productivity of the more than 20,000 'maladjusted' Hawthorne employees.

By now, the manipulative possibilities created by the Hawthorne counselling programmes should be clear. While such manipulation may not have been part of any deliberate management strategy at Hawthorne, the potential for refined employee control was not missed by academic commentators at the time. The article of Wilensky and Wilensky (1951) set the tone of this commentary in their study based on the participant observation by the first author, Jeane L. Wilensky, who was employed as a personnel counsellor at Hawthorne from 1947 to 1950. As Wilensky and Wilensky noted, the counselling programme allowed the Hawthorne management to explore the souls of their employees: 'Western Electric . . . has not only entered the worker's social life, his financial life, and his intellectual life, but now, through personnel counseling, his most intimate thoughts, deeds, and desires may be laid bare to a representative of the company' (1951: 266). They noted that the effectiveness of counselling was judged by the ability of the counsellor to reduce feelings of grievance and aid efficient production and job performance. They quoted at length from an internal Hawthorne report which explicitly attempted to sell the counselling programme on the basis of its ability to control workers. By letting out frustrations and 'irrational demands', counselling guarded against any threat of militancy, and helped to guard against 'grievances that might otherwise find expression in other channels' (1951: 276). As Lasch somewhat later put it, this kind of 'personnel management treats the grievance as a kind of sickness, curable by means of therapeutic intervention' (1977: 184).

Though Wilensky and Wilensky were careful to point out that there was no firm evidence that elements of the Western Electric management used counselling as a strategy to avoid union militancy, they nevertheless noted the fact that there had never been any threat of a strike in Hawthorne's history. As they observed: 'If we assume that grievance handling is the core of an active local union's function, we must conclude that the connection between "good employee relations" and a "tame" union is more than coincidental' (1951: 277). Wilensky and Wilensky concluded that the Hawthorne management had used 'a battery of manipulative devices' in order to cope with 'the challenge to its power'.

Following Hawthorne, there were very few developments in counselling up to the Second World War. However the war saw a 'mushrooming of personnel counselling organizations' (Wilensky and Wilensky, 1951: 278). There has been no detailed analysis of the context of this rapid wartime development in counselling. For example, Wilensky and Wilensky simply explain it as being due to 'special dislocations of the war' (1951: 278), whilst Baritz declares that counselling expanded because of the 'tremendous production and engineering demands of the war', and owing to the employment of women workers who 'troubled managers' since 'they had neither the time nor the skill necessary to deal with their problems' (1960: 163). After the war, a few organizations introduced employee counselling programmes. For example, in 1945, Caterpillar Tractor set up a mental health programme with the aid of a team of psychologists and psychiatrists. Three years later Prudential Life Insurance instituted a programme headed by a psychologist which aimed to give employees an improved 'understanding of themselves and others' (Levinson, 1956: 78). Around the same time, Standard Oil also formed a counselling programme in order to provide 'a safety valve for the angry, a stimulant for the bored, an escape for the frustrated, a refuge for the fearful' (Baritz, 1960: 164). However, beyond such documented examples, the post-war expansion of the kind of employee counselling witnessed at Hawthorne appears to have been relatively limited. In addition there was a shift in focus from counselling normal employees towards treatment of troubled employees, especially those with alcoholic problems. The reasons for this shift appear unclear. Baritz (1960) suggests three influences: (1) the decline of women workers after the war; (2) the high cost of well-trained counsellors; and (3) the feeling that supervisors should be able to do their own counselling without the need for outside help. Murphy (1988) cites the survey of industrial mental health programmes conducted by the Menninger Foundation in 1954, which suggested that companies were uncomfortable with the idea of becoming involved with employee mental health.

Whilst this provides some limited explanation as to why Hawthorne-style employee counselling did not expand at this time, it does not explain why alcoholic counselling gradually did. Weiss (1986) cites the first alcohol treatment programme as being instituted at Du Pont in 1942, staffed by company physicians as well as by employees who had 'recovered' from alcoholism through following the programme of Alcoholics Anonymous (AA). Further alcohol programmes followed at companies such as Eastman Kodak, Consolidated Edison, Illinois Bell, Allis Chalmers as well as Western Electric (Weiss, 1986: 68). However the real expansion in alcohol counselling appears to have taken place during the 1970s. In the US, the Department of Health and Human Services (1980) reported an expansion of programmes from 500 to 1973 to 2400 in 1977 and to 4400 in 1979–80 (Murphy, 1988: 306). During this time, the term 'employee assistance programme' gradually appears to have become the label for alcohol counselling. Blum and Roman (1987) argue that the US National Institute on Alcohol Abuse and Alcoholism (NIAAA: a US government agency founded in 1970) played a pivotal role in the development of EAP methods. Although the EAPs dealt with behavioural problems outwith alcoholism, Murphy argues that in general 'EAPs continue to focus on the alcoholic employee' (1988: 307).

Weiss (1986) has provided a detailed critical analysis of alcoholic counselling and EAPs. His starting point is interesting in relation both to EAPs and to the work stress discourse more generally. Weiss draws on Bendix (1956) to argue that EAPs enshrine a convenient managerial ideology, since they relate to ideas which are difficult to assess but which have broad applicability. For example, the definition of who is or is not an alcoholic tends to be extremely vague, yet anyone has the potential to be an alcoholic, and the consequences of alcoholism are seen as extremely grave (so that a policy of 'tough love' is warranted). Defining alcoholism is difficult for a number of reasons. Firstly, models of alcoholism tend to assume that alcoholics will deny their alcoholism, so the fact that someone says that they are not an alcoholic cannot be taken as evidence that they are non-alcoholic. As Weiss noted: 'according to this Catch-22-type-tenet, the best basis on which to positively identify someone as an alcoholic is for that person to deny having problems with alcohol' (1986: 126). In consequence, it can be very easy to convert suspicions that, say, a subordinate is an alcoholic into near confirmation. A second problem with defining alcoholism is where you draw the cut-off point between alcoholism and non-alcoholism. Weiss provided a number of examples in order to illustrate how the cut-off point is often set very low. One example is that of a widely used alcoholism test, based on yes/no answers to 26 questions. The test includes a lot of fairly innocuous items such as 'Do you drink because you are shy with other people?' Yet even if a respondent gives only one yes answer on the test, it is usually taken as a definite warning of alcoholism; if they score two yeses, they are defined as probably an alcoholic. As Weiss pointed out, if a respondent admits that she drinks alone, and drinks at the same time every day, then following the test she would probably be classed as an alcoholic. Whilst the test may 'detect' alcoholics, it is likely to produce an awful lot of false positives, since drinking when one is feeling shy or when one is alone can hardly be taken as proof of alcoholism.

Such dubious tests are used to classify an employee as an alcoholic. Once such a classification has been made, the next step is 'confrontation'. Weiss cited the approach described by Wagner, a former Hawthorne counsellor turned EAP counsellor. Having used the 26-item test described above to establish alcoholism, Wagner then confronts the employee with the following question: ' "Do you want to do something about your alcoholism?" If the answer is no, the employee is on his own regarding his job future' (Wagner, 1982: 61). Given that your job is already in jeopardy, how do you answer? Whilst this scenario appears as an extremely coercive way to extract a 'confession', the alcohol counselling programme described by Wagner is actually more refined than it need be. At least some attempt was made to assess whether alcoholism existed, even if the validity of that assessment was highly dubious. In other EAPs, such assessments may not even be made, the detection of alcoholism being entirely on the basis of an employee's job performance. And in the US, such an approach is actually in line with the recommendations of the NIAAA. In a paper funded by an NIAAA grant,

Blum and Roman noted that what distinguished the new EAP model of the NIAAA from earlier AA programmes was that 'confrontation (a replacement for the term coercion) was to be based on documentable job performance decrement' since this helped to 'minimize the employee's opportunities for denial' (1987: 18). Weiss (1986) documented how organizations took this advice to heart through an examination of company literature describing EAP programmes. For example, Weiss quotes from a 'widely distributed pamphlet' from the Kemper Insurance Companies entitled *What to Do about the Employee with a Drinking Problem*. The pamphlet quotes Trice, a widely known researcher into occupational alcoholism, as stating that: 'Recurrent poor job performance due to the use of alcohol becomes a simple, direct, clear definition of alcoholism . . . Alcoholism is simply repeated poor work.' As Weiss observed: 'To some this definition might read like a Marxist's caricature of occupational medicine in capitalist society – constructing a pernicious disease *whose only symptom* is a loss of productivity and profits for the company. Nevertheless it has considerable currency' (1986: 116, my italics). Focusing on the 'illness' of alcoholism lends great weight to EAP powers of surveillance over potential problem employees, because it rationalizes the doctrine of 'tough love'. Because alcoholism is popularly thought to be a 'killer', company EAP literature appears justified in, for example, stating: 'Do not let friendship or sympathy mislead you into covering up for the employee with the idea that you are being helpful' (Weiss, 1986: 125). Given the supposedly dire consequences of alcoholism, protecting a colleague becomes the only sensible course of action to take. And whilst this colleague may deny her alcoholism, this is only to be expected since, as the EAP brochure of a chemical firm summarizes, 'alcoholism is an illness of denial' (Weiss, 1986: 127).

The Stress Discourse, Stress Counselling and Stress Management Training

Weiss (1986) presents an interesting analysis of the catch-22 dynamic of alcoholic counselling. But what is also interesting are the similarities between alcoholic counselling and other forms of stress management. Like alcoholism, stress is very difficult to define. Even established measures such as the General Health Questionnaire are of questionable validity (Newton, 1989), so that classification is not straightforward. As with alcoholism, sure signs of stress are a deterioration in an employee's job performance, and other personnel problems such as absenteeism: such employee behaviour provides a strong indication of an employee's 'inability to cope'. Thus the stress discourse also provides for a pernicious disease whose only symptom may be loss of productivity and profits for the company. The justification to intervene is provided by such 'evidence' of coping inability, as well as by the 'evidence' that stress, like alcoholism, is a killer. As was noted in chapter 2, an essential argument of the stress literature is that stress is linked to illness, and illness which may be of a terminal variety, such as coronary heart disease and cancer. The anthropological research of Pollock (1988) also supports a lay understanding of stress as potentially lethal (see chapter 1). As with alcoholism, company interventions to 'confront' stress therefore also appear as a caring policy with the employee's best interests at heart.

The stress metaphor may also be seen as having some advantages over that of alcoholism for a 'caring' management. Firstly, it implies love rather than tough love, since the employee is not generally seen as being weaned off a drug (though there are some exceptions here, as we shall see). Referring a colleague for SMT or employee counselling does not therefore imply pain and suffering for said colleague. Secondly, the stress metaphor has the advantage that there is a reasonable likelihood that a confronted employee will accept that he is suffering from stress. As we saw in chapter 1, stress appears as a widespread phenomenon suffered by many people, an argument portrayed by both the general media and academic literature (for example, see Fletcher, 1988). With alcoholism, a non-alcoholic employee may be made to feel that she is alcoholic through a redefinition of alcoholism: for example, 'it's true I do have a drink every day, and I suppose it would be hard to give this up – maybe I am addicted.' However such redefinitions may not lead to belief in all cases. Employees may well not be alcoholic, and they may rile against the argument that any denial of alcoholism is just part of the 'dependency profile', so that even when they submit to the tough and caring love of alcoholic treatment, it may be done with a less than whole-hearted conviction. In contrast, the stress metaphor is arguably more persuasive because it is perceived to have a far wider effect on the general populace than alcoholism (Pollock, 1988). It therefore has a particular power deriving from its difficulty of assessment, combined with a wide applicability (Weiss, 1986). So whilst there may be a stigma attached to stress, once confronted, employees are more likely to admit that they are a bit stressed than to confess to being an alcoholic. And, interestingly, any stigma attached to stress is linked directly to its perceived association with job performance (the dreaded inability to cope), thus reinforcing job performance as the criterion in assessing stress.

There are notable similarities between the SM practices of employee counselling and SMT. For example, with both there may be an element of coercion deriving from the tacit acceptance that job promotion is consequent upon the ready participation of the employee in development programmes (Salaman, 1979). Both are designed to relieve tensions and reduce frustrations, with the consequence that the employee who is counselled or practises SMT may be less likely to express grievances. By helping their employees to learn SM skills, organizations promote workforces who are committed to being effective copers, the definition of which is directly related to their job performance, again resulting in a happy union of the interests of the individual and the organization. Through an introduction to stress concepts, the employee is taught to be wary of getting stressed (stress leads to heart attacks), whilst also being shown how stress is chiefly a function of the individual and of outmoded patterns of behaviour such as that engendered by fight or flight reactions, instincts suitable to the cave-dweller but not to modern business environments. The message is that a stressful work environment is not necessarily bad, but that the psychosocial nature of human beings hasn't caught up with the modern technological world we have built (see chapter 2). Thus the reason we get frustrated and feel like expressing our grievances is not because our work environment is overly stressful, but because our own in-built technology is inappropriate. Help is at hand however in the form of counselling or SMT which provides the basis to overcome these inbuilt handicaps so common to everyone, so that, rather than getting stressed by the nature of the work organization in which we find ourselves, we are brought up to date. A new, improved human being can supplant her phylogenetically outmoded patterns of behaviour with, say, SMT coping skills, so that what were seen as job stressors can become the exciting challenges of the modern business world (see chapter 2). Managing stress is also, conveniently, a private affair, conducted off-stage (e.g. through meditation, counselling). As such it supports the tacit constraints on the expression of emotion at work (see chapter 3), a support which can also be seen as helpful to human resource management. After all, if employees did openly express their feelings of anger, distress, upset or frustration in the workplace, they might be more likely to notice the commonality amongst their feelings, and *even* to express collective grievances in relation to them.

For a supervisor worried about a stressed employee, there is also a persuasive logic to the stress argument. As a supervisor you should not be surprised to find that one or more of your subordinates is suffering from stress. You can diagnose this by any indications of inability to cope – such as poor job performance – augmented by the observation of symptoms which are common among the general populace, for example headaches, feelings of worry, anxiety, trouble over sleeping. You must intervene not only because of the implications for your unit or department, but because your subordinate may be on a 'downhill path'. Some anecdotal evidence is worth including here, deriving from the SMT courses which I have run for both private and public sector organizations. A frequent concern of the course participants is with the question of how they identify the stressed subordinate. When this question is put back to them, the immediate reply tends to be that of 'poor work performance' or 'seeming as though they can't cope'. Such a reply is hardly surprising since it acknowledges that people may experience headaches, or sometimes feel anxious, without there being any implication that they are suffering from any kind of 'serious' stress. Something else is needed to nail the diagnosis, and that something can be provided by the 'hard' evidence of an individual's inability to cope with the job. The stress metaphor can thus be seen as having a persuasive and easily verifiable internal logic which directs attention to job performance.

Stress Management and Organizational Change

The power of SM metaphors is further illustrated in a book by Schaef and Fassel, entitled *The Addictive Organization* (1988). Their work is interesting because of the way in which they apply the language of EAPs as a basis for organizational change. The target of their interventions is what they call failing or addictive organizations, which are characterized by maladaptive and, in the long term, 'fatal' behaviour patterns. At the root of the addictive organization is the problem of employees with an 'addictive personality'. In other words, the complexity of the social and power relations surrounding organizations are, for Schaef and Fassel, reducible to questions of individual personality traits. At the same time they employ the kind of quasi-medical metaphor referred to in chapter 4, wherein the organization is reified to the extent that it appears as an organic entity suffering from a dire disease, for which the only cure is to remove the pathological element, the addictive personality.

They take the notion of addictive personalities from the leadership styles identified by Kets deVries and Miller (1984) in *The Neurotic Organization*: the depressive, the paranoid, the compulsive and the schizoid. Whilst Schaef and Fassel thank Kets deVries and Miller for gathering 'valuable data', they conclude that the latter authors 'made a wrong interpretation' (1988: 81). Where they went wrong is that they didn't recognize that all four of these leadership styles could happily exist in one person, that of the 'addictive personality'. This individual can be depressive in harbouring 'feelings of guilt and inadequacy and a diminished ability to think clearly', paranoid in exhibiting the 'frozen feelings of the addict', compulsive in the tendency to be 'perfectionist and controlling', as well as schizoid through 'exhibiting ethical deterioration and out-of-touch feelings' (1988: 82).

For Schaef and Fassel the addictive personality is a major problem for organizations, which if left untreated is likely to result in serious dysfunctional consequences. What is striking about their definition of the addictive personality is that, by bringing together all four of Kets deVries and Miller's leadership styles, Schaef and Fassel provide an extremely wide definition potentially capable of classifying anyone as an addict. For example, the person who shows strong leadership might be seen as compulsive because of their 'controlling' tendencies. If they showed concern, this might simply reflect 'feelings of guilt'; whereas if they are detached, their 'frozen' and possibly 'out-of-touch' feelings indicate that they are probably also paranoid and schizoid. Given the wide range of characteristics that Schaef and Fassel attribute to addicts, it seems safe to assume that there are an awful lot of them about. And Schaef and Fassel go on to illustrate how this is precisely the case, and how there are consequences so dire for most organizations that it is a wonder that any survive. Witness the vice-president of whom an 'internal consultant' noted, 'I'm afraid this guy is going to wipe out, but he'll take the division down with him before he goes' (1988: 83). More revealing though is the case of 'Sue', an employee at a psychiatric treatment centre that formed part of 'a major metropolitan hospital complex' (1988: 85). This centre had been 'experiencing increasing problems with organizational structure personnel' (1988: 85). Through their 'assessment interviews' Schaef and Fassel became aware that there was a problem with Sue, 'a key team member'. They identified Sue as a 'dry drunk' exhibiting 'addictive personality' behaviour because of the following criteria: (1) 'she was deeply dishonest'; (2) 'she refused to speak to us about her concerns'; (3) she spread 'gossip and rumour'; and (4) 'Very early in the process, [she] let it be known that she had a "personality conflict" with the consultants [Schaef and Fassel]' which reflected her addict behaviour of 'setting up a me (us)–you (they) situation in which people believe they have to take sides' (1988: 85–7). Having diagnosed Sue as the key source of the centre's difficulties, Schaef and Fassel confronted her with her behaviour and recommended:

'relapse treatment . . . with her continuation in the organization being contingent upon her going for treatment; she chose not to go; the administrator accepted her resignation' (1988: 87). They concluded: 'As consultants we have exhibited concern for the organization and concern for Sue. . . In this case an employee chose to leave rather than get better' (1988: 87–8).

There are three remarkable things about Schaef and Fassel's analysis. Firstly, Sue appears to have had only one choice: accept her guilt or be fired (that she took the latter course might be taken as a sign of authenticity). The second is that Schaef and Fassel seem to give very little consideration to alternative explanations. For example, they appear to operate within what might be loosely described as a psychodynamic framework, particularly influenced by writers such as Kets deVries and Miller. It seems surprising given this theoretical orientation that they did not consider the possibility that Sue might have provided a convenient scapegoat for the centre's problems, an individual on to whom the rest of the team could project their 'internal bad objects' and obtain (unconscious) relief from paranoid anxiety (Klein et al., 1955; Jaques, 1955). Operating within this *social* psychodynamic tradition, projection appears as one obvious interpretation, since it seems unlikely that the centre's problems were chiefly related to just one person. Equally some of the other behaviours of which Sue stood accused do not seem remarkable. For example, that she saw an us/them situation is hardly surprising given that she was being accused, in effect, of dishonesty and gossip-mongering. And by the style of their intervention, Schaef and Fassel appear just as likely to encourage an atmosphere of gossip and rumour. Indeed their own portrayal of Sue as resorting to us/them tactics can itself be seen as a defence by Schaef and Fassel against Sue's dislike and seemingly justifiable mistrust of them.

The final remarkable feature of Sue's case is that in her 'trial', Schaef and Fassel do not appear (as with their many other cases) to reveal the source of their prosecution evidence or the names of prosecution witnesses. In addition, any evidence which she or her colleagues put forward in her favour would be treated as inadmissible. Indeed, in most of the cases that Schaef and Fassel describe, they appear to be both judge and jury. This is a consequence of central elements of their theory of the addictive personality. Firstly, like the alcoholic, the addictive personality will always tend to deny the addictive behaviour, and so their statements are immediately suspect. But in addition any supportive statements which are made about a supposed addictive personality by colleagues would also be treated as circumspect. This derives from Schaef and Fassel's importation of the alcohol-related concept of the co-dependent – someone who lives or works with the alcohol addict who may become part of, and supportive of, the 'disease'. So, where colleagues defend the addict, they are accused by Schaef and Fassel of covering up the behaviour of the addict, whilst the addict becomes 'sicker with a progressive and fatal disease' (1988: 84). Additionally, because it is assumed that the addict will tend to create us/them situations, co-determinants feel they have to choose between supporting the addict and accepting the advice of Schaef and Fassel. This supposedly occurred in Sue's case where the 'practicing co-dependents in the organization immediately felt they had to take sides, and it was easy to see the panic in their faces' (1988: 87). Given this interpretation, if colleagues speak in favour of the 'accused', they are likely to be seen as 'non-recovering organization co-dependents', and as such their evidence, like that of the accused, is inadmissible. If they speak ill of the accused, they are likely to be seen as breaking free of their co-dependence, and therefore to be encouraged in this behaviour. Indeed Schaef and Fassel see their role as interventionists as being to 'educate the group [of immediate colleagues] about the progress and characteristics of the [addictive personality] disease' (1988: 185). To the extent that they are successful in such education, the colleagues of a supposed addict are also likely to doubt the validity of anything she says since addictive personality behaviour is seen as being characterized by dishonesty and denial. Their success in education also implies an isolation of the supposed addict, since Schaef and Fassel will try and 'educate' 'family, friends, workers, and managers or supervisors' (1988: 186). When all significant others have been convinced of your disease, when there is no support for an alternative version of reality, it may be difficult to resist the argument yourself. Everything points to one conclusion: you are guilty, you are diseased, own up and admit it.

In sum, the whole process appears likely to heavily stack the cards against the accused, and appears as a more or less self-fulfilling prophecy once the sinner has been identified. As with any good inquisitor the aim of Schaef and Fassel is of course to help the sinner overcome their addictive personality behaviour, and so get out of their cycle of denial, dishonesty, rumour-mongering and so on. Borrowing directly from Alcoholics Anonymous, they argue that others 'must show that they care about the *person* and will not tolerate the *disease*' (1988: 185–6); in other words, the soul of the heretic must be saved by punishing his sins. Such imagery of the Spanish Inquisition may seem a little far-fetched, yet it is entirely appropriate since Schaef and Fassel apply the key elements described by commentators on the inquisitorial mode of judgement. Thus in the Spanish Inquisition: (1) like Schaef and Fassel, 'the inquisitors were both judge and jury' (Kamen, 1985: 182); (2) the definition of a heretic, like that of the addictive personality, was very widely drawn, and often relied on dubious evidence (Turberville, 1932; Burman, 1984; Kamen, 1985); (3) as with Schaef and Fassel's trial of Sue, 'the names of all prosecution witnesses [against the heretic] were suppressed' (Kamen, 1985: 180) with 'accusations apt to be very deficient in precise details' so that the accused heretic was 'very much in the dark and had to proceed largely by guesswork' (Turberville, 1932: 89); and finally (4) the inquisitors also pursued a policy of tough love:

> With the Holy Office to plead guilty was to obtain mercy; of what other court could that be said? The inquisitor was as much a father-confessor as a judge, aiming not at condemnation but at ending an estrangement, at restoring lambs to the fold. The accused was . . . therefore adjured to seek salvation through confession. This attitude presupposed that there was some degree of guilt to be confessed. (Turberville, 1932: 98)

As in the Spanish Inquisition, the problem with Sue was that she persisted in her heresy, and therefore could not open herself up to the salvation which Schaef and Fassel offered.

This analysis of Schaef and Fassel may appear to be an extreme case. Yet their approach has much in common with other forms of SM. With EAP work, for example, there is usually the assumption of a latent function, derived from some loose affiliation to psychoanalytical theory. Linked to this assumption is the idea that employees will usually exhibit resistance to the latent, and will therefore tend to deny the 'underlying problems'. This central assumption of denial on the part of the accused means that the whole framework is likely to lead to a highly selective treatment of data, with limited opportunity for any serious consideration of discordant evidence. It is hard not to feel pity for any employee who, having been identified as a problem performer, is subject to this kind of caring treatment. In addition, if one views such EAP counselling from a social control perspective, it appears to be both subtle and brutal in its delivery. Yet arguably, from the same perspective, SMT is more subtle, because there is less of the coercion, less of the inquisitorial style. There is likely to be less resistance to SMT, since the employee is not being accused, but is merely being given a set of stress management skills which should both help herself, and help her to do her job. In moving from alcohol counselling to SMT, there therefore appears to be a shift from the utilization of extrinsic motivation, based on 'constructive' coercion, to an intrinsic motivation wherein the employee 'sees' the benefits of SMT and actively engages with them, their identity being constituted as a person who is a coper and who, after SMT, will be stress-fit.

The influence of SMT and EAPs is also reinforced because of the individualism of the models upon which they are based. The Hawthorne counselling programme provided a dramatic example of this individualism, since success was based on shifting attention from job factors to personal concerns in order to gain 'deeper insight' (see above). This emphasis has continued in employee counselling programmes. For example, the UK Post Office counselling service illustrates the individualism, as well as its links to models of occupational stress. In documenting the Post Office service, Allinson et al. summarized the model that guided the counselling: 'The model from which we work is that certain individuals perceive that events have arisen in their psychosocial environment, and that they lack the capacity to cope with them adequately' (1989: 387). This kind of approach is entirely compatible with the emphasis of Selye and of Lewinian-influenced role stress theory on the primacy of the individual's perception, rather than the real objective world (see chapter 2). Not surprisingly, in reducing stress, the emphasis is again on the individual: 'In providing a counselling resource, the Post Office has attempted to provide a service whereby the clients can be guided to discover or create *within themselves* the capacity to cope more effectively with their present problems, and ideally with future problems' (1989: 388).

This same emphasis is apparent throughout much of the SM literature. Its compatibility with aspects of (what would traditionally be seen as) management ideology is illustrated in the US study by Neale et al. (1982) conducted for the National Institute of Occupational Safety and Health (NIOSH). As noted above, their study compared management and union perspectives on stress, and as such provides an appropriate reference point by which to draw this chapter to a close. Their illustration of the union perspective is worth quoting at length, since this kind of analysis has been studiously ignored within most of the occupational stress literature:

> union spokesmen [sic] were adamant in rejecting a Lazarus/coping style approach to work place stressors. [Lazarus's model of] Cognitive appraisal is an attractive strategy with its stoic belief in the power of human expectations to alter the stress value of stimuli. If the worker changes his/her perception of the job demands, the stress level will be accordingly diminished. Unions reject this perspective. . . They argue that their members would learn more relaxed styles if the demands and deadlines, job-loss threats and speedups, were diminished to a more

acceptable level. To adjust the worker to these stressors is to make them more bearable. The more bearable they become, the less motivation the rank-and-file will have to alter the institutions that impose these stressors. For the more adversarial representatives with whom we spoke, coping is tantamount to accepting and thus only blurs the battlelines. (1982: 22–3)

There is anecdotal evidence to suggest that this perspective is shared by UK trade unions. For example, the resource pack accompanying a video on stress (Team Video Productions, undated) sponsored by a number of white collar British unions (BIFU, CPSA, NALGO, NUCPS) defines the causes of stress as 'environmental' (noise, overcrowding, poor childcare facilities), due to 'job design' (boring work, no control over pace of work, lack of discretion and decision-making, working with VDUs), as well as being 'contractual' (low pay, shift work and unsocial hours, job insecurity) and due to 'relationships' (racism, sexism, ageism, impersonal treatment at work).

With Neale et al.'s findings, the corporate perspective stood in stark contrast to that of the union in defining stress, emphasizing individual characteristics (type A, lifestyle, family problems, etc.) as the major factors behind work stress. Whilst there may have been some variation within management groups, the aggregate data suggest that the predominant management perspective was that stress arises because individual patterns of behaviour are inappropriate for the demands of the contemporary work environment. Such observations suggest a close correspondence between the stress discourse, SM practice and predominant management perspectives on stress. In addition, Neale et al. noted how corporate literature frequently references individualistic models of stress and stress management that closely reflect the occupational stress literature. As they noted, 'Little of the corporate material focused on stressors, discussed enhancement of individual control through structural change' (1982: 35).

Neale and his colleagues attempted to build on this research by explicitly acknowledging the differences between union and management perspectives. In addition, in their subsequent study of stress amongst hotel employees (Neale et al., 1987; Singer et al., 1987) they found that, as researchers, they were more aligned with the union's position because they obtained the union's consent to the project, but not that of the hotel management. At the outset the researchers appear to have been aware that the union might 'turn our findings into a vehicle for organizational change' (Singer et al., 1987: 8), through helping the union to raise awareness amongst its members of political issues. To many stress researchers, their alignment with the union might be seen as casting doubt on the validity of their research results, since the union-sponsored pro-motion of their study may have encouraged respondents to voice greater management antagonism than would normally be the case. Yet all Neale and his colleagues did was to acknowledge the political context of stress research, wherein the notion of an apolitical 'normal' response can only be a myth. For example, the more common scenario of stress researchers' identification with management means that, in most stress studies, respondents may be *less likely* to voice management antagonism. And in any case, the construction of the research within individualistic models of stress means that the research is biased away from socio-political issues from the outset. As Singer et al. concluded:

> we saw our role for the union as functionally equivalent to that of a stress consultant for management. The stress consultant, who asks questions about diet and exercise and offers training in relaxation, promulgates a certain 'management' conception of what stress is and how it should be treated. In the same vein, we asked questions about job characteristics, organizational policies, and working conditions. These questions encour-aged workers to conceive of organizational stressors that they might not have considered previously. The fact that our approach appears unortho-dox and politically-slanted may be more a statement about the lack of labor-oriented stress consultants than an indictment of our method. (1987: 26)

Conclusion

This chapter has been concerned to present an alternative to the traditional anodyne image of SM, wherein it is seen as an impartial practice which can be applied by a caring progressive management. Against this kind of construction can be drawn an image of SM as having political effects arising from the constitution of individuals within a discourse which ties their job performance to intimate concerns about their psychological and physical health. From a traditional ('Bravermania') labour process perspective, SM deploy-ment may be seen as nakedly coercive, as a tool of a cunning homogeneous management intent upon the total domination and control of their employees (see chapter 3). However, more recent labour process accounts might emphasize that though SM is chiefly significant as a technology of manufacturing consent, it nevertheless may not form part of a deliberate management strategy. Rather its effects need to be understood in relation to its broad consonance with the constitution of employees' identities in ways convenient to controlling the labour process: for example, the emphasis in SM upon individual responsibility, the tying of psychophysical health to job performance (the good coper), and in consequence the connecting of intimate concerns and anxieties to the job and the organization. At the same time SM articulates well with other human resource management approaches which both individualize and probe more intimate details of the employee's life (e.g. performance appraisal: see chapter 7).

From a Foucauldian perspective, SM can be seen as a series of practices which invite individuals to 'see' a certain view of themselves (wherein they, say, become anxious about stress, and learn a vocabulary of stress). SM invites a differentiation between the normal and the abnormal (most graphically illustrated above with the case of Sue), and offers a variety of observational techniques (interviews, questionnaires, observation) whereby the 'danger' signs of stress may be identified, and the stress 'case' 'treated'. Indeed, as noted in chapter 3, employee counselling may represent the closest thing to the panopticon in the workplace, with its ability not just to observe behaviour but to explore the intimacies, anxieties, anger, hopes, ambitions and dreams of the employee. Not only can it gaze upon the soul of the miscreant and sinner, but it offers the promise of redemption through showing the problem employee that they can cope with the stresses and strains of the 'ever busy' modern business life. Like other forms of SM, it thus promises a 'bio-power', an opportunity to maximize the enjoyment of a healthy, (suitably) adaptive living. As also noted in chapter 3, SM practices articulate with other economic, social and psychological practices of the 1970s and 1980s (e.g. those associated with neo-liberal economics, corporate culture, human growth) which emphasize the sovereignty of self-actualizing autonomous subjects.

Whilst SM practices can thus be fairly easily written into a Foucauldian text, they also point to some of the difficulties in applying Foucault that were discussed in chapter 3 – particularly the lack of attention by a Foucauldian treatment to issues of agency and social relations. The analyses presented in this chapter illustrate the need to examine discursive practices in the context of social and power relations. Otherwise, how are we to account for the observation that the stress discourse is so managerialist? Or that the bottom-line interest in SM investment derives from its potential to curtail labour costs? Or that, in their deployment, SM practices may be used in a highly coercive and manipulative fashion? As Mouzelis notes, 'Foucault has no ways of showing how practices of coercion/ subjugation and/or practices of freedom vary in their complex articulation from one institutional situation to another' (1993: 686).

Without attending to the social and power relations of particular situations, it is difficult to begin to analyse why SM practice appears as a subjugatory rather than a liberatory device. Equally, there is a need to explore the commonality across situations such as those of employment settings, where there may be notable similarities in the way in which power relations are socially structured. Whilst a Foucauldian account rightly points to the relativity of the truth effects we seek to create – for example, seeing SM as a liberatory device in conventional stress discourse, or as more of a subjugatory device in the present analyses – this does not mean that we can let go of the question of how human agency and power relations may affect the terms under which particular discursive practices are evolved and deployed (Newton, 1994a).

As we saw in chapter 3, Elias provides one entry into this kind of analysis, particularly since the employee still does bear some resemblance to the image of the courtier witnessed in Elias's analysis of the aristocratic court. In this light SM practices can be seen as part of the deference that is expected of the courtier/employee, a reflection of the unequal power relations of the workplace. In return for the privilege of economic favour, the employee is expected to show appropriate grace and, in particular, to control her emotions so that they do not upset either her superiors or her peers. Whilst Elias's work may not have the power of labour process theory in accounting for the seeming subjugatory image of SM presented in this chapter, it nevertheless does provide a means to analyse how power relations, emotion and subjectivity interrelate. Thus drawing on Elias, SM can be seen to provide a means of ensuring appropriate civility and deference, of maintaining emotional restraint through an individualization and privatization of emotion based on off-stage techniques such as meditation or counselling. In this way individuals learn new ways to go on (Giddens, 1984) that rearticulate and reinforce existing tacit understandings about appropriate codes of emotion and behaviour at work. SM also supports a formalization of affect and behaviour that reflects the unequal power relations of the workplace, illustrated through distinctions such as those between employer and employee, superior and subordinate, men and women. These themes are discussed further in chapter 7.

In the next two chapters we shall further explore this last perspective through a more explicit focus on the relation between power, stress and emotion. In chapter 6 Stephen Fineman provides a detailed social constructionist analysis of some tacit rules of emotional expression, exploring the relationship between implicit and explicit 'feeling rules' at work. He then relates this analysis to a consideration of the difficulties of undertaking organizational inter-ventions which either account for, or challenge, the management of emotion. In addition to pursuing this theme, chapter 7 will also draw together our earlier discussions, and consider how we might reconstruct the stressed subject.

6

Stress, Emotion and Intervention

Stephen Fineman

This chapter explores the social and political features of the feelings we label as stress, with particular accent on intervention and change. I focus a large part of my inquiry through an emotion lens – a powerful, although less conventional, way of examining how the dynamics of the socially constructed world can regulate individual stress.

Politics and Stress Intervention: the General Case

Though the personal experience of stress is decidedly individualistic, it is influenced and expressed through the cultural and political milieu of the organization. By this, I mean firstly the differences in power, status and control that socially structure an organization, elements of which emanate from the broader society of which the organization is a part. Secondly, I refer to the product of competing and colliding interests of organizational members (e.g. Pfeffer, 1981; Morgan, 1986). Actors differ in their commitments to different social orders and will be motivated to protect their own territory and projects – necessarily a passionate process, sometimes a stressful one (Hosking and Fineman, 1990).

Individualistic stress interventions may assist with personal coping, but they are likely to miss the social reproduction of working patterns which contribute to, and define, stress. This is partly because stress interventionists often fail to look in the social direction. If they did, however, not all would be plain to see. Organized life proceeds on the basis of many taken-for-granted assumptions; the distressed individual cannot simply articulate what he or she has never been aware of, or tacitly accepts (Fineman, 1983a). For example, there are the legal and hierarchical controls over work methods which become part of the unnoticed or unquestioned backdrop to the job. There are the pressures from customers, clients and administrators that seem inevitable. And it is often self-evident that it is improper to admit to, or talk about, one's stresses.

A social/political analysis of stress and intervention opens yet other windows. It raises questions about who defines stress for whom. A particular interest group is likely to choose a stress meaning which most favours its cause. For example, as we saw in chapter 5, Singer et al. (1987) report on the tendency of management to regard workers' stress as 'maladaptive person–environment fit'. Contrast the union's perspective, where the stress is defined in terms of poor working conditions, lack of workers' control over their work, and overload. The partiality frame can be extended a little further to encompass the stress managers or interventionists themselves. Stress interventions are usually well cloaked in symbols of apparent neutrality (tests, questionnaires, personal advice), but, as we also saw in chapter 5, the interventionist's position may be far from unaligned. A paid external consultant can be hired by management to report just to management; an internal consultant will be very keen to 'produce results' for the boss; an academic may have a hidden agenda, such as gathering stress data to test out a particular theory. Added to this, the organization's gatekeepers, such as key managers, union officials or influential shareholders, can markedly influence who takes part in a stress intervention, the form of the study, and the nature of the reported discoveries (Buchanan et al., 1988). This point was forcefully brought home to me in an independently funded study on employee role stress in a nuclear research establishment. So alarmed by the results were the line managers that the findings were immediately suppressed, and attempts were made to discredit the analysis (Fineman and Payne, 1981).

In contextualizing and politicizing the person at work I am suggesting that stress has much to do with the organization and social context of the job. This is likely to be problematic for helpers who seek to counsel individuals out of their stresses, but not surprising to some theorists and practitioners of organizational change who have for some time argued that change has to be seen beyond just the individual, that it has to incorporate the influence of coalitions of power, informal group processes, and the bargaining positions of various stakeholders in the organization's well-being (Cyert and March, 1963). Through the 1980s, a number of writers on organizational change advocated a 'cultural' approach (see chapter 4). Change, they claim, should be seen in terms of the meaning that people place upon the subtle and not so subtle interactional activities and physical props (buildings, office arrangements, communication literature) of organized life. 'Managing the meanings' through specific executive actions can create new symbols of purpose and value, *ergo* organizational change (Schein, 1985;

Deal and Kennedy, 1982; Fineman and Mangham, 1987). This particular kind of culture approach comes closest to an organization-wide change effort which attempts systematically to influence the way people feel about their work lives, so it appears especially relevant to stress management. However, changing an organization's culture beyond adjustments to its rational rhetorics (e.g. statements of mission, goals, tasks and scripts) means that shared, tacit meanings and feelings have to be accessible, and amenable to manipulation. The culture change studies are not reassuring in this respect (Smith and Peterson, 1988; Carrahan and Stewart, 1989). I shall return to this point.

The Emotions of Stress

Emotions, like ideas, can be regarded as cultural artefacts (Geertz, 1973). Our personal experience of stress as private *feeling* is well documented. Phenomenologically our feelings signal to us, sometimes clearly, sometimes inchoately, something of the quality of our interactions, performances and involvements in the world about us. Feelings are self-validating; they are what they are for those who feel. There may be a pre-linguistic knowing of feelings (Sandelands, 1988); however, it is when feelings become linguistically tagged – as anger, fear, love and so forth – that we have emotion. More importantly, though, we here have a social product, potentially amenable to various forms of social influence and intervention (Sugrue, 1982; Harré, 1986).

The feelings that people call stress have been variously described: doubt, despair, panic, worry, tension, frustration, confusion, depression, fear, insecurity. Psychologists have tried to explain them as intrapsychic and physiological phenomena, but my interest is rather different. I will view stress as an emotional product of the social and political features of work and organizational life. I will also explore the particular social/political interventions which follow from this perspective, with relevant field illustrations. Our analysis will relate to a number of points already indicated in the first section of this chapter.

Social Structure and Construction

Kemper (1978; 1981) argues the case for regarding emotions as a direct consequence of structural characteristics of the social world. In strident positivistic tone, Kemper appeals to Durkheim's (1938) notion of constraining 'social facts' which cue the cognitive appraisals of actors as they perform and interact. These 'facts' reside in power and status arrangements. Kemper proposes that 'an extremely large class of human emotions results from real, anticipated, imagined or recollected outcomes of human relationships' (1978: 32), and he boils down the pattern of relationships to the extent of control by one actor over another (power), and how positively (in status terms) they relate to one another. Kemper's treatment of power is both unidimensional and mechanistic – something some people have, by virtue of their social position, and can use over other people. The powerful can coerce, force or dominate others to get from them what they will not relinquish willingly. The problem with this mechanistic representation of power is that it does not consider power relations which are based, not on positional or status differences, but on how people present, negotiate and reproduce their realities. That said, one can defend Kemper's view of power as dominance to the extent that there are relatively enduring social structures (e.g. labour markets) which do appear to symbolize the dominance of some groups of people over others (e.g. men over women, whites over ethnic minorities); and, because such social structures do help to define real and anticipated outcomes, they also stage our emotions.

Kemper develops his views to account for 'distressful emotions' (i.e. what an actor claims to really feel), which includes the stress-related emotions (although stress is not a term Kemper uses) of anxiety, despair, fear, dread, anger, hostility and sense of worthlessness. To take anxiety as an example, this is regarded as a consequence of a power imbalance between actors. Anxiety is the anticipation by a person that a more powerful other will use his or her power to invade, or otherwise encroach, on the person's self or space. If the person feels that he or she personally holds the responsibility for the power deficit (because of personal incapacities or deficiencies) then anxiety, according to Kemper, is turned inwards, and is expressed in terms of feelings of dread or doom. The actor feels helpless in the face of the protagonist. If, on the other hand, the other party is seen as responsible, the anxiety is turned outwards in the form of anger, resistance or rebellion.

Kemper's somewhat simplistic definition of power and status asks a lot of just two social dimensions, but he is not entirely rigid in his usage:

> The ineluctable fact is that social relations of power and status, sometimes crystallized into an enduring structure, sometimes fluid and evanescent, determine our feelings at funerals, parties, weddings and similar occasions of interaction. I refer here to real emotions, not forced smiles at parties when we feel bored, or put-on tragic miens at funerals

where we feel indifferent. It is what our fellow participants do to us and what we do to them – the social relations that constitute the existing structure – that evoke our emotions. (1981: 345)

Following Kemper, analysing the social relations of power and status provides a distinctly different view of stress emotions. For example, feelings of stress are likely to be affected not only by how well individuals are able to control their jobs, but also by the kind of social structures within which their organization operates (the mainstream stress literature regards control almost exclusively as a personality problem, or as confined to local, immediate job issues: see Newton, 1989). I will examine this argument further by using two stress studies: firstly, through a further examination of the research of Handy (see chapter 4), and secondly, through illustrating work by Sugrue (1982).

As we saw in chapter 4, Handy's (1990; 1991) study of psychiatric nurses illustrates the relationship between the structure and ideology of the psychiatric system and the actions, world-view and subjective experiences of the nurses. She found that stress was best explained by the nurses' struggles to come to terms with the inherent contradictions within psychiatry: to legally control certain patients, while also helping them; to support people in the community, while also spotting who might be a new 'case'; to institutionalize patients for care purposes, while also encouraging patients towards autonomy. Such conflicting expectations could be interpreted as mightily confusing the power/status relations, to use Kemper's simple distinction. The nurses found themselves bewildered about their relative standing with their patients, and about their own competence to achieve what they were expected to achieve. The nurses felt unable to influence the institutional rules which set the expectations in the first place, so their attention turned to their patients. The patients were seen as the power threat; they could consume or disable the workers with their demands. One nurse explains:

> I often find I want to pull away from clients – this year I've been listening to clients and experiencing symptoms myself when a little voice inside of me has been saying 'I must get out' . . . We have no way of escaping . . . and sometimes if I've put a lot of effort in and they demand more and more then it begins to feel like 'You're taking my blood' . . . and you find it really difficult to go on working with them. (Handy, 1991: 827)

Such despair contrasts with the patient-directed anger experienced by another nurse. She notes in her diary:

> Mad at the thought of admitting this lady again as it has only been six weeks since her discharge. Always admitted after her bi-sexual boyfriend

has found another girlfriend. X cannot cope with this – always plays the psychiatric sick role and always warrants admission. Since her arrival has been kissing the walls, lifting clothes up in the lounge. Counselled her re this but to little effect. Maintains it is through (boyfriend) she has ended up coming in. Given prescribed injection to calm her. (1991: 823)

Handy's accounts can be read as consistent with the power deficiency features of Kemper's theorizing on anxiety. The nurses' emotional responses are linked to how relations between nurses and patients are maintained and reproduced in hospital settings – in ways which sometimes leave the nurse powerfully in charge, but at other times expect a relinquishment of such control. The nurses become bewildered, can feel a loss of control and a threat to their power and status. The form of the organization's policies and social structure is, therefore, critical in comprehending stress – as, indeed, would be the wider community policies and laws which frame the direction of the organization. If either remained unexplored, there may be little alleviation of the sources of the nurses' stresses.

Noreen Sugrue's (1982) study is also of a medical setting. She set out to describe and evaluate the 'emotional context' of an interactional situation. Building on Strauss's (1978) negotiated order in interpersonal encounter, she examined how the specific emotional standpoint of actors can become part of the substantive negotiative reality. In her introduction, Sugrue briefly mentions political issues, but she does not consider them in her main analysis on emotional framing. The study, nevertheless, can be seen as a strong demonstration of how intense, negative emotions can be experienced within asymmetrical power relations.

Sugrue tells the story of one very frightened patient, Kathy, who was admitted on Christmas Eve to the emergency room of a hospital. She had a bleeding ulcer. She eventually underwent surgery but recovered slowly following post-operative complications. Kathy's passage through the hospital was a turbulent one. Her doctors denied her a pass to go home for Christmas for a few hours (presumably for 'sound' medical reasons) which left her feeling isolated and scared. Despite her requests to the contrary, the doctors insisted on inserting a nasal gastric tube which gave her much pain and a dreadful sense of choking. She began to fear death and was convinced that the medical staff were inhumane and incompetent. Her clinical notes described her as an agitated, uncooperative, depressed and neurotic patient; and each time there was an entry to this effect, there was a statement that she requested Valium. However, Kathy claims she patently refused Valium because of her fear of the side effects and the loss of faculties associated with its use. Valium, nevertheless, was injected into her intravenous tube. The nurses told her that she 'had to take the medication because the doctors had left orders'.

By this time Kathy's fear and distress turned into open anger and non-cooperation. Her alienation, states Sugrue, was 'not only from the staff, the interactions, and the treatment of her disease, but also from her body. She said that she never forgave the nurses' and doctors' incompetence, and that her hatred for them framed all interactions with them' (1982: 284). As matters progressed from bad to worse, Kathy declared open war on the medical staff. She writes in her diary:

> Well it's been 10 days since I started my war with the staff and it drives them nuts. I'm getting some satisfaction out of it, but they still don't seem really miserable. I'm scared and angry and worried, but I have to get even with them for being jerks and stupid. I'll never forget being left alone for 3 hours with no way to call for help . . . My family and friends tell me I should be nice to the nurses. After all, I need them and they might ignore me or hurt me. This just makes me more mad – to think they would hurt or ignore a sick and vulnerable person, they're no better than pigs and I really hate them. (1982: 287)

Faithful to her interpretative frame, Sugrue speaks of Kathy 'negotiating for her mental competence' as she came to realize that her behaviour was regarded as evidence of mental instability. However, we can also see in Kathy's anxiety an almost perfect expression of Kemper's emotional paradigm. She was convinced from her interactions with the hospital doctors and attendants that they meant her psychological and physical harm, and they had the power to impose their will on her. This anticipation evoked a deep anxiety which came to overshadow all of her encounters with hospital staff. In her initial attempts to cope she saw the fault to lie in herself; she needed to improve herself in some way to restore her self-esteem. But she failed, with an increasing sense of helplessness. She then switched to laying the blame squarely on the shoulders of her protagonists, and fought them furiously.

Sugrue's account offers only occasional glimpses of what the medical staff themselves felt about what was happening. There is a hint that their own anxiety ironically mirrored Kathy's. How could they feel competent caring professionals, with a clear place within the medical community to define the rules, if the patient simply refused to accept the basic premise that the staff knew what they were doing, and it was OK? They appeared to reinforce their professional status by blaming the patient, and fighting her bureaucratically and medically: freezing her out, minimizing contact, and labelling her a suitable case for psychiatric treatment. As with Handy's distressed nurses, Sugrue's analysis suggests that the most tangible target for the professionals' frustration was the non-conforming patient. But what is unquestioned in Sugrue's account is the kind of bind that exists in hospitals where often overloaded professional carers are expected to attend 'efficiently' to a mass throughput of patients, make sound professional judgements and also be caring to the individuals in their charge. Ultimately, it seems that such an organizational apparatus cannot operate without production-line control, which includes patients who are well socialized into accepting whatever they get. The Kathys of the world threaten to upset a fragile social order and balance of power; but they also expose the often impossible or contradictory premises upon which the system is erected.

Stress interventions – such as relaxation, empathy training and counselling – may succeed in ironing out some of the interactional wrinkles, but they act as a cosmetic in social structures within which people continually reproduce the same forms of stress. Kemper's framework successfully points us in this direction, although our discussion of Handy's and Sugrue's studies suggests that he sometimes does not go quite far enough; we may need to peer further both within and beyond the organization's boundaries to understand why stress is continually reproduced.

Beneath the Structures

There is a case to be made for the relatively independent impact of social structures – be they related to power, policies, contradictory expectations or legal constraints – on the job holder's emotional life. Even though the individual is actively involved in the reproduction of social structures, there may be little that they can do to materially affect them, either because they are tacit and taken-for-granted features of organizational life (see chapter 2), operating at a more or less pre-conscious level (cf. Giddens's notion of practical consciousness), or because the individual is relatively powerless to affect them (e.g. the formal rule of law). More generally, though human agency is essential to organizational reproduction, that agency may be severely constrained by existing forms of social structure. To this extent it is important to try and probe further into the way in which social structures relate to the experience of stress.

The detail of such responses can be regarded as a product of more specific social rules and personal interpretative processes. We here enter the realm of the politics of emotional expression. The thesis, as expressed by writers such as Schachter (1959), Eckman (1971), Hochschild (1975) and Averill (1980), runs thus. In society and in organizations we learn particular, socially defined, 'feeling rules'.

These prescribe or discourage certain types of emotional display: our appearance, demeanour, facial expression, words used and intonation. Different societies and different organizations have various rules of emotional display. Some of the rules will reflect the mores associated with specific societal groups, such as what men or women, the old or the young, the working class or the middle class, should show of their feelings; others will tie in more directly with the nature of the business in which the actor performs. Crucially though, to comply with the emotional codes (and avoid the discomfort of embarrassment or censure – emotions fine for social control), people will privately *labour* with, or *do work on*, their feelings in order to create the socially desired emotional expression and impression.

From this perspective, stress feelings such as anxiety, fear, dread and so forth, the 'real feelings' alluded to by Kemper (1981), often will be transmuted, or dressed up, into a form that the actor judges acceptable for public consumption (e.g. for customers, managers, clients or colleagues). The personal labour associated with this may itself introduce additional feelings of stress. We are, in Goffman's (1961) terms, doing face work: managing the risk inherent in any interpersonal encounter. In pleasing the audience by dealing with our stress feelings we are working at camouflage, a process which can create new tensions – which also must be kept from our audience if the act is to continue successfully.

In Hochschild's (1979) eloquent account of the social construction of emotion, she notes the peculiarity of modern urban culture which, unlike 'traditional' cultures, puts people outside the cultural frame of feeling rules and distances them more from their private feelings. We 'look on' and make more specific choices about what to reveal of our feelings, to whom and when. In this sense, emotional labour is part institutional and part interpretative. The actor's definition of the situation, their reading of the emotional cues, is germane to the quality and quantity of emotional labour invested in a social act (Shott, 1979).

Emotional labour at work may be slight, well internalized and relatively stress free: the polite and automatic smile of the waitress as she serves the food (a smile that vanishes the instant she turns away); the mechanically effusive response of the telephone operator thanking us so much for our inquiry. But the psychological costs of emotional labour rise sharply when the waitress begins to hate her work and the people she serves, and when the telephone operator's care and concern are directed at people whom she finds irritating to the extreme.

It is important, both analytically and for stress intervention purposes, to distinguish between two classes of feeling rules. Firstly, there are those that are explicit: deliberate, managerially contrived ways of serving the organization's commercial or supposed strategic ends. Secondly, there are the rules implicit to the organization's informal culture, the procedures which help people to get by in everyday social interaction; they help protect or save face.

Explicit Feeling Rules
Explicit feeling rules have become a significant feature of employment contracts in many mass-service industries – especially fast food, leisure and travel. For example, McDonald's 'Hamburger University' instructs its managers to ensure that 'all-American traits' are displayed by its counter staff, namely 'sincerity, enthusiasm, confidence and a sense of humour' (Boas and Chain, 1976). That equally all-American institution, Walt Disney World, has recently exported its mega enterprise to Europe, along with its uncompromising feeling rules:

> First we practice a friendly smile at all times with our guests and among ourselves. Second, we use friendly courteous phrases. 'May I help you' . . . 'Thank you' . . . 'Have a nice day' . . . 'Enjoy the rest of your stay', and many others are all part of our working vocabulary. (Walt Disney Productions, 1982: 6)

The notion of personality as a market-place commodity has been with us for some time (Mills, 1956); however, we are now witnessing an increase in the sophistication of social technologies designed to support the commercialization of human feelings (see Newton, 1992). New techniques of personnel selection, training and surveillance help to cultivate company-appropriate emotional appearances (see Newton, 1994a). Hochschild (1983) provides an example of a major American airline which insists on recurrent training for its flight attendants, aimed at reinforcing the mandatory 'inside-out' smile. What people call stress may emerge when the emotional labour required eventually outstrips the flight attendant's capacities or inclinations:

> A young businessman said to a flight attendant, 'Why aren't you smiling?' She put her tray back on the food cart and said, 'I'll tell you what. You smile first, then I'll smile.' The businessman smiled at her. 'Good,' she replied. 'Now freeze and hold that for fifteen hours.' (Hochschild, 1983: 127)

Hopfl offers a similar illustration from her study of a British airline:

> You try saying 'hello' to 300 people and sound as though you mean it towards the end. Most of us make a game of it. Someone – probably a manager – said 'This business is all about interpersonal transactions.' He

was wrong. It's all about bullshit. If life is a cabaret, this is a bloody circus. (1991: 5–6)

Stressful feelings may occur in two ways. The first is when, as illustrated, the mask cracks. The tension between inner feeling and the requirement of outward display is simply too great. The second is when the mask and the inner feeling become fused; the company's message is taken to heart to the extent that people begin to lose touch with their own feelings. It is as if one's feelings have been given over to a third party to manage. Hochschild (1983) describes the personal anxiety produced by this, especially the flight attendant's confusion over her sexual identity (as we saw in chapter 4, it is not uncommon for airlines to sexualize the flight attendant's image in their advertising). Generally, the more emotional labour put into a job, the more problematic becomes work and personal identity. The best copers, it seems, are those who see the job as all about acting; they treat the emotional performance as a game into which they switch in or out (see chapter 4). Some will acquire a protective layer of cynicism to help them through.

We can conclude that for some people, company-prescribed feeling rules are positively harmful. For many others they force a separation between private feeling and public face in a way which promotes insincerity and cynicism – exactly the opposite sentiments desired by the company. But in so far as employees are able to maintain face, there is little incentive for an organization's management to worry too much; Taylorized feelings sell the goods. Indeed the very large and powerful transnational corporations can, in hegemonic fashion, begin gradually to dilute the influence of the host's own national culture when it is contrary to their own expectations of emotional performance. For example, we see British workers, known historically for their indifference to the customer, now cheerfully dispensing American hamburgers, pizzas and airline tickets. Even Russian workers who, as legend has it, would serve with a grimace, now smile as they present American fast food to their compatriots. (A few, according to newspaper reports, have found the expressive clash too great and have left their jobs, despite very high unemployment. There are, however, plenty of others to take their places.)

If we must have company rules of emotion display, a step towards second-order 'stress reduction' would be to ensure that the rules do not invade private feelings. In other words, they should be un-coupled from the ethically dubious practice of insisting that workers really *should* love the customer, product, service or whatever, and have the 'right' affective personality characteristics when they join. It might be, as some labour process theorists argue, that emotional labour is a logical development of the need to control labour (Thompson and McHugh, 1990). Another argument is that, even accepting the constraints of capitalist production, there may be *some* convergence of company and employee interest when feeling rules are explicitly made those of good maskmanship, and that alone. More or less explicit feeling rules are already part of the world of some professionals, especially helpers. For example, police officers are instructed and trained to curb their anger when under provocation (e.g. see Novaco, 1977); the clergy are expected to show compassion, whatever; probation officers are expected to work sympathetically with clients, regardless of what they feel about their misdemeanours; and doctors are supposed to react coolly and dispassionately to whatever ailments their patients bring. Indeed, the very notion of being professional has come to imply a set of rules about doing a job at an emotional distance from the client/ customer, with heavy sanctions against getting 'too personally involved'.

When helping professionals enter their occupations they are agreeing, in effect, to do a lot of emotional labour, and often hard labour at that, judging from the stress and burnout associated with these groups (Pines and Aronson, 1989; Fineman, 1985a). As members of large, regulated, professional institutions they are now less able to claim a place within the wider cultural/community framework of feeling rules. This, ironically, insulates them from their own clients while also closing off more conventional channels through which they could normally express their own stresses. Significantly, stress programmes for such groups rarely question the professional/feeling rules as such, or the social structures through which the professional operates. They favour more individualistic regimes of stress management – off site and largely detached from actual work practice.

Implicit Feeling Rules

Feeling rules are not exclusively of managerial or occupational prescription. People create their own as, in Strauss's (1978) terms, they negotiate organizational order. By trial and error, revealing too much or too little, in one situation or another, a tacit cultural framework for emotional expression is created. The framework is pinned together by rules on what, for example, should remain as private doubt and worry, and what can be openly expressed – and how. Fineman's study of social workers provides an apposite illustration:

> In one of our meetings a social worker spoke with poignancy about her difficulties in coping with the demands of a particular client, when added

to her home pressures. I asked her if she had shared her concerns with any of her colleagues. 'Oh no!', she retorted, 'I wouldn't want to be social worked by them.' She then recoiled with a look of horror on her face, 'God, what am I saying? I can use my social work skills on clients but I can't accept them for myself?' (1985a: 100)

A supervisor in the study added that social workers 'played a charade' with each other's stresses. They would not admit their own stresses, and would overtly fail to care for colleagues. We see here in operation a feeling rule of the following sort: 'never show you can't cope; disguise your feelings of stress; remember, a competent social worker should be able to handle her own stress' (the irony in this is that clients were expected to do just the opposite). In fact, what the social workers 'did' with their stress was to go sick or absent. This was organizationally acceptable. The very high sickness and absenteeism statistics in the agency were taken for granted by management, as if in unspoken collusion with the feeling rule.

It is one of the paradoxes of the helping professions that they often seem unable to help themselves. The very nature of the professionalization process contains the seeds of this difficulty: a rational framework to apply to others; a helper–client divide; a power and status imbalance which can give the professional a sense of invulnerability; a dependence on the professional's services. The helper expects to be able to cope and, importantly, the client expects that of the helper. Unexpected feelings of disquiet, uncertainty, alienation or stress are handled in a way which will preserve the professional's persona as a good coper (Fineman, 1990; Sarason, 1977).

Sometimes the emotional labour required to sustain an *explicit* feeling rule is so great that the rule is informally recoded. For example, the social workers in Fineman's (1985a) study talked of their struggle not to get too fond of their clients; and to 'be professional, as we are told in social work training'. 'This doesn't do much about your feelings, though', said one social worker dolefully (1985a: 58). And another explained:

> I get protective feelings towards my clients if somebody here appears to be attacking them. I shouldn't let this confuse the goal of a meeting, so I suppress the feelings; this is stressful. Also, with clients it's so hard, and so important to decipher that part of the emotional response which comes from the effect of the client, and that part which comes from one's own biography – or the row with the wife last night. What can I do with these feelings? (1985a: 58)

A response to this dilemma was to recast the 'being professional' feeling rule into a form that the social workers considered to be politically correct for *themselves*. They firmly argued that a good relationship with a client was inevitably a close one, and they would feel closer to some clients than to others. This cognitive somersault relieved the guilt and stress that accompanied their feelings for their clients and their welfare. But it did not obviate the considerable emotional effort to be put into presenting the orthodox face of emotional control – for their managers and supervisors. For example, some would be involved in elaborate supervision games, figuring out what was safe to reveal and what should be avoided:

> I have regular meetings with my supervisors, but always steer clear of my problems in coping with my report work. Can I trust her? I need her backing for my career progress, but will she use this sort of thing as evidence against me? There are some painful areas that are never discussed but need discussing so much. It's an awful dilemma for me. (Fineman, 1985a: 52)

Echoed in these comments is the uneasy mix of help and inspection to be found in many formal supervision situations. There is, however, added poignancy when the politics of self-revelation prohibit the expression of deep distress.

Change and Implicit Feeling Rules

Implicit feeling rules are woven into the fabric of working and organizing processes. They cannot simply be picked out for examination or change. Many are not reflected in conscious deliberation but are expressed automatically, in routine and habit-bound responses (Averill, 1980). There are likely to be strong social pressures on the individual to go along with a myriad of impression management behaviours, of which the appearance or otherwise of specific emotions, including stress, is just one part. Furthermore, we need to address how implicit feeling rules are socially constructed, and why they are continually maintained, if we are seeking change towards stress alleviation/management (Fineman, 1993).

This is methodologically problematic. The tacit assumptions of working are not going to fall out neatly from the questions and answers of interviews or questionnaires. The feeling rules identified in the Fineman social work study were an unintended product of an inordinately lengthy process of contracting and relationship building. It is, furthermore, arguable that much of what is revealed by an *in*-work study is necessarily inhibited by the taken-for-granted nature of that very frame; people will be more able to see what they take for granted when they are shaken out of the frame – such as when unemployed (Jahoda, 1979; Fineman, 1983a; 1983b).

The inherently political aspect of implicit feeling rules adds further complexity to the question of change. The codes meet the emotional interests of different stakeholders in the organization; there is a division of emotional labour. Van Maanen and Kunda (1989) suggest that it is easier for those at the very top and those at the bottom of the organization to express what they feel as they have the least to risk by such openness. On the other hand, it is perhaps more realistic to expect the 'tycoons and temps' to be bound by their own social constituency, or reference group, which makes for *different* clusters of feeling rules. And both groups, one would suppose, would be inclined to labour harder at emotion management in the midst of a job-restrictive recession than when times are good and jobs plentiful.

There are examples of change programmes which set out to alter an organization's culture by encouraging, or impressing, a particular set of managerial beliefs or values (Peters and Waterman, 1982; Schein, 1985). These employ an array of social technologies which influence organizational rites, rituals, ceremonies and loyalties, and their proponents argue that they can have a remarkable effect on the programming of emotional display. They are unashamedly unilateral and indoctrinating (the making of an IBM, M&S, McDonald's or Disneyland person) and, as we have seen, they can leave their own legacy of distress. The extent to which these efforts result in a genuine sharing of values and meanings (the heart of a 'strong' culture) between management and labour is, however, questionable. There are only a few examples of successful, persisting, cultural changes, and many that claim to be so are revealed to be too coercive to validly represent a value consensus (Smith and Peterson, 1988). What we do observe is the *appearance* of a cultural uniformity with its explicit feeling rules. A surface scratch can reveal other, more significant, subcultures – with different rules of feeling which help people to get by (Fineman, 1985b; Anthony, 1990).

At present, we can only imagine what an intervention programme might look like which would comprehensively examine and change the interplay between formal and informal feeling rules. Such a programme would need to delve deeply in examining the way meaning is constructed within the enterprise, and offer negotiative rights to all constituent groups. A possible model is that of participatory action research, variants of which can be found in the work of Whyte (1991) and Israel et al. (1989). In participative action research the researchers and workers are supposed to work together, jointly conceptualizing and theorizing organization – how it is and how it might be. Strategies for possible change are devised, and are negotiated within and between interest groups. This approach is meant to give voice and power to all groups, an essential pluralistic vision of the enterprise.

That is the theory. But some feeling rules are likely to be highly resistant to change. For example, many administrations proclaim an open door policy, ready, indeed eager, to hear employees' anxieties about aspects of their organization that bother them. Yet, as demonstrated by the ruthless treatment of some whistleblowers, such an offer is often very much less open than it appears, being constrained by an implicit rule of the sort: 'never embarrass your management, especially in public' (Whitehead, 1990; Jackall, 1988). The feeling rules (explicit and implicit) serve to preserve managerial control and prerogative, interests that are not easily negotiated away (see chapter 7). This is amplified many times when the organization's business is deemed to be secret, such as with research and development activities, or in some departments of government or the military. In these settings the state may prescribe the dominant feeling rules (with official secrets acts, confidentiality clauses, loyalty oaths) which will smother local attempts to do things differently. And there is a further disincentive to change: the *realpolitik* of organizational life suggests that, where valued corporate rewards are dispensed with partiality, ambitious individuals should smile often at the people they need most to please. Participatory action research, and other democratic forms of organizational change, are appealing in their potential to directly address the micro-politics of emotion. What we see, however, is that such attempts can be weakened by organizational members who have a powerful vested interest in maintaining particular patterns of emotional deference, or by the influence of 'external' agents, or by social structures that support emotional control.

The question therefore remains as to how we intervene in relation to issues of subjectivity such as those associated with stress. Answering this question depends also of course on how we view the stressed subject. It is to this issue that we turn in our final chapter, drawing on and attempting to summarize some of the points already discussed. Specifically, the chapter will try to show how the stressed subject might look if it were historicized, emotionalized, gendered, collectivized and managed through a publicizing rather than a privatizing of emotion. In addition, we shall return to the question of how the stress discourse relates to other discourses, and why it seems so powerful.

7

Conclusion: Rewriting the Stressed Subject

This chapter will consider alternatives to the conceptualization of stress in mainstream discourse, exploring other ways in which the discourse might be written in relation to both analysis and change.

In rethinking stress, our primary concern in this book has been with the image of the stressed subject contained within stress discourse. In a similar fashion, when we begin to consider alternatives, the central issue is to write a different kind of subject. Put very simply, this subject is one which might be historicized, politicized, collectivized and gendered. At the same time this subject needs to be seen in the context of wider discourse. In what follows, the aim will be to try and illustrate what this might mean through the writing of different images of the stressed subject, and through examining both how the stress discourse contrasts with other discourses, and why it appears to be so comparatively powerful.

Historicizing the Stressed Subject

In historicizing the subject, one point of reference comes from the work of Foucault (see chapter 3). Loosely applying a Foucauldian framework, the stress discourse applies largely psychological discourse and practice to the stress 'epidemic'. In so doing it attempts to explain why people experience certain types of distressing emotion such as worry, anxiety, frustration and anger. These are of course emotions which people probably experienced long before the development of stress discourse. What the discourse can be seen as doing is 'capturing them', through re-explaining their significance to both social and medical scientists, and to lay people. Within the discourse, these emotions are portrayed as potentially dangerous, since if they are continually aroused, they may set up psychophysiological maladaptation (e.g. heightened adrenalin, noradrenalin levels) which may result in serious illnesses, such as those of heart disease and cancer. So these emotions, as well as patterns of 'ineffective' coping behaviour, are problematized by the discourse, and their 'danger' calls out for a solution.

Given this historical perspective, one question is that of whether there really is an epidemic of stress. Have 'stress levels' really changed, or has psychophysiological discourse merely succeeded in problematizing one further area of human life? As noted in chapter 1, there is no reliable way of answering this question since any apparent rises in stress levels may reflect the increasing spread of the stress discourse (and the routine utilization of its language and concepts), rather than any 'real', 'objective' increase in stress. But, for the sake of argument, let us assume that what we now call stress has increased through the twentieth century. Why might this be the case? If we look to the stress discourse, we find only fairly bland answers such as the 'rapid pace of change', with hardly anything resembling a detailed historical or sociological account. For example, Allinson et al. provide one such account:

> Many stress and stress-related conditions are related to change. In Orlans' and Shipley's survey of large organisations in the UK, respondents cited 'change' as being the most important current stressor in the context of their organisation . . . Many employees are grimly beginning to acknowledge the fact that stability (in the sense of freedom from constant change) is a thing of the past, but this in itself is not helping them to cope any better. (1989: 385–6)

There is plenty of scope to sociologically develop this sort of account. We have already examined some examples, applying the work of Foucault and Elias (see chapter 3). In order to illustrate further what a socio-historic account of stress might look like, I shall now briefly explore the implications of some of the work of Giddens. The aim here is not to establish the validity of the account that follows (which could be debated), but rather to illustrate how it is possible to give accounts of stress that are alternative to the ahistorical and asocial view that currently predominates.

Within Giddens's theorizing, stress could be seen as in part a consequence of the increasing uncertainty of modern life. As Giddens points out, we no longer have clear sources of authority, such as those traditionally provided by religious authorities. Instead there is an 'indefinite pluralism of expertise' (1991: 195) which 'some individuals find it psychologically difficult or impossible to accept' (1991: 196). For most people, 'A self-identity has to be created and more or less continually reordered against the backdrop of shifting experiences of day-to-day life and the fragmenting tendencies of modern institutions' (1991: 186). Giddens contrasts this situation with that of feudal Europe where there were only a few and relatively unwavering sources of authority. These sources were the relatively stable traditions, the local community and kinship systems, and the religious authorities. By stark contrast, in modernity there are no clear sources of traditional authority, no compelling guides as to how we should lead our lives. In addition, we are all increasingly 'disembedded', with relationships no longer defined by local contexts (e.g. the traditional image of the village) but taking place across time and space:

> Consider some examples. A person may be on the telephone to someone twelve thousand miles away and for the duration of the conversation be more closely bound up with the responses of that distant individual than with others sitting in the same room. The appearance, personality and policies of a world political leader may be better known to a given individual than those of his next-door neighbour. (Giddens, 1991: 189)

Lichfield, in an article in *The Independent on Sunday*, provides a popular media illustration of the sense of distress and alienation which may accompany disembeddedness. The article reports his research into the phenomenon of edge cities – the semi-urban developments where the professional classes of the US have relocated away from the problems of race, poverty and crime associated with large American cities. He quotes a resident of one of these edge cities, 'a successful highly paid executive', who admits to 'a sense of bewilderment, even loss' in living in an urbanization that has no generally accepted name, but is known to local real estate agents as '287–78, after the two interstate freeways which intersect nearby'.

> *We are less and less involved in other people and more and more involved in ourselves* . . . People compensate by making their own communities, nationwide communities of family or friends. *But they are scattered communities, of people living in places like this hundreds of miles apart,* connected by airlines and the interstate and faxes and telephones. (*The Independent on Sunday, Sunday Review,* 15 November 1992: 9; my italics)

Images similar to those created by Giddens can be found in the stress discourse, especially within its popular media representation. *Good Housekeeping* provides one example:

> Stress, anxiety, depression, phobias – all are part of the accepted fallout of the 'busyness' of modern life, in which technology, far from freeing time for leisure, only seems to accelerate the pace. Those we tradition-ally turned to for emotional support – priests, family doctors, wise old relatives and neighbours – are lost in our mobile, secular society, where families are scattered hundreds, even thousands, of miles apart. We scuttle breathlessly with no time for those leisurely confidences that can unravel so much anguish. (*GH,* October 1992: 76)

Yet, as noted above, this kind of account has not been subject to any detailed analysis by academic stress researchers, which is hardly surprising given the individualistic and ahistorical nature of the discourse (see chapter 2). Applying Giddens, however, it is possible to construct a historical image of the stressed subject which sees stress as related to changing patterns of social relations where little is fixed, where 'the signposts established by tradition are now blank' (1991: 82).

It is also possible to reframe the kind of socio-historic account of stress presented above. For example, in Giddens's account, the problem of stress is likely to appear as fundamentally social, moral and institutional. Yet equally it is possible to develop an account which explains modern *Angst* through an emphasis upon the relation between discourse and subjectivity.[1] For example, in a medieval village, news from abroad is limited to a small number of agents such as priests, soldiers, journeymen, wandering mendicants and traders. Such communicative constraints bear little relation to the modern situation. People are bombarded with different ways of seeing our world – the physical, the mathematical, the literary, the biological, the psychological – and these discourses relate to a diverse range of practices carried out through media, schools, hospitals and workplaces (Gergen, 1991). The technological products of these discourses, whether hard technology such as microchips, or human technology such as psychotherapy, appear to develop on an ever accelerating curve. It is because of the multiplicity of such discursive developments that our modern world seems far less certain than that of the village serf. And ironically, because of this very uncertainty, we appear more in need of the help of discourse, so that we know how to lead our lives. For example, to avoid being duped by 'green' advertising, we must delve further and further into the environmental discourse so that we can discover the right and true way to be green. To take another example, sex can never be taken for granted since psychological and demographic discourse tells us that relationships are increasingly unstable, whilst also revealing how important sex is to 'committed relationships'. A plethora of statistics tell us about how fast our world is changing, and reveal its inherent unpredictability. To cope we need to be not just sex-fit but stress-fit, diet-fit, green-fit and so on.

Within this kind of analysis, the stress discourse, like other discourses of fitness, appears important because of the uncertainty of modern life, an uncertainty itself promoted by the array of discourse, and the continually competing priests of authority and expertise. Stress appears almost as a necessary kind of comfort discourse, a tranquilliser to cope with the diversity of competing messages about the truth of this world, and the dreadful uncertainty of our times. The stress discourse reassures us by explaining how it is *normal* to feel stressed in these conditions, and it provides strategies to help us cope with them by being vigilant and stress-fit.

The above exploration of some of the work of Giddens illustrates how it is not difficult to find ways in which we might historicize the stressed subject. The current ahistoricism does not therefore derive from a lack of theoretical opportunity but rather reflects the narrowness with which stress and distress are presently conceptualized, a narrowness which largely precludes the possibility of a historical analysis of stress and subjectivity.

Politicizing the Stressed Subject

Currently the best-known theoretical approach relevant to politicizing stress is perhaps that of Hochschild, and her analysis of the strong affect control that is required by the commercialization of feeling in modern business (see chapters 4 and 6). Her work has been subject to some valid criticism, most notably that it relies on a notion that there is a true self: that is, her argument that employees' feelings are commercialized implicitly relies on some notion that there is 'true' or 'real' self that exists somewhere beyond the one that has been commercialized and 'distorted' in the modern era (Wouters, 1989). The problem here is very similar to that involved in traditional Marxist arguments about false consciousness (see chapter 1), in that both false consciousness and true selves rely on tenuous notions that in some blissful happy land we can find our real consciousness and our real selves. Another limitation of Hochschild's work is that it is not placed in a broad historical context, and in consequence it might benefit considerably from some integration with the kind of perspective provided by Elias.

Wouters (1989) also criticizes Hochschild's work for understating the extent of informalization that has characterized the twentieth century, and overstating the degree of alienation that arises from the commercialization of feeling (see chapter 3). However these criticisms seem more questionable. Firstly, as was argued in chapter 3, the workplace does not appear to have been subject to the same degree of informalization as the home. It has never really begun to resemble a place where you could let it all hang out. Secondly, it is not too hard to find examples which resonate well with Hochschild's images of the alienation of commercialized feelings, with the consequence that it is debatable whether she is really overstating her case. For example, in a five-year study of six British supermarkets, Ogbonna and Wilkinson found that supermarket checkout operators were expected to carefully tailor their affective and behavioural responses in order to please the customer. At one supermarket company, a store manager commented that they tell their checkout operators 'not to let out their emotion and to be as polite as possible and to tell themselves that the customers are not having a go at them but at the company and the system' (1990: 516). At another, a supervisor commented that 'We are able to tell when a checkout operator is not smiling or even when she is putting on a false smile . . . we call her into a room and have a chat with her' (1990: 517).

This is not stress in the sense traditionally encompassed by the stress discourse (see chapter 2), but as Hochschild's work illustrates, there may be considerable pressure associated with maintaining the appropriate affective and behavioural response, with keeping up the continual smile (particularly if there is a lack of access to back-stage and off-stage arenas where the mask can more safely slip). And it is not just airline or supermarket workers who appear subject to maintaining appropriate civility in the face of the customer. For example, if you visit a McDonald's restaurant, you may notice that their workers wear badges with stars on them. The number of stars reflects how their performance has been rated, and is linked to their pay and promotion prospects. The performance rating is made on the basis of an assessment which lists criteria such as:

Greeting the customer:
1 There is a smile.
2 Greeting is pleasant, audible and sincere.
3 Looks customer in the eyes.
(from McDonald's 'Counter observation check list')

McDonald's staff, or crew members, are rated on such items on a 0–4 scale, where 0 is unsatisfactory and 4 is outstanding. Such rather panoptic observation indicates how even fairly low-paid service workers do not appear immune from commercial demands to control affect. Such analyses of emotional labour do not of course represent the only form of stress and distress in the workplace, but they are clearly relevant to broadening our conceptualization of stress, and to beginning to politicize the stressed subject.

Throughout this book we have tried to explore other images of the way in which the stressed subject is inevitably a politicized one, through illustrating the relationship between the current stress discourse and issues of power and subjectivity. For example:

1 At worst the stress discourse appears as a Marxist caricature, a means of getting workers to squeeze the last drop of surplus value out of themselves.
2 It can be seen to articulate with views of the entrepreneurial self-improving subject glorified in neo-liberal discourse.
3 It facilitates the privatization and containment of distress at work.

4 It provides a representation which appears far closer to the views of management groups than that of organized labour.

5 The deployment of stress management practices can also provide a means to scapegoat and witch-hunt anyone seen as a problem employee, or even anyone who admits to the heresy of not believing or conforming to the terms of stress management practice (see chapter 5).

6 It denies the relation between stress and social stratification (Pearlin, 1989), and the possibility that stress might itself reflect a containment of emotion that arises from the power relations between employer and employee, superior and subordinate, or men and women (Hearn, 1993; Parkin, 1993).

These kinds of criticism generate their own alternatives. In the remainder of this chapter, I shall explore some of them.

Emotionalizing the Stressed Subject

Once we acknowledge, following Elias, that emotion is historically and socially variable, it becomes important to consider how it is historically and socially constructed in employment settings. In general, the workplace appears as a setting which still requires a fair degree of emotional restraint (see above and chapter 3). By individualizing both the supposed causes of stress and its treatment (relaxation, meditation etc.), stress discourse and practice appear to support emotional restraint by privatizing distress and keeping it off limits. The stress discourse is not the only discourse supportive of emotional restraint, but rather it can be seen to be built into the seeming scientism of much of current human resource management. For example, Parkin (1993) notes how supervisory feedback and performance appraisal are portrayed within HRM as something which should be seen as a disciplined and objective task. In consequence, if a subordinate is given negative feedback, or a poor appraisal, it can be argued that they should not take it personally, as it is part of the rational, semi-scientific procedures of modern-day management (Newton and Findlay, 1994). But as Parkin argues, such approaches are premised on a questionable notion of human emotionality, an 'idea that one can separate off part of oneself' (1993: 174) even when given a negative feedback or appraisal. And the inability to not 'take things personally' is only likely to compound the feelings of distress and vulnerability that arise from negative feedback, as well as reinforcing the message that such distress should remain private (since, after all, it shouldn't be 'taken personally' in the first place).

In contrast to these explicit or implicit demands for emotional restraint, it can be argued that we should take things personally, that we should let off and ventilate our feelings rather than feel that they must be contained or dealt with off-stage through meditation, relaxation and so on. That said, of course, any employee who chooses to do this is in grave danger of ignoring power relations within organizations, and the way these are structured around employer–employee, superior–subordinate, men–women and so on. Most of us are aware that the kind of demands for emotional restraint and civility identified by Elias within the circles of courtly aristocracy have still not disappeared from a workplace where we still need to maintain economic 'favour'. At the same time, Parkin's comments about the denial of emotion within performance appraisal can itself be seen as a symbol of the power relations which it enacts. For example, employees may well maintain the front of 'not taking it personally' since emotional expression (of anger, frustration, sorrow etc.) would be seen as unprofessional behaviour likely to damage their employment prospects. Grey (1994) provides an example of this within a Foucauldian analysis of the performance appraisal of trainee accountants (Newton and Findlay, 1994 reinterpret this analysis with reference to Elias). He notes that although those appraised were invited to comment on their appraisal ratings, they rarely did so because ' "it wouldn't be good for your career" (newly qualified accountant)' (Grey, 1994). The sensible courtier thus knows her place.

Alternatives to this individualization and privatization within HRM could proceed in both a theoretical and a practical direction. Theoretically, there is a need to explore further the relation between emotion and work since the Industrial Revolution. Elias provides one starting point here, but as noted in chapter 3, his work focuses far more on the courtly aristocracy than on capitalist production. However, there are a number of interesting avenues that might be followed: the relation between discourse and emotional expression (e.g. the psychoanalytical legacy: see chapter 2); the changing nature of private versus public emotional display; the divide between the expression of affect in the home and the workplace, and the historical development of this divide (see chapter 3).

At a practical level, interventionists might begin to challenge the explicit and implicit feeling rules that apply in different work settings. For example, in chapter 6 Stephen Fineman noted an implicit feeling rule associated with the work of some social workers: 'never show you can't cope; disguise your feelings of stress; remember, a competent social worker should be able to handle her own stress.' One approach would be to try and challenge such rules through group-focused interventions. Yet, as was also noted in chapter 6, this is not an approach without constraints and problems. Firstly, exploring the emotional landscape is likely to require lengthy in-depth study, rather than the use of questionnaires or small numbers of interviews. One can also analyse the 'emotional map' of an organization (Hochschild, 1993), and Nurse (1994) has provided an example of such mapping, exploring which individuals and groups within the organizational hierarchy emotionally 'talk to' each other (Nurse illustrates such maps by literally laying them over the top of an organizational chart). Yet by themselves, such approaches are unlikely to reveal the *tacit* emotional codes which different groups in an organization may follow. As the work of Menzies (1959) and Satyamurti (1981) suggests (see chapters 2 and 4), emotion work may often involve collective denial of difficulties and threats within the workplace. Not only may emotional codes be tacit then; there may also be considerable defence against acknowledging them.

Such problems do not however mean that this kind of work is impossible. Emotion maps of an organizational hierarchy may provide a focusing technique through which to narrow in on what in chapter 6 we referred to as different clusters of feeling rules. Participant or non-participant observation, individual and group interviews, may then provide more in-depth understanding of how tacit and explicit emotional codes relate to the historical and socio-political context of particular work settings. These approaches are of course far more time consuming and costly than traditional stress management programmes. Besides which, to the extent that they challenge the existing socio-political context, they are unlikely to be adopted by stress management consultants, given that their clients are management groups, not those of organized labour or other (e.g. women's) collectives. At the same time, this is in itself an argument for independent researchers to pursue this kind of research and intervention.

Gender and the Stressed Subject

Parkin and Hearn have illustrated the way in which the expression of emotion is gendered, arguing that the dominant emotional and sexual codes in organizations are those of men, and that such codes promote images of order and rationality, underwritten by tight emotional constraint. Their work also suggests that women may experience greater stress because of the way in which emotionality and sexuality in organizations are at the same time both denied and projected on to women (a kind of splitting in a Kleinian sense). Thus 'men who express emotion are seen as weaker and "like women" ' (Parkin, 1993: 1984). If women express emotion in organizations, they may therefore both intrude on (male) rationality, and support the sexual splitting of emotion that allows men to deny emotions. At the same time, such emotional expression breaches the tacit codes of emotional restraint within organizations, and reinforces an image of women as problematic and as having a semi-neurotic emotionality. As Parkin puts it, her feelings of distress in organizations are 'not just because of different structures, kinds of work, management styles, public and private, but because of the problematized construction of me as an emotional, sexualized woman' (1993: 186).

Clark also argues that women's experience of stress is directly related to the predominance of male attitudes, values and behaviour, and she illustrates how gender issues are generally marginalized in stress research (Clark, 1994; see also chapter 4). One exception, however, is provided in the work of Hall (1989) who has used mainstream stress discourse to present some research data which suggest that women generally occupy jobs with lower levels of discretion and control than men.[2] What is particularly interesting about Hall's research is her finding that even in occupations where women predominate, they still report lower levels of discretion than men. Part of the reason for this finding may be that men predominate in the upper echelons of 'women's jobs' (e.g. nursing), which in itself is related to the lack of organizational support for women's careers (Collinson et al., 1990). So this argument brings in many of the issues raised in the study of the gendered nature of work, such as adequate childcare, maternity and paternity leave, career breaks, access to training and so on. In sum, low levels of control and discretion experienced by women in employment appear likely to relate both to broader issues of power, distress and emotion, and to the politics surrounding the gendered nature of organizations.

Collectivizing the Stressed Subject

An obvious response to the over-individualization of the stressed subject is to try and collectivize her. We have already examined examples of this endeavour at various points in this book. For example, Scandinavian research and the work of Menzies (1959; see chapter 2), Satyamurti (1981) and Handy (1990; see chapter 4) indicate that coping may often be a collective process, whilst some of this work also suggests that such collective processes may help in maintaining stress and distress (through a collective denial). Working from a view of stress as a collective process may also imply a changed role for the stress interventionist. For example, in choosing to act through organized labour, Neale and his colleagues not only obtained a very different view of stress to that of conventional researchers (see chapters 5 and 6), but also clearly identified with the difficulties of labour rather than management. The work of Israel and her colleagues (see chapter 6) also shows how analysis and intervention can take a more collective orientation by adopting a participatory research approach. Whilst participatory research may not guarantee any equality between researcher and researched,[3] this work does illustrate group processes relating to stress, and provides examples of stress management interventions that are less individualistic than those which currently predominate (even if they are not politically very radical).

The denial of the collective is apparent in both stress discourse and practice. The point made by Wilensky and Wilensky (1951) relating to their experience of employee counselling at Hawthorne still has relevance: that Hawthorne had extensive employee counselling and a tame union is probably not a coincidence. Rather than expressing problems and grievances through a collective channel, through stress management practices they become individualized, a 'personal problem' rather than one which may be shared by a large number of employees. Stress management can be seen as part of a number of other human resource management approaches which individualize employee experience. For example, performance appraisal can also be seen to write collective problems (of say an entire unit or even an organization) as though they were individual problems (Newton and Findlay, 1994). Though there may be scope for (individual) bargaining in performance appraisal, it nevertheless tends to move the focus away from the shared nature of employee experience. The gaze remains upon the individual and as a result intervention is targeted at the individual, and the relevance of collective action tends to be obscured. The primary underlying concern is often with employee performance, and to the extent that there are welfarist considerations, it is once again individual, not collective, welfare that is at stake.

Publicizing Stress?

A significant part of the problem with the management of stress may derive from the fact that employees are generally not expected to express their feelings of distress at work, and certainly not front-stage (Hochschild, 1983). They are instead expected to 'own their own stuff', 'keep cool' and so be 'professional'. This exhortation is also to a large extent written into the stress discourse with its encouragement of stress-fit employees who can handle the tough pressures of their jobs, and deal with the tensions *privately*, through say letting off steam at home, or through the use of stress management techniques.

In contrast, emotional restraint when in private can be considerably relaxed. As was argued in chapter 3, there can be seen to be an inversion of the demand to maintain a stiff upper lip through the twentieth century (Newton, 1994c). Indeed within some discourses (e.g. that relating to family therapy), emotional restraint has become pathologized, reflective of an 'unhealthy repression'. The easing of emotional restraint when in private raises the question of why a similar relaxation has not occurred in public and workplace settings. This question is also partly of interest since one way to radically tackle stress would be to try and remove the restraints on the expression of distress (and emotion more generally) within organizations. Yet such a stress management solution is likely to be difficult to implement for a number of reasons. Firstly, the distinction between the private and the public expression of emotion can be so taken for granted that it is simply the natural way of behaving. To some, it can seem crazy to question it. The idea of people expressing, say, their anger, pain, job, love, hurt or distress at work may seem very odd and rather threatening. Whilst it is one thing to acknowledge that emotion is historically and socially variable, it may therefore be quite another to expect any radical change in the tacit codes of emotionality that apply in the workplace. Secondly, as was argued in chapter 3, organizational emotionality does need to be seen in the context of the relationship between employer and employee, and between superior and subordinate, wherein employees and subordinates are still generally expected to maintain civility. As was illustrated with regard to social workers in chapter 6, the power relations within many organizations may mean that subordinates are very wary of revealing their feelings of stress and anxiety to their superiors (and may be equally wary of sharing such feelings with their peers). Thirdly, most management discourse promotes an ideal of management as being governed by a seeming masculine rationality, epitomized by approaches such as that of management information systems with its goal of an organized objective data system.

Together these issues provide pointers as to why there remains a rigidity in the divorce between emotional expression in private, public and especially organizational settings. But so long as stress remains a private matter, it is more likely to remain depoliticized, because it is seen as something that individuals are meant to deal with by themselves. The prospects of a more radical approach to stress management are constrained because of this very individualization and privatization. Yet it might be expected that the growing body of discursivities which challenge the rationality, sexuality and emotionality of organizations will have some influence on the way in which we all experience life in organizations. As Giddens argued, over time the 'original quality' of social science discourse may be lost, since it 'may become all too familiar. The notion of sovereignty and associated theories of the state were stunningly new when first formulated: today they have in some degree become part of the very social reality which they helped to establish' (1984: xxxiv). Such an argument appears at first sight to suggest that relatively novel discourses such as those relating to gender and sexuality may one day appear as the 'natural' way to see things. But of course we must not forget the need to examine discourse in the context of broader power relations. For example, it may be that the notion of sovereignty was rather more attractive in its day to dominant groups than are current theories of sexuality and emotionality to the 'white male hegemony' (Parkin, 1993: 187). While domination may not be as linear and monistic as this last quote would imply, if we follow Elias, we might not expect discourse that threatens existing power relations to be readily received. And emphasizing power relations once again underlines the need to understand the stress discourse in the context of other discourses that are concerned with the government of the self, since such contrasts provide further pointers to the political convenience of its present form.

Relating Stress to Other Discourses

Throughout this book we have related the stress discourse to other discourses with which it appears to articulate. In general we would argue that such an approach is necessary when looking at any particular discourse, since discourses cannot exist in isolation, and they may rely on a conceptualization of the subject which is very similar to that contained in other discourses. For example, notions of stress-fitness applied to the workplace foster images of the managerial subject as a 'real *man*ager' who isn't afraid of the pressures, keeps his cool, owns his stuff, and doesn't whinge or moan. Implicitly this subject is one who is autonomous and enterprising, who owns their own problems, and gets on with it. A complementary kind of text is written into many other discourses, especially those concerned with human growth (Rose, 1990). They tend to project an image of individuals as very powerful, if only they will accept the 'power' inside them.

For an example of this complementarity, I shall briefly refer to the bestseller by Susan Jeffers, *Feel the Fear and Do It Anyway*. In this book Jeffers encourages her readers to identify with the statement, 'I am powerful and I love it' (1987: 35). The consequences of accepting this power are portrayed as immense; almost anything can be achieved if only we just accept our own power. Power inequalities related to, say, gender, class or race would appear to pale into relative insignificance compared with the power that comes from within, and the willingness to take responsibility.

> It's better to take responsibility for whatever happens to you in life than always to be the victim. 'It's not my fault I got sick'; 'It's not my fault I lost my job.' If you are willing to take responsibility, then you might see what you can change in the future. Relative to illness, say, *'I'm totally responsible* for my illness. Let's see what I can do to prevent it from happening again. I can change my diet. I can stop smoking. I can get enough sleep.' (1987: 40–1)

In this brave new world, feeling that we are victims should have nothing to do with the fact that we have just been made redundant, or we have got cancer. We just need to think positive, to eliminate our destructive negativity (Jeffers even advises her readers to drop negative friends, and avoid 'complaint mates': 1992: 104). And there is a clear correspondence with this text and that of the stress discourse where once again the problems of stress are often seen as a problem of attitude; instead of complaining and whinging about our work (or worst of all perhaps, lodging a formal grievance), we need to see the challenges, the opportunities, the excitement. As Jeffers again explains: ' "It's a problem" is another deadening phrase. It's heavy and negative. " *It's an opportunity*" opens the door to growth' (1987: 41). As Rose and Miller (1992) have noted, this promotion of an autonomous, entrepreneurial subject has clear consonances with the government of the state and the organization through the neo-liberalism associated with Thatcher and Reagan, and the promotion of a go-getting on-your-bike citizen (and as noted in chapter 3, this may in part explain the phenomenal rise of the stress discourse in the 1980s). Whinging, moaning and grievances are part of the sad litany of trade unions and collectivism, a bygone era that has thankfully passed now that we are all willing to use the power within, and 'see the gift in life's obstacles' (Jeffers, 1987: 41).

From a labour process perspective, applying these images of empowerment in the workplace does appear awfully convenient for 'squeezing the last drop of surplus value', and comes pretty close to a Marxist caricature. It encourages employees to believe that a can't-do attitude is very 'negative', and that instead they can ride any pressures provided they just put their minds to it, and take steps to, say, 'reduce stress'. If employees adopt a can-do attitude, they should also become more committed and productive workers who, even when they are made redundant, still realize that it is up to them to take responsibility (see Jeffers quote above). The stress discourse both embodies notions of this kind of productive pressure-relishing subject, and incorporates assumptions which articulate with those of managerialism – that is, its individualization, apoliticism, ahistoricism and so on. Similarly stress management practice strongly emphasizes the individual's responsibility for exercising control and restraint: 'Don't whinge to your colleagues, or worst of all, break down. See your employee counsellor, or take up meditation.'

Analysis of the kind of positive thinking discourse exampled by Jeffers illustrates how it may be helpful to examine the similarities in the image of the subject created in differing discourses, even though our focus may remain on a particular discourse and its practices. In addition, relating the stress discourse to other discourses raises another interesting question: why is the stress discourse so 'successful' when compared with other social science discourses? Why does it appear so much part of the language of not just academic, but also lay understanding? And more generally, why is it that some discourses appear more powerful than others in their ability to constitute individuals within their orbit?

The Power of the Stress Discourse

Examine the following questions:

1 Will the idea of 'emotional labouring' become part of everyday discourse?
2 Will there be any practitioners of Hochschild's theory who will apply it to analysis and intervention in organizations?
3 Will a stream of magazine articles appear about it, alerting us to the commercialization of our feeling in our everyday work?

My guess is that the most likely answer to all these questions is 'no'. I don't expect to overhear discussion of emotional labouring on the bus. Nor do I expect to see a plethora of media examinations of the subject. Even within academic circles, it is noticeable that Hochschild's theory has had a slow take-off compared, say, with Khan et al.'s definitive study of role stress. One explanation for this answer along social constructionist lines is that the more politicized notion of emotional labouring will not supplant that of work stress because it relies on a view of emotion and the self which is at variance with the West's cultural attachment to individualization and decontextualization. Equally, from a labour process perspective, it might be argued that the promotion of the idea of emotional labouring is at variance with the interests of capital, and that, as the work of Neale et al. illustrates (see chapter 5), management groups appear to favour an individualized definition of employee subjectivity. But such explanations beg the additional question of whether the power of the stress discourse is reducible purely to questions of cultural assimilation, or to more powerful interests within the labour process. For there are other discourses which are equally individualistic and apolitical which have not been so well diffused. Most of organizational psychology meets these criteria, yet other topics in organizational psychology are not so well 'spread over the surface of things', with an ability to 'cover' both organizational and domestic life.

Throughout this book, a number of reasons have been put forward as to why the stress discourse appears powerful in its articulation with, say, eugenicist, militaristic and managerial concerns. Following a strictly Foucauldian line, one could also argue that the power of stress discourse derives principally from its bio-power, its ability to gaze upon life, death and health, and to provide 'methods of power capable of optimizing forces, aptitudes, and life in general without at the same time making them more difficult to govern' (Foucault, 1981: 141). One could further argue, again following Foucault, that it is this celebration of life, and the normalization of attention to life, that particularly distinguishes the stress discourse from other discourses relating to work and organizations. It gains an existential power from its ability to frame what is important in life (e.g. the promotion of psychological and physical health) thereby helping to answer 'the only important question for us: what shall we do and how shall we live?' (Rose, 1990: 255, quoting Weber quoting Tolstoy). The stress discourse thus appears as part of the panoply of bio-power that celebrates and normalizes life. Whilst the same can be said of other areas of social science discourse, within organizational discourse, work on stress is particular in the way that it stands as a kind of rubric for the normalization of psychophysiological health and well-being.

Yet attention to the bio-power of the stress discourse does not detract from the need to analyse its political significance. For example, as noted in chapter 5, is it a mere coincidence that the stress discourse is phrased in managerialist terms? If subjectivity is just a matter of our constitution in language and discourse, and the self-surveillance so produced, why do organizational definitions of that subjectivity (such as work stress) appear so politically one-sided (managerial, male etc.)? There does appear to be a relative *stability* in power relations such that one voice is favoured. Within organizations, this is classically that of 'management', but it can be those of whites rather than ethnic minorities, or of men rather than women. And though, say, equal opportunities discourse may seek to destabilize gender and race discrimination in the labour market, nevertheless such discrimination appears relatively enduring, and is rationalized in the language of capital–labour relations. In sum, understanding power and discourse in the workplace does still appear to need an attention to how it relates to relatively stable social structures.

Some writers argue however that stability is not so stable. For example, Knights and Vurdubakis (1994) maintain that:

> specific power relations, procedures, apparatuses, etc., may at certain times and in particular sites achieve together some measure of stability. Nevertheless this stability needs to be understood in terms of the specific conditions that made it possible in a given site (Knights and Collinson, 1987). We cannot *a priori* assume, as Foucault [in an interview in 1984] has pointed out, that any such stability is anything more than contingent and precarious.

They further argue that:

> Discourses do not simply produce, transmit and reinforce power relations, they also threaten, expose and render them fragile.

Yet while there may be no *a priori* reason to assume stability, there nevertheless would appear to be a fair degree of stability in the relations of, say, capital and labour, or of a gendered labour market. And though some sociological and social psychological discourse may, say, render managerialist discourse more fragile, it is my bet that it is this latter variant of management studies which will surround management decision-making for some time. To put it bluntly, Peters and Waterman are likely to be better received than Braverman. Stability seems more apparent than instability.

Conclusion

The alternative ways of looking at stress that have been presented in this chapter represent a summary of the arguments made in the previous chapters of this book. Essentially they are about changing our view of the subject that we see as 'stressed', so that she is not one whose stressful emotions are somehow divorced from other emotions, or whose stress is placed outside any historical or political context. Similarly stress needs to be related to gender, sexuality and other social stratification issues, as well as to collective experience within private, public and organizational settings. Those researchers and practitioners whose work is closely tied to the mainstream discourse might object that such an emphasis aims to change the stress discourse out of all recognition. We would have to agree that this is in many ways a fair assertion, for it is difficult to salvage much of the existing mainstream stress discourse from our present perspective. It seems to us simply to be far too narrowly written.

As a final point, we should also note that, like others (e.g. Hollway, 1991), part of our difficulty in this book has been in hanging on to central aspects of the project of organizational psychology, since the work stress discourse is heavily associated with it (and represented one of the main growth areas in organizational psychology in the 1980s). The problem with organizational psychology as an academic discipline is that it seems remarkably resistant to change, at least judging by the academic journals associated with it. For example, though there have been criticisms of the stress discourse within organizational psychology (e.g. Newton, 1989), these have very largely operated from within the functionalist and individualistic perspective that still surrounds the discipline (see chapters 2 and 4). And furthermore, the most common reaction to such criticisms has been to either almost carry on regardless, or retreat into even more individualistic explanations such as those of dispositional psychology, the safety of the familiar wherein workplace subjectivity is reduced to questions of 'neuroticism', or enduring traits of 'positive or negative affect' (see Davis-Blake and Pfeffer, 1989 and Newton and Keenan, 1991 for a critique of the re-emergence of such dispositional arguments). This is not to deny the relevance of individual differences or 'dispositions', but it does appear as a narrowing rather than a broadening of discourse.

It will be interesting to see the way in which psychology departments and organizational psychology practitioners react in relation to current critiques. Previously, institutionalized psychology has shown a remarkable ability to suppress strong critique (as with earlier generations of 'radical' psychologists), and it remains to be seen whether this will apply in the case of new onslaughts upon its apolitical and positivist orientation. Some organizational psychologists may feel that through deconstructing a mainstay of organizational psychology we have also been highly critical of most of the other assumptions of 'their' discourse (one which is more often celebrated than criticized: see for example Newton, 1994a; 1994b). But, as other writers such as Hollway have persuasively argued, these assumptions are strongly in need of reappraisal. More to the point, mainstream work psychology does seem rather open to criticism. For example, it remains remarkable how work stress researchers of the 1960s to the 1980s adopted a largely sociological concept, that of role, along with its functionalist methodology, and continued to publish article upon article that appeared as though they were stuck in a time warp of *circa* 1960 (see chapter 2).

We are uncertain as to whether Hollway is right to 'err on the side of pessimism' (1991: 183) with regard to future developments in organizational psychology. Certainly there have been some attempts to emancipate the discipline by devolving it from its neo-positivist legacy, such as that recently provided by Steffy and Grimes (1992), and to broaden its research methodology to (at last) take qualitative research more seriously (Cassell and Symon, 1994). We would argue that there is a clear need for further analysis of this kind, analysis which needs to take place far more inside than outside the pages of organizational psychology journals.

Notes

1 Giddens's interest appears more focused around moral and social issues than with the relation between discourse and subjectivity. A central part of his argument is the assertion that the deployment of such discursive expertise and professionalism raises fundamentally *moral* questions. The problem, according to Giddens, is that a 'sequestration of experience' arises whereby ordinary people are sheltered from some basic moral questions relating to issues such as sickness, madness, criminality, sexuality and death. We are no longer confronted with the sick, the insane, the criminal and the dying (as say a feudal peasant might have been) since they are contained in the hospital, the mental asylum and the prison. In consequence, these modern institutions *'repress a cluster of basic moral and existential components of human life* that are, as it were, squeezed to the sidelines' (1991: 167). In attempting to answer the question of why we have allowed such moral impoverishment, Giddens draws on psychodynamic discourse. He argues that underneath our complicity with this sequestration of basic moral issues lie deep-rooted individual concerns with maintaining a sense of continuity and order in our personal world, the desire for what Giddens calls 'ontological security'. He further asserts that we maintain a kind of 'protective cocoon' which screens out the dangers of the external world, and that our ability to do this relies on a feeling of basic trust in our world that is developed in 'normal' childhood. If we fail to develop this protective cocoon, or if it is seriously ruptured, chaos may threaten with the 'prospect of being overwhelmed by anxieties that reach to the very roots of our "being in the world" ' (1991: 37). But the maintenance activities of our protective cocoon are difficult in the modern age because 'by comparison with the generality of pre-modern cultures, the framework of ontological security becomes fragile' (1991: 167).

Giddens's analysis presents an image of life in an increasingly unanchored and less certain age, where relationships and self-identity have to be continually worked at.

Yet this relationship between subjectivity, discourse and expertise appears problematic. The problem arises in part because of the amount of theoretical work which the concept of ontological security is asked to do. It is through the evoking of this latent function, whose secrets lie buried in our childhood, that Giddens ultimately makes sense of how our subjectivity and identity are formed (even though elsewhere Giddens is highly critical of functionalist accounts). But this notion of ontological security is one that precludes further analysis. As Burkitt (1992) has noted, Giddens desocializes feelings of anxiety and existential loneliness by naturalizing them, making them an inevitable development of the supposedly natural process of childhood, and one which therefore doesn't need to be further explained. From the present perspective though, the problem is that not only are existential and moral questions desocialized by invoking latent childhood accounting mechanisms, but also the inquiry into the relationship between subjectivity, expertise and discourse is foreshortened. For example, Giddens pays attention to the environmental discourse and feminist discourse, seeing these as the emergence of 'life politics' which addresses the kind of moral dilemmas that have arisen from the sequestration of experience. But the relationship between the individual and such discourses is again ultimately reduced to whether they have attained 'a framework of basic trust' (1991: 215) which, as we have seen, is dependent upon notions of ontological security. There is only a limited elaboration of how and why it is that people become attached to feminist/environmentalist discourse, that is the relation between discourse and subjectivity remains somewhat obscure.

Elsewhere, Giddens appears ambivalent on the relationship between discourse and subjectivity. On the one hand, the calling up of discourse and experts (e.g. of psychotherapeutic discourse) can appear helpful in maintaining routines that guard against the chaos and hellish anxiety that would rise up were our protective cocoon to be seriously punctured. On the other hand, they provide the pool of knowledge upon which expert systems may sequester experience and deny us morally meaningful lives. In a similar fashion some discourses are posited as morally enhancing by engaging us in life politics (e.g. environmental/feminist discourse), whilst others appear as morally alienating through their sequestration of meaningful experience (e.g. psychiatry, medicine). Following Giddens, whether discourse is morally enhancing or alienating would appear to depend on the context of its delivery: for example, therapy in private counselling appears as enhancing, but when institutionalized in psychiatric hospitals it is portrayed as a more morally alienating experience – an argument which implicitly points to the need to consider power relations within the institutionalization of discourse.

2 Though the relationship between job discretion and distress/strain is contentious within mainstream stress discourse, it seems unlikely that reliance on questionnaire methodology could reveal much of the complex relationship between control, power and emotion (admittedly, Hall's own research was based on a questionnaire application of Karasek's measures, but her focus was largely on perceptions of job control).

3 Central to participatory research, and to the similar but more managerialist 'action research', is an attempt to establish 'co-learning' relationships involving researcher–subject collaboration. As Morgan and Ramirez comment on action research, 'no one individual or group [including researchers] is given a role that suggests they have a monopoly on insight and knowledge' (1984: 18), or as Hamnett et al. suggest with participatory research, there is a 'free and creative dialogue' which avoids 'an authoritarian process' (1984: 102). Yet the problem with this emphasis on

researcher–subject equality is that, rather than acknowledging the political relationship of research activity, it is in danger of trivializing it. The emphasis on collaboration assumes that researcher and subject will evolve a similar perspective. But there is no guarantee that this should be the case. In particular, it seems unlikely that the espousal of an equal relationship with organizational members is attainable in practice. For example, the outcomes of participatory research and action research would appear to be remarkably consonant with their particular discursive approaches. With its more managerialist orientation, action research has tended to produce outcomes that are consistent with management objectives. In contrast, participatory research is constituted within a discourse which advocates an oppositional stance to those who hold power, and has tended to produce outcomes which aim to alleviate the position of oppressed groups (Hamnett et al., 1984). In sum, the discursive allegiance of both groups of researchers appears to be notably associated with the analyses they produce, suggesting that, rather than there being an equal collaboration, the influence of the researchers (and their favoured discourse) is paramount in the direction taken by interventions. They may empower their respondents by seeming to speak for them, but all the while have the upper hand in the definition of discourse, research problem and solution (Bhavnani, 1990).

References

Ager, B. (1975) *Arbetsmiljön i sågverk* (Work environment in the saw-mill industry). Stockholm: Arbetarskyddsstyrelsen.

Ahrenfeldt, R.H. (1958) *Psychiatry in the British Army in the Second World War*. London: Routledge and Kegan Paul.

Air Ministry (1947) *Psychological Disorders in Flying Personnel of the Royal Air Force Investigated during the War 1939–1945*. Air Publication 3139. London: HMSO.

Allinson, P., Cooper, C.L. and Reynolds, P. (1989) Stress counselling in the workplace: the Post Office experience, *The Psychologist*, 2 (9): 384–8.

Angell, N. (1933) *The Great Illusion*. London: Heinemann.

Anthony, P.D. (1990) The paradox of the management of culture, or 'He who leads is lost', *Personnel Review*, 19 (4): 3–8.

Appley, M.H. and Trumbull, R. (1986) *Dynamics of Stress: Physiological, Psychological and Social Perspectives*. New York: Plenum.

Arroba, T. and James, K. (1987) *Pressure at Work: A Survival Guide*. London: McGraw-Hill.

Averill, J.R. (1980) A constructivist view of emotion. In R. Plutchik and H. Kellerman (eds.), *Theories of Emotion*. New York: Academic Press.

Baritz, L. (1960) *The Servants of Power*. Middletown, CT: Wesleyan University Press.

Beehr, T.A. and Franz, T.M. (1987) The current debate about the meaning of job stress. In J.M. Ivancevich and D.C. Ganster (eds.), *Job Stress: From Theory to Suggestion*. New York: Haworth Press.

Bendix, R. (1956) *Work and Authority in Industry*. New York: Harper and Row.

Benhabib, S. (1992) *Situating the Self: Gender, Community and Postmodernism in Contemporary Ethics*. Cambridge: Polity.

Benson, H. (1979) Your innate asset for combating stress. In *Harvard Business Review: On Human Relations*. London: Heinemann.

Bertera, R.L. (1990) The effects of workplace health promotion on absenteeism and employment costs in a large industrial population, *American Journal of Public Health*, 80: 1101–5.

Bhavnani, K.K. (1990) What's power got to do with it? Empowerment and social research. In I. Parker and J. Shotter (eds.), *Deconstructing Social Psychology*. London: Routledge.

Blackler, F. (1982) Job redesign and social policies. In J.E. Kelly and C.W. Clegg (eds.), *Autonomy and Control at the Workplace*. London: Croom Helm.

Blackler, F.H. and Brown, C.A. (1978) *Job Re-design and Management Control*. Farnborough: Saxon House.

Blum, T.C. and Roman, P.M. (1987) Aesculapian control in the workplace. Unpublished manuscript.

Boas, M. and Chain, S. (1976) Big Mac: The Unauthorized Story of McDonald's. New York: Dutton.

Bogner, A. (1987) Elias and the Frankfurt School, Theory, Culture and Society, 4: 249–85.

Bolveg, J. (1976) Job Design and Industrial Democracy: The Case of Norway. Leiden: Nijhoff.

Bowlby, J. (1969) Attachment and Loss. Volume 1: Attachment. London: Hogarth Press.

Braverman, H. (1974) Labor and Monopoly Capital. New York: Monthly Review Press.

Brief, A. and Atieh, J. (1987) Studying job stress: are we making mountains out of molehills?, Journal of Occupational Behaviour, 8: 115–26.

Briner, R.B. and Reynolds, S. (1993) Bad theory and bad practice in occupational stress, The Occupational Psychologist, 19.

Buchanan, D., Boddy, D. and McCalman, J. (1988) Getting in, getting on, and getting back. In A. Bryman (ed.), Doing Research in Organizations. London: Routledge.

Burawoy, M. (1979) Manufacturing Consent: Changes in the Labour Process under Monopoly Capitalism. Chicago: University of Chicago Press.

Burkitt, I. (1991) Social Selves. London: Sage.

Burkitt, I. (1992) Beyond the 'iron cage': Anthony Giddens on modernity and the self, History of the Human Sciences, 5: 71–9.

Burkitt, I. (1993) Overcoming metaphysics: Elias and Foucault on power and freedom, Philosophy of the Social Sciences, 23: 50–72.

Burman, E. (1984) The Inquisition: The Hammer of Heresy. Wellingborough: Aquarian Press.

Burrell, G. and Morgan, G. (1979) Sociological Paradigms and Organisational Analysis: Elements of the Sociology of Corporate Life. London: Heinemann.

Burrows, R. (ed.) (1991) Deciphering the Enterprise Culture. London: Routledge.

Burt, C. (1977) The Subnormal Mind (3rd edn). Oxford: Oxford University Press.

Cannon, W.B. (1914) The interrelations of emotions as suggested by recent physiological researches, American Journal of Psychology, 25: 256–82.

Cannon, W.B. (1932) The Wisdom of the Body. London: Kegan Paul, Trench, Trubner.

Cannon, W.B. (1935) Stresses and strains of homoeostasis, American Journal of the Medical Sciences, 189: 1–14.

Cannon, W.B. (1939) Bodily Changes in Pain, Hunger, Fear and Rage (2nd edn). New York: Appleton-Century.

Carrahan, P. and Stewart, P. (1989) Working for Nissan, Science and Culture, October.

Cassell, C. and Symon, G. (1994) Qualitative Research Methods in Organizational Psychology. London: Sage.

Clark, H. (1994) Patriarchy, alienation and anomie: new directions for stress research. In H. Clark, J. Chandler and J. Barry (eds), Organisation and Identities. London: Chapman and Hall.

Cofer, C.N. and Appley, M.H. (1964) Motivation: Theory and Research. New York: Wiley.

Cohen, S. and Williamson, G.M. (1991) Stress and infectious disease in humans, Psychological Bulletin, 109: 5–24.

Collinson, D.L., Knights, D. and Collinson, M. (1990) *Managing to Discriminate.* London: Routledge.

Conrad, P. (1986) Wellness in the workplace: potentials and pitfalls of worksite health promotion. Unpublished manuscript, Brandeis University.

Conrad, P. (1988) Health and fitness at work: a participant's perspective, *Social Science and Medicine*, 26: 545–50.

Cooper, C. (1986) Job distress: recent research and the emerging role of the clinical occupational psychologist, *Bulletin of the British Psychological Society*, 39: 325–31.

Creedon, P.J. (ed.) (1989) *Women in Mass Communication: Challenging Gender Values.* Newbury Park, CA: Sage.

Crozier, M. and Friedberg, E. (1980) *Actors and Systems: The Politics of Collective Action.* Chicago: University of Chicago Press.

Cyert, R.M. and March, J.G. (1963) *A Behavioral Theory of the Firm.* Englewood Cliffs, NJ: Prentice-Hall.

Dahrendorf, R. (1968) *Essays in the Theory of Society.* London: Routledge and Kegan Paul.

Danziger, K. (1990) *Constructing the Subject: Historical Origins of Psychological Research.* Cambridge: Cambridge University Press.

Davis-Blake, A. and Pfeffer, J. (1989) Just a mirage: the search for dispositional effects in organizational research, *Academy of Management Review*, 14: 385–400.

Deal, T.E. and Kennedy, A.A. (1982) *Corporate Cultures.* Reading, MA: Addison-Wesley.

De Board, R. (1978) *The Psychoanalysis of Organizations.* London: Tavistock.

Department of Health and Human Services (1980) *Fourth Special Report to Congress on Alcohol and Health.* Washington, DC: Public Health Service, National Institute of Alcohol Abuse and Alcoholism.

Derrida, J. (1992) Jacques Derrida: interview transcript from Channel 4 programme, 'Talking Liberties'. London: Channel 4 Television.

Dewe, P., Guest, D. and Williams, R. (1979) Methods of coping with work-related stress. In C. Mackay and T. Cox (eds.), *Response to Stress: Occupational Aspects.* Guildford: IPC Business Press.

Dews, P. (1987) *Logics of Disintegration: Post-Structuralist Thought and the Claims of Critical Theory.* London: Verso.

Dickson, W.J. (1945) The Hawthorne plan of personnel counselling, *Journal of Orthopsychiatry*, 15: 343–7.

Dickson, W.J. and Roethlisberger, F.J. (1966) *Counselling in an Organization.* Boston: Harvard University Press.

Dohrenwend, B.P. (1961) The social psychological nature of stress: a framework for causal inquiry, *Journal of Abnormal and Social Psychology*, 62: 294–302.

Dubin, R. (1956) Industrial workers' worlds: a study of the central life interests of industrial workers, *Social Problems*, 3: 131–42.

Durkheim, E. (1938) *The Rules of Sociological Method.* Chicago: University of Chicago Press.

Eckman, P. (1971) Universals and cultural differences in facial expressions of emotion. In J.K. Cole (ed.), *Nebraska Symposium of Motivation*, vol. 19. Lincoln: University of Nebraska Press.

Edwards, R. (1979) *Contested Terrain: The Transformation of the Workplace in the Twentieth Century.* London: Heinemann.

Eichenbaum, L. and Orbach, S. (1984) *What Do Women Want?* London: Fontana.

Elden, M. (1986) Sociotechnical systems ideas as public policy in Norway: empowering participation through worker-managed change, *Journal of Applied Behavioral Science*, 22: 239–55.

Elias, N. (1978) *The Civilizing Process*, vol. 1. Oxford: Blackwell.

Elias, N. (1982) *The Civilizing Process*, vol. 2. Oxford: Blackwell.

Elias, N. (1987) The balance of power between the sexes – a process sociological study: the example of the ancient Roman state, *Theory, Culture and Society*, 4: 287–316.

Ellery, R.S. (1945) *Psychiatric Aspects of Modern Warfare*. Melbourne: Reed and Harris.

Emery, F. and Thorsrud, E. (1969) *Form and Content in Industrial Democracy*. London: Tavistock.

Emery, F. and Thorsrud, E. (1976) *Democracy at Work: Report of the Norwegian Industrial Democracy Programme*. Leiden: Nijhoff.

Emery, F.E. and Trist, E.L. (1969) Socio-technical systems. In F.E. Emery (ed.), *Systems Thinking*. Harmondsworth: Penguin.

Faulder, C. (1977) Women's magazines. In J. King and M. Stott (eds.), *Is This Your Life? Images of Women in the Media*. London: Virago.

Filby, M.P. (1992) 'The figures, the personality and the bums': service work and sexuality, *Work, Employment and Society*, 6: 23–42.

Fineman, S. (1983a) Work meanings, non-work and the taken for granted, *Journal of Management Studies*, 20 (2): 143–57.

Fineman, S. (1983b) *White Collar Unemployment*. Chichester: Wiley.

Fineman, S. (1985a) *Social Work Stress and Intervention*. Aldershot: Gower.

Fineman, S. (1985b) The skills of getting-by. In A. Strati (ed.), *The Symbolics of Skill*. Trento: Dipartimento di Politica Sociale.

Fineman, S. (1990) *Supporting the Jobless*. London: Routledge.

Fineman, S. (1993) *Emotion in Organizations*. London: Sage.

Fineman, S. and Mangham, I.L. (1987) Change in organizations. In P.B. Warr (ed.), *Psychology at Work*. Harmondsworth: Penguin.

Fineman, S. and Payne, R.L. (1981) Roles stress – a methodological trap?, *Journal of Occupational Behaviour*, 2: 51–64.

Firth, J. (1985) Personal meanings of occupational stress: cases from the clinic, *Journal of Occupational Psychology*, 58: 139–48.

Firth, J. and Shapiro, D. (1986) An evaluation of psychotherapy for job-related distress, *Journal of Occupational Psychology*, 59: 111–20.

Firth-Cozens, J. (1992) Why me? A case study of the process of perceived occupational stress, *Human Relations*, 45: 131–42.

Fletcher, B. (1988) The epidemiology of occupational stress. In C.L. Cooper and R. Payne (eds.), *Causes, Coping and Consequences of Stress at Work*. Chichester: Wiley.

Fletcher, B. and Jones, F. (1993) A refutation of Karasek's demand-discretion model of occupational stress with a range of dependent measures, *Journal of Organizational Behaviour*, 14: 319–31.

Fletcher, B. and Payne, R. (1980) Stress at work: a review and theoretical framework, part 1, *Personnel Review*, 9: 19–29.

Foucault, M. (1979) *Discipline and Punish*. Harmondsworth: Penguin.

Foucault, M. (1980) *Power/Knowledge: Selected Interviews and Other Writings*, trans. C. Gordon. Hemel Hempstead: Harvester Wheatsheaf.

Foucault, M. (1981) *The History of Sexuality*, vol. 1. Harmondsworth: Penguin.

Foucault, M. (1982) Afterword: the subject and power. In H.F. Dreyfus and

P. Rabinow (eds.), *Michel Foucault: Beyond Structuralism and Hermeneutics.* Brighton: Harvester Press.

Foucault, M. (1984) Nietzsche, genealogy, history. In P. Rabinow (ed.), *The Foucault Reader.* Harmondsworth: Penguin.

Foucault, M. (1988) *Technologies of the Self: A Seminar with Michel Foucault,* ed. by L.H. Martin, H. Gutman and P.H. Hutton. London: Tavistock/University of Massachusetts Press.

Frankenhaeuser, M. (1989) A biopsychosocial approach to work life issues. *International Journal of Health Services,* 19: 747–58.

Frankenhaeuser, M. and Gardell, B. (1976) Underload and overload in working life: outline of a multidisciplinary approach, *Journal of Human Stress,* 2: 35–46.

Fraser, R. (1947) *The Incidence of Neurosis among Factory Workers.* Industrial Health Research Board Report 90. London: HMSO.

French, J.R.P. and Kahn, R.L. (1962) A programmatic approach to studying the industrial environment and mental health, *Journal of Social Issues,* 18: 1–47.

French, J.R.P., Kahn, R.L. and Mann, F.C. (1962) Work, health and satisfaction, *Journal of Social Issues,* 18: preface.

Friedman, A. (1977) *Industry and Labour: Class Struggle at Work and Monopoly Capitalism.* London: Macmillan.

Fromm, E. (1942) *The Fear of Freedom.* London: Routledge and Kegan Paul.

Gardell, B. (1971) Technology, alienation and mental health in the modern industrial environment. In L. Levi (ed.), *Society, Stress and Disease,* vol. 1. London: Oxford University Press.

Gardell, B. (1976) Reactions at work and their influence on nonwork activities: an analysis of sociopolitical problems in affluent societies, *Human Relations,* 29: 885–904.

Gardell, B. (1983) Worker participation and autonomy: a multilevel approach to democracy at the workplace. In C. Crouch and F. Heller (eds.), *Organisational Democracy and Political Process,* vol. 1. Chichester: Wiley.

Gardell, B. and Gustavsen, B. (1980) Work environment research and social change: current developments in Scandinavia, *Journal of Occupational Behaviour,* 1: 3–17.

Geertz, C. (1973) *The Interpretation of Culture.* New York: Basic.

Gergen, K.J. (1991) *The Saturated Self: Dilemmas of Identity in Contemporary Life.* New York: Basic Books.

Giddens, A. (1984) *The Constitution of Society.* Cambridge: Polity Press.

Giddens, A. (1991) *Modernity and Self-Identity.* Cambridge: Polity Press.

Gillespie, R.D. (1942) *Psychological Effects of War on Citizen and Soldier.* London: Chapman and Hall.

Goffman, E. (1961) *Asylums.* Harmondsworth: Penguin.

Goffman, E. (1971) *The Presentation of Self in Everyday Life.* London: Pelican.

Goldthorpe, J.H., Lockwood, D., Bechhofer, F. and Platt, J.(1968) *The Affluent Worker: Industrial Attitudes and Behaviour.* Cambridge: Cambridge University Press.

Goode, W.J. (1960) A theory of role strain, *American Sociological Review,* 25: 483–96.

Grey, C. (1994) Career as a project of the self and labour process discipline, *Sociology,* 28: 479–98.

Gustavsen, B. (1983) The Norwegian work environment reform: the transition from general principles to workplace action. In C. Crouch and F. Heller (eds.), *Organisational Democracy and Political Process,* vol. 1. Chichester: Wiley.

Gustavsen, B. (1988) Democratising occupational health: the Scandinavian experience of work reform, *International Journal of Health Services*, 18: 675–89.

Gustavsen, B. and Hunnius, G. (1981) *New Patterns of Work Reform – the Case of Norway*. Oslo: Oslo University Press.

Hall, E.M. (1989) Gender, work control, and stress: a theoretical discussion and empirical test. *International Journal of Health Services*, 19: 725–45.

Hall, S. (1988) The toad in the garden: Thatcherism amongst the theorists. In C. Nelson and L. Grossberg (eds), *Marxism and the Interpretation of Culture*. Basingstoke: Macmillan.

Hamnett, M.P., Porter, P.J., Singh, A. and Kumar, K. (1984) *Ethics, Politics, and International Social Science: From Critique to Praxis*. Hawaii: University of Hawaii Press.

Handy, J. (1990) *Occupational Stress in a Caring Profession*. Avebury: Aldershot.

Handy, J. (1991) The social context of occupational stress in a caring profession, *Social Science and Medicine*, 32 (7): 819–30.

Harré, R. (1986) *The Social Construction of Emotions*. Oxford: Blackwell.

Hearn, J. (1993) Emotive subjects: organizational men, organizational masculinities and the (de)construction of emotions. In S. Fineman (ed.), *Emotion in Organizations*. London: Sage.

Hearnshaw, L.S. (1964) *A Short History of British Psychology, 1840–1940*. London: Methuen.

Hearnshaw, L.S. (1987) *The Shaping of Modern Psychology*. London: Routledge and Kegan Paul.

Herbst, P. (1976) *Alternatives to Hierarchies*. Leiden: Martinus Nijhoff.

Hinkle, L.E. (1973) The concept of social 'stress' in the biological and social sciences, *Science, Medicine, and Man*, 1: 31–48.

Hirschhorn, L. (ed.) (1989) *Organisational Psychodynamics*. Special issue of *Human Resource Management*, 28 (2).

Hochschild, A. (1975) The sociology of feeling and emotion: selected possibilities. In M. Millman and R. Kanter (eds.), *Another Voice*. New York: Anchor.

Hochschild, A. (1979) Emotion work, feeling rules, and social structure, *American Journal of Sociology*, 39: 551–75.

Hochschild, A. (1983) *The Managed Heart*. Berkeley: University of California Press.

Hochschild, A. (1993) Preface. In S. Fineman (ed.), *Emotion in Organizations*. London: Sage.

Hollway, W. (1989) *Subjectivity and Method in Psychology: Gender, Meaning and Science*. London: Sage.

Hollway, W. (1991) *Work Psychology and Organizational Behaviour*. London: Sage.

Hopfl, H. (1991) Nice jumper Jim!: dissonance and emotional labour in a management development programme. Paper presented at the 5th European Congress on the Psychology of Work and Organizations, Rouen, 24–7 March.

Hosking, D. and Fineman, S. (1990) Organizing processes, *Journal of Management Studies*, 27 (6): 583–604.

Israel, B.A., Schurman, S.J. and House, S.J. (1989) Action research on occupational stress: involving workers as researchers, *International Journal of Health Services*, 19 (1): 135–55.

Jackall, R. (1988) *Moral Mazes*. New York: Oxford University Press.

Jackson, S.E. and Schuler, R.S. (1985) A meta-analysis and conceptual critique of research on role ambiguity and role conflict in work settings, *Organizational Behavior and Human Decision Processes*, 36: 16–78.

Jacobsen, E., Charters, W.W. Jr and Lieberman, S. (1951) The use of the role concept in the study of complex organizations, *Journal of Social Issues*, 7 (3): 18–27.

Jahoda, M. (1955) Toward a social psychology of mental health. In R. Kotinsky and Helen Witmer (eds.), *Community Programs for Mental Health*. Cambridge, MA: Harvard University Press.

Jahoda, M. (1958) *Current Concepts of Positive Mental Health*. New York: Basic Books.

Jahoda, M. (1979) The impact of unemployment in the 1930s and in the 1970s, *Bulletin of the British Psychological Society*, 32: 309–14.

Janis, I.L. (1951) *Air War and Emotional Stress. Psychological Studies of Bombing and Civilian Defense*. Westport, CT: Greenwood Press.

Jaques, E. (1955) Social systems as a defence against persecutory and depressive anxiety. In M.L. Klein, P. Heimann and R. Money-Kyrle (eds.), *New Directions in Psychoanalysis*. London: Tavistock.

Jeffers, S. (1987) *Feel the Fear and Do It Anyway*. London: Random Century.

Jeffers, S. (1992) *Dare to Connect: How to Create Confidence, Trust, and Loving Relationships*. London: Judy Piatkus.

Johansson, G. (1979) Psychoneuroendocrine reactions to mechanized and computerized work routines. In C. Mackay and T. Cox (eds.), *Response to Stress: Occupational Aspects*. London: IPC Science and Technology Press.

Johansson, G., Aronsson, G. and Lindstrom, B.O. (1978) Social psychological and neuroendocrine stress reactions in highly mechanized work. *Ergonomics*, 21: 583–99.

Johansson, G. and Aronsson, G. (1984) Stress reactions in computerized administrative work, *Journal of Occupational Behaviour*, 5: 159–81.

Johnson, J.V. and Johansson, G. (1989) Introduction: the need for new directions in research on work organization and health, *International Journal of Health Services*, 19: 721–4.

Johnson, J.V. and Johansson, G. (eds.) (1991) *Psychosocial Work Environment: Work Organization, Democratization and Health*. Amityville, NY: Baywood.

Kahn, R.L., Wolfe, D.M., Quinn, R.P., Snoek, J.D. and Rosenthal, R.A. (1964) *Organizational Stress: Studies on Role Conflict and Ambiguity*. New York: Wiley.

Kamen, H. (1985) *Inquisition and Society in Spain*. London: Weidenfeld and Nicolson.

Karasek, R.A. (1978) A stress management model of job strain. Working paper, Swedish Institute for Social Research, Stockholm University.

Karasek, R.A. (1979) Job demands, job decision latitude, and mental strain: implications for job re-design, *Administrative Science Quarterly*, 24: 285–308.

Karasek, R. (1989) The political implications of psychosocial work redesign: a model of the psychosocial class structure, *International Journal of Health Services*, 19: 481–508.

Karasek, R., Gardell, B. and Lindell, J. (1987) Work and non-work correlates of illness and behaviour in male and female Swedish white collar workers, *Journal of Occupational Behaviour*, 8: 187–207.

Kasl, S.V. (1978) Epidemiological contributions to the study of work stress. In C.L. Cooper and R. Payne (eds.), *Stress at Work*. Chichester: Wiley.

Kasl, S.V. (1983) Pursuing the link between stressful life experiences and disease: a time for reappraisal. In C.L. Cooper (ed.), *Stress Research: Issues for the Eighties*. Chichester: Wiley.

Katz, D., Maccoby, N. and Morse, N.C. (1950) *Productivity, Supervision and Morale in an Office Situation*, part 1. Ann Arbor, MI: Survey Research Center, Institute for Social Research, University of Michigan.

Katz, D. and Kahn, R.L. (1966) *The Social Psychology of Organizations*. New York: Wiley.

Kelly, J.E. (1982) *Scientific Management, Job Redesign and Work Performance*. London: Academic Press.

Kelly, J.E. (1985) Management's redesign of work. In D. Knights, H. Willmott and D. Collinson (eds.), *Job Redesign: Critical Perspectives on the Labour Process*. Aldershot: Gower.

Kemper, T.D. (1978) Towards a sociological theory of emotions: some problems and some solutions, *The American Sociologist*, 13: 30–41.

Kemper, T.D. (1981) Social constructionist and positivist approaches to the sociology of emotions, *American Journal of Sociology*, 87 (2): 336–62.

Kessler, R.C. (1987) The interplay of research design strategies and data analysis procedures in evaluating the effects of stress on health. In S.V. Kasl and C.L. Cooper (eds.), *Stress and Health: Issues in Research Methodology*. Chichester: Wiley.

Kets deVries, M.F.R. and Miller, D. (1984) *The Neurotic Organization*. San Francisco: Jossey-Bass.

Klein, M., Heimann, P. and Money-Kyrle, R. (eds.) (1955) *New Directions in Psycho-analysis*. London: Tavistock.

Knights, D. and Collinson, D.L. (1987) Shop floor culture and the problem of managerial control. In J. McGoldrick (ed.), *Business Case File in Behavioural Science*. London: Van Nystrand.

Knights, D. and Morgan, G. (1991) Strategic discourse and subjectivity: towards a critical analysis of corporate strategy in organizations, *Organization Studies*, 12: 251–73.

Knights, D. and Vurdubakis, T. (1994) Foucault, power, resistance and all that. In J. Jermier, W. Nord and D. Knights (eds.), *Power and Conflict in Organizations*. London: Routledge.

Kornhauser, A. (1960) Toward an assessment of mental health of factory workers: a Detroit study. Paper presented to the American Psychological Association, Chicago, September.

Kornhauser, A. (1965) *Mental Health of the Industrial Worker: A Detroit Study*. New York: Wiley.

Kotinsky, R. and Witmer, H. (eds.) (1955) *Community Programs for Mental Health*. Cambridge, MA: Harvard University Press.

Kronenfeld, J.J., Jackson, K.L., Davis, K.E. and Blair, S.N. (1988) Changing health practices: the experience from a worksite health promotion project, *Social Science and Medicine*, 26: 515–23.

Lanier, L.H. (1952) *Handbook of Experimental Psychology*: a special review by nine psychologists, *Psychological Bulletin*, 49: 156–8.

Lasch, C. (1977) *Haven in a Heartless World: The Family Besieged*. New York: Basic Books.

Lazarus, R.S., Deese, J. and Osler, S.F. (1952) The effects of psychological stress upon skilled performance, *Psychological Bulletin*, 49: 293–317.

Lazarus, R.S. and Eriksen, C.W. (1952) Effects of failure upon skilled performance, *Journal of Experimental Psychology*, 43: 100–5.

Lazarus, R.S. and Launier, R. (1978) Stress related transactions between person and environment. In L.A. Pervin and M. Lewis (eds.), *Perspectives in Interactional Psychology*. New York: Plenum.

Lennon, M.C. (1989) The structural context of stress: an invited response to Pearlin (vol. 30, no. 3), *Journal of Health and Social Behavior*, 30: 261–8.

Levi, L. (1974) Stress, distress and psychosocial stimuli. In A. McLean (ed.), *Occupational Stress*. Springfield, IL: C.C. Thomas.

Levi, L. and Kagan, A. (1980) Psychosocially induced stress and disease – problems, research strategies and results. In H. Selye (ed.), *Selye's Guide to Stress Research*. New York: Van Nostrand Reinhold.

Levinson, H. (1956) Employee counselling in industry: observations on three programs, *Bulletin of the Menninger Clinic*, 20: 76–84.

Levinson, H. (1961) Industrial mental health: progress and prospects, *Menninger Quarterly*, Winter.

Lewin, K. (1952) *Field Theory in Social Science: Selected Theoretical Papers*, ed. by D. Cartwright. London: Tavistock.

Likert, R. (1961) *New Patterns of Management*. New York: McGraw-Hill.

Likert, R. and Campbell, A. (1951) Preface to volume 7, part 3 of the *Journal of Social Issues*: 2–3.

Lysgaard, S. (1961) *Arbeiderkollektivet* (Worker Collectivity). Oslo: Oslo University Press.

McGregor, D. (1960) *The Human Side of Enterprise*. New York: McGraw-Hill.

Macleod, A.G.S. (1985) EAPs and blue collar stress. In C. Cooper and M.J. Smith (eds.), *Blue Collar Stress*. Chichester: Wiley.

Mason, J.W. (1975) A historical view of the stress field: part I, *Journal of Human Stress*, 1: 6–12.

Matteson, M.T. and Ivancevich, J.M. (1982) The how, what and why of stress management training, *Personnel Journal*, 61: 768–74.

Meichenbaum, D. (1975) A self-instructional approach to stress management: a proposal for stress-inoculation training. In C.D. Spielberger and I. Sarason (eds.), *Stress and Anxiety*, vol. 1. Washington, DC: Hemisphere.

Melton, A.W. (1947) *Apparatus Tests*. Army Air Forces Aviation Psychology Program Research Report 4. Washington, DC: US Government Printing Office.

Menzies, I.E.P. (1959) The functioning of social systems as a defense against anxiety: a report on a study of the nursing service of a general hospital, *Human Relations*, 13: 95–121.

Menzies Lyth, I.E.P. (1988) *Containing Anxiety in Institutions: Selected Essays*, vol. 1. London: Free Association Books.

Merton, R.K. (1957) The role-set: problems in sociological theory, *British Journal of Sociology*, 8: 106–20.

Miller, P. and Rose, N. (1988) The Tavistock programme: the government of subjectivity and social life, *Sociology*, 22: 171–92.

Miller, P. and Rose, N. (1990) Governing economic life, *Economy and Society*, 19: 1–31.

Mills, C.W. (1956) *White Collar*. New York: Oxford University Press.

Morgan, G. (1986) *Images of Organization*. Beverly Hills, CA: Sage.

Morgan, G. and Ramirez, R. (1984) Action learning: a holographic metaphor for guiding social change, *Human Relations*, 37: 1–28.

Mouzelis, N. (1993) The poverty of sociological theory, *Sociology*, 27: 675–95.

Munsterberg, H. (1913) *Psychology and Industrial Efficiency*. Boston: Houghton Mifflin.

Murphy, L.R. (1987) A review of organizational stress management research: methodological considerations. In J.M. Ivancevich and D.C. Ganster (eds.), *Job Stress: From Theory to Suggestion*. New York: Haworth Press.

Murphy, L.R. (1988) Workplace interventions for stress reduction and prevention. In C.L. Cooper and R. Payne (eds.), *Causes, Coping and Consequences of Stress at Work*. Chichester: Wiley.

Muscio, B. (1920) *Lectures on Industrial Psychology* (2nd edn). London: Routledge.

Neale, M.S., Singer, J.A., Schwartz, G.E and Schwartz, J. (1982) Conflicting perspectives on stressor reduction in occupational settings: a systems approach to their resolution. Unpublished paper, Department of Psychology, Yale University.

Neale, M.S., Singer, J.A. and Schwartz, G.E. (1987) A systems assessment of occupational stress: evaluating a hotel during contract negotiations. In A.W. Riley and S.J. Zaccaro (eds.), *Occupational Stress and Organizational Effectiveness*. New York: Praeger.

Newton, T.J. (1989) Occupational stress and coping with stress: a critique, *Human Relations*, 42: 441–61.

Newton, T.J. (1992) Stress management in caring services. In C. Duncan (ed.), *The Evolution of Public Management: Concepts and Techniques for the 1990s*. Basingstoke: Macmillan.

Newton, T.J. (1994a) Discourse and agency: the example of personnel psychology, and 'assessment centres', *Organization Studies*, 15 (6).

Newton, T.J. (1994b) Reply to Bernard Ungerson, *The Psychologist*, 7 (3): 105–6.

Newton, T.J. (1994c) Postmodernism and action, *Organization*, forthcoming.

Newton, T.J. (1994d) *Agency and Discourse: Recruiting Consultants in a Life Insurance Company*. University of Edinburgh, Department of Business Studies, Working Paper Series.

Newton, T.J. and Findlay, P. (1994) *Playing God? The Performance of Appraisal*. University of Edinburgh, Department of Business Studies, Working Paper Series 94/5.

Newton, T.J. and Keenan, A. (1985) Coping with work-related stress, *Human Relations*, 38: 107–26; translated into Arabic in the *Arab Journal of Administration*, 1986, 10 (4).

Newton, T.J. and Keenan, A. (1987) Role stress re-examined: an investigation of role stress predictors, *Organisational Behavior and Human Decision Processes*, 40: 346–68.

Newton, T.J. and Keenan, A. (1991) Further analyses of the dispositional argument in organizational behavior, *Journal of Applied Psychology*, 76 (6): 781–7.

Novaco, R. (1977) A stress-inoculation approach to anger management in the training of law enforcement officers, *American Journal of Community Psychology*, 5: 327–46.

Nurse, J. (1994) Researching emotion in organisations. Paper presented at 'Emotion and organisations', a study day of the British Sociological Association Study Group for the Sociology of Emotions, 5 February, Social Science Research Unit, 18 Woburn Square, London, WC1H 0NS.

Ogbonna, E. and Wilkinson, B. (1990) Corporate strategy and corporate culture: the view from the checkout, *Personnel Review*, 19 (4): 9–15.

OSS Assessment Staff (1948) *Assessment of Men*. Office of Strategic Services. New York: Rinehart.

Parker, I. (1989) Discourse and power. In J. Shotter and K.J. Gergen (eds.), *Texts of Identity*. London: Sage.

Parkes, K. (1982) Occupational stress among student nurses: a natural experiment, *Journal of Applied Psychology*, 67: 784–96.

Parkes, K.R. (1985) Stressful episodes reported by first year student nurses: a descriptive account. *Social Science and Medicine*, 20: 945–53.

Parkin, W. (1993) The public and the private: gender, sexuality and emotion. In S. Fineman (ed.), *Emotion in Organizations*. London: Sage.

Payne, R. (1978) Epistemology and the study of stress at work. In C. Cooper and R. Payne (eds.), *Stress at Work*. Chichester: Wiley.

Pearlin, L.I. (1989) The sociological study of stress, *Journal of Health and Social Behavior*, 30: 241–56.

Peters, T. (1988) Leadership excellence in the 1990s: learning to love change, *Journal of Management Development*, 7: 5–9.

Peters, T. and Waterman, R.H. (1982) *In Search of Excellence*. New York: Warner.

Pfeffer, J. (1981) *Power in Organizations*. Marshfield, MA: Pitman.

Pines, A. and Aronson, E. (1989) *Career Burnout*. New York: Free Press.

Pollert, A. (1981) *Girls, Wives, Factory Lives*. London: Macmillan.

Pollert, A. (1991) The orthodoxy of flexibility. In A. Pollert (ed.), *Farewell to Flexibility?* Oxford: Blackwell.

Pollock, K. (1988) On the nature of social stress: production of a modern mythology, *Social Science and Medicine*, 26: 381–92.

Postman, L. and Bruner, J.S. (1948) Perception under stress, *Psychological Review*, 55: 314–23.

Pronko, N.H. and Leith, W.R. (1956) Behavior under stress: a study of its disintegration, *Psychological Reports*, 2: 205–22.

Rabinow, P. (1984) *The Foucault Reader*. Harmondsworth: Penguin.

Ramsay, H. (1983) Evolution or cycle? Worker participation in the 1980s. In C. Crouch and F. Heller (eds.), *Organisational Democracy and Political Process*, vol. 1. Chichester: Wiley.

Ramsay, H. (1985) What is participation for: a critical evaluation of 'labour process' analyses of job reform. In D. Knights, H. Willmott and D. Collinson (eds.), *Job Redesign: Critical Perspectives on the Labour Process*. Aldershot: Gower.

Roman, P.M. and Blum, T.C. (1988) Formal intervention in employee health: comparisons of the nature and structure of employee assistance programs and health promotion programs, *Social Science and Medicine*, 26: 503–14.

Rose, M. (1985) *Re-working the Work Ethic*. London: Batsford.

Rose, M. (1988) *Industrial Behaviour* (2nd edn). Harmondsworth: Penguin.

Rose, N. (1985) *The Psychological Complex*. London: Routledge and Kegan Paul.

Rose, N. (1990) *Governing the Soul: The Shaping of the Private Self*. London: Routledge.

Rose, N. (1991) Governing the enterprising self. In P. Heelas and P. Morris (eds.), *The Values of the Enterprise Culture – The Moral Debate*. London: Unwin Hyman.

Rose, N. and Miller, P. (1992) Political power beyond the state: problematics of government, *British Journal of Sociology*, 43: 173–205.

Ryan, T.A. (1947) *Work and Effort: The Psychology of Production*. New York: Ronald Press.

Sahlins, M.D. (1972) *Stone Age Economics*. Chicago: Aldine-Atherton.

Salaman, G. (1980) Roles and rules. In G. Salaman and K. Thompson (eds.), *Control and Ideology in Organizations*. Milton Keynes: Open University Press.

Salaman, G. (1979) *Work Organisations: Resistance and Control*. London: Longman.

Sandelands, L.E. (1988) The concept of work feeling, *Journal of the Theory of Social Behavior*, 18: 437–57.

Sarason, S.B. (1977) *Work, Aging and Social Change*. London: Macmillan.

Satyamurti, C. (1981) *Occupational Survival*. Oxford: Blackwell.

Schachter, S. (1959) *The Psychology of Affiliation*. Stanford, CA: Stanford University Press.

Schaef, A.W. and Fassel, D. (1988) *The Addictive Organization*. San Francisco: Harper and Row.

Schein, E. (1985) *Organizational Culture and Leadership*. San Francisco: Jossey-Bass.

Selye, H. (1936a) A syndrome produced by diverse nocuous agents, *Nature*, 138: 32.

Selye, H. (1936b) Thymus and adrenals in the response of the organism to injuries and intoxifications, *British Journal of Experimental Pathology*, 17: 234–48.

Selye, H. (1937) Studies on adaptation, *Endocrinology*, 21: 168–88.

Selye, H. (1946) The general adaptation syndrome and the diseases of adaptation, *Journal of Clinical Endocrinology*, 6: 117–230.

Selye, H. (1950) *Stress*. Montreal: Acta.

Selye, H. (1952) *The Story of the Adaptation Syndrome (Told in the Form of Informal, Illustrated Lectures)*. Montreal: Acta.

Selye, H. (1956) *The Stress of Life*. New York: McGraw-Hill.

Selye, H. (1971) The evaluation of the stress concept – stress and cardiovascular disease. In L. Levi (ed.), *Society, Stress and Disease*, vol. 1. London: Oxford University Press.

Selye, H. (1976) *Stress in Health and Disease*. Boston: Butterworth.

Selye, H. and Collip, J.B. (1936) Fundamental factors in the interpretation of stimuli influencing endocrine glands, *Endocrinology*, 20: 667–72.

Selye, H. and McKeown, T. (1935) Studies on the physiology of the maternal placenta in the rat, *Proceedings of the Royal Society of London, Series B*, 119: 1–30.

Sennett, R. (1977) *The Fall of Public Man*. Cambridge: Cambridge University Press.

Sewell, G. and Wilkinson, B. (1992) Someone to watch over me: surveillance, discipline and just-in-time labour process, *Sociology*, 26: 271–89.

Shott, S. (1979) Emotion and social life: a symbolic interactionist analysis, *American Journal of Sociology*, 84 (6): 317–34.

Singer, J.A., Neale, M.S. and Schwartz, G.E. (1987) The nuts and bolts of assessing occupational stress: a collaborative approach with labour. In L.R. Murphy and T.F. Schoenborn (eds.), *Stress Management in Work Settings*. US Department of Health and Human Services (DHHS), National Institute for Occupational Safety and Health (NIOSH), Robert A. Taft Laboratories, 4676 Columbia Parkway, Cincinnati, Ohio 45226. DHHS (NIOSH) Publication 87–111.

Smith, P.B. and Peterson, M.E. (1988) *Leadership, Organizations and Culture*. London: Sage.

Steffy, B.D. and Grimes, A.J. (1992) Personnel/organization psychology: a critique of the discipline. In M. Alvesson and H. Willmott (eds.), *Critical Management Studies*. London: Sage.

Stevens, S. (1951) *Handbook of Experimental Psychology*. New York: Wiley.

Stone, M. (1985) Shellshock and the psychologists. In W.F. Bynum, R. Porter and Michael Shepherd (eds.), *The Anatomy of Madness*, vol. II. London: Tavistock.

Strauss, A. (1978) *Negotiations*. San Francisco: Jossey-Bass.

Sugrue, N. (1982) Emotions as property and context for negotiation, *Urban Life*, 11 (3): 280–92.

Sutherland, J. (1960) Prevention and treatment of psychiatric reactions to stress by psycho-social means. In J.M. Tanner (ed.), *Stress and Psychiatric Disorder: The Proceedings of the Second Oxford Conference of the Mental Health Research Fund*. Oxford: Blackwell.

Symonds, C.P. (1947) Human response to flying stress. In Air Ministry Air Publication 3139, *Psychological Disorders in Flying Personnel of the Royal Air Force Investigated during the War 1939–1945*. London: HMSO.

Tancred-Sheriff, P. (1989) Gender, sexuality and the labour process. In J. Hearn, D.L. Sheppard, P. Tancred-Sheriff and G. Burrell, *The Sexuality of Organizations*. London: Sage.

Tanner, J.M. (ed.) (1960) *Stress and Psychiatric Disorder: The Proceedings of the Second Oxford Conference of the Mental Health Research Fund*. Oxford: Blackwell.

Tanner, J., Davies, S. and O'Grady, B. (1992) Immanence changes everything: a critical comment on the labour process and class consciousness, *Sociology*, 26: 439–53.

Team Video Productions (undated) *Stress: Work Place Education Resource Pack and Guidance Notes* (accompanying the video 'Stress'). Team Video, Canalot, 222 Kensal Road, London, W10 5BN.

Theorell, T. (1993) On the end of the Swedish system, *Work and Stress*, 7: 201–2.

Thompson, P. (1983) *The Nature of Work: An Introduction to Debates on the Labour Process*. London: Macmillan.

Thompson, P. (1990) Crawling from the wreckage: the labour process and the politics of production. In D. Knights and H. Willmott (eds.), *Labour Process Theory*. Basingstoke: Macmillan.

Thompson, P. (1992) *The Nature of Work* (2nd edn). Basingstoke: Macmillan.

Thompson, P. and McHugh, D. (1990) *Work Organisations*. Basingstoke: Macmillan.

Trist, E. (1981) *The Evaluation of Socio-Technical Systems*. Ontario: Ontario Ministry of Labour.

Trist, E.L. and Bamforth, K.W. (1951) Some social and psychological consequences of the longwall method of coal-getting, *Human Relations*, 4: 3–8.

Trist, E.L. and Murray, H. (1990) *The Social Engagement of Social Sciences – A Tavistock Anthology*, vol. 1: *The Social-Psychological Perspective*. Philadelphia: University of Pennsylvania Press.

Tuchman, G., Daniels, A.K. and Benet, J. (1978) *Hearth and Home: Images of Women in the Mass Media*. New York: Oxford University Press.

Tufts, E.M. (1955) The field of mental health promotion. In R. Kotinsky and Helen Witmer (eds.), *Community Programs for Mental Health*. Cambridge, MA: Harvard University Press.

Turberville, A.S. (1932) *The Spanish Inquisition*. London: Thornton Butterworth.

Van Maanen, J. and Kunda, G. (1989) 'Real feelings': emotional expression and organizational culture, *Research in Organizational Behavior*, 11: 43–103.

Viteles, M.S. (1932) *Industrial Psychology*. New York: Norton.

Wagner, W.G. (1982) Assisting employees with personal problems: the bottom line is increased productivity and money saved, *Personnel Administrator*, November (27): 59–64.

Walker, C.R. and Guest, R.H. (1952) *The Man on the Assembly Line*. Cambridge, MA: Harvard University Press.

Wallas, G. (1914) *The Great Society: A Psychological Analysis*. London: Macmillan.

Walt Disney Productions (1982) *Your Role in the Walt Disney World Show*. Orlando, FL: Walt Disney Productions.

Weiss, R.M. (1986) *Managerial Ideology and the Social Control of Deviance in Organizations*. New York: Praeger.

Wetherell, M. and Potter, J. (1992) *Mapping the Language of Racism: Discourse and the Legitimation of Exploitation*. Hemel Hempstead: Harvester Wheatsheaf.

Whitehead, M. (1990) *Minding Your Own Business*. London: Social Audit.

Whittingham, C. and Holland, R. (1985) A framework for theory in social work, *Issues in Social Work Education*, 5: 25–50.

Whyte, W.F. (ed.) (1991) *Participatory Action Research*. Beverly Hills, CA: Sage.

Wilensky, J.L. and Wilensky, H.L. (1951) Personnel counselling: the Hawthorne case, *American Journal of Sociology*, 17: 265–80.

Willmott, H. (1989) Subjectivity and the dialetics of praxis: opening up the core of labour process analysis. In D. Knights and H. Willmott (eds.), *Labour Process Theory*. London: Macmillan.

Wolff, H.G., Wolf, S.G. and Hare, C.G. (1950) *Life Stress and Bodily Disease*. New York: Hafner.

Wouters, C. (1977) Informalization and the civilizing process. In P. Gleichman, J. Godsblom and H. Korte (eds.), *Human Figurations: Essays for Norbert Elias*. Amsterdam: Amsterdams Sociologisch Tijdschrift.

Wouters, C. (1986) Formalization and informalization, changing tension balances in civilizing process, *Theory, Culture and Society*, 3: 1–19.

Wouters, C. (1987) Developments in the behavioural codes between the sexes: the formalization of informalization in the Netherlands, 1930–1985, *Theory, Culture and Society*, 4: 405–27.

Wouters, C. (1989) The sociology of emotions and flight attendants: Hochschild's *Managed Heart*, *Theory, Culture and Society*, 6: 95–123.

Zuboff, S. (1988) *In the Age of the Smart Machine*. Oxford: Heinemann.

Index

Compiled by Jackie McDermott